I HEAR HIS

Whisper

Encounter God's Heart for You

BroadStreet
PUBLISHING

BroadStreet Publishing® Group, LLC
Savage, Minnesota, USA
BroadStreetPublishing.com

I HEAR HIS *Whisper*: Encounter God's Heart for You

Printed in China
19 20 21 22 23 5 4 3 2 1

Introduction

It is good to be alone with Jesus in the early morning hours. Many mornings before the sun is up, we spend time hearing and listening to the voice we have come to love. God whispers to those who seek him. Yes, he will thunder with a mighty sound, but he will also whisper his words of love into our hearts.

We love and serve a God who delights in hearing our voice in prayer. How grateful we can be that the God of glory hears our sighs and our cries. Even our tears are liquid words, and he can read them all. Our God answers prayer. He whispers to us his messages of love and truth.

Prayer can be two-sided. We call out to him, and he answers us with tremendous love, whispering into our hearts, "I know you. I see what you are going through, and I am there for you." Today, you can lean in to his heart and hear for yourself the words of grace he may speak to you.

This is a compilation of the messages of love we have heard spoken to our hearts. While God has spoken these words personally, each whisper will also have application for life. For example, God welcomes each of us to know that he is enough, and to respond to his invitation to give our hearts to him. God is not silent. He has a voice, and we can hear it for ourselves. We trust these whispers will spark a desire to hear God's gentle voice.

The whispers are not meant to replace God's eternal, inspired Word. The Bible speaks clearly and gives unfiltered truth. Have your Bible close at hand as you read through these pages. Search the Scriptures to ensure the whispers agree with God's Word. God loves his people and longs for them to know him, to hear his voice, and to obey his Word.

Dedication

I wish to thank Gretchen Rodriguez for writing alongside me on this project. Our publishers and friends at BroadStreet Publishing Group also deserve my heartfelt thanks. And of course, I want to thank Father God, Holy Spirit, and my Lord, Jesus Christ, for their endless love that I'm only beginning to dive into. Thank you, thank *you*, my God!

Brian Simmons

January

I love you because you are my child.

I love you simply because you are my child. I enjoy you for the same reason. I didn't create you so I could have a world full of minions running around doing my bidding. I created you because I wanted to share my love with you. I desired you and held you in my heart before you were formed in your mother's womb.

Husbands and wives don't want children so they can create someone to *do* something. They desire children simply because they want someone to pour their love into. They want a piece of themselves to love without reservation. It's a love so deep, it is hard to put into words. This is how I feel about *you*. You weren't born with a to-do list from me. I didn't create you on a mass production line, like a bunch of robots! I started pouring love into you from the beginning. When you were in your mother's womb, I took my time and weaved every detail of your being. I love you, simply because I love you.

This is how much God loved the world—
he gave his one and only, unique Son *as a gift*.
So now everyone who believes in him
will never perish but experience everlasting life.
God did not send his Son into the world
to judge and condemn the world,
but to be its Savior and rescue it!

JOHN 3:16–17

I want every part of you to be free.

I want you to be one with me. You've known this. You've aimed to let this be the theme of your life—living in union with me— but you have been neglecting one area. In order for you to truly be one with me, you must allow yourself to be fully consumed with me. Fully consumed—spirit, soul, and body. That means not only is your spirit aware of me and sensing my presence, but so is your soul, and ultimately your body.

Today, I remind you that I want every part of you to be free. The issue is that when your mind is consumed with your problems, you're not experiencing the fullness of my love. I want you to find true freedom in complete oneness with me. So let your mind come into agreement with me. Trust me and completely resign your will to mine. Release those cares into my hands. Either you can be in control of them or I can. But if you let me have control, you will finally experience the freedom and unity with me that you desire. You'll finally have peace.

The mind-set of the flesh is death,
but the mind-set controlled by the Spirit finds life and peace.

ROMANS 8:6

See yourself through my eyes.

I want you to see yourself through eyes of love and acceptance. You believe in me and my love for you, but it's time for you to believe in yourself. Let your confidence in me grow greater, especially in the areas you feel inadequate and afraid. I see your weaknesses, but I still believe in you!

Instead of looking in the mirror and doubting yourself, trust my judgment. If I say that you can do all things through me, and you don't believe it, then you are not just doubting yourself, you're not trusting me. You are more powerful than you know. The wisdom of the ages lives inside of you. You are bursting with my favor! Don't stare at others with a heart of jealousy, as if they have it better than you. They have their own path to walk with me. I have anointed you. You are my radiant bride, full of my glory. Be confident and vulnerable. Do not wear a mask to cover who you are. Be real and authentic. Feel each moment. Discover me in greater depths, and in turn, you will discover more about yourself.

We have come into an intimate experience with God's love,
and we trust in the love he has for us. God is love!
Those who are living in love are living in God,
and God lives through them.

1 JOHN 4:16–17

I offer you true vision.

From today forward, I am calling you to lay aside your blindness and take my healing eye salve—the revelation of my love—and see everything differently. You will be known as sons and daughters of the living God as you speak with purity and clear vision. I will show you the secrets of what is to come when your eyes have been healed and you look upon my throne.

I give you this day *true vision* that springs from revelation and understanding. Your eyes will be anointed to see beyond the moment with the faith that will call things that are not as though they are. You were created to see clearly, past the illusions the enemy seeks to distract you with. I have given you this gift of discerning grace that you might bring hope where others have lost courage. To stand in confidence, knowing my truth will prevail, when swirling chaos abounds. Take this healing eye salve of love to the people, and watch what I will do as you speak my words and see with my eyes.

"Purchase eye salve to be placed over your eyes
so that you can truly see.
All those I dearly love I unmask and train.
So repent and be eager *to pursue what is right.*"

REVELATION 3:18–19

I enjoy the kiss of your worship.

Your worship is your kiss to me. Your deepest affection. Never withhold what I treasure most: your kiss, your voice, your songs of adoration. For these are my reward. Your worship is specially perfumed to bring me delight. As it rises from your heart, I carry it to my throne—such a beautiful offering of love.

Today, I will open up a brand new dimension, a new element of your worship. It will flow from you in waves of praise and will rise from depths of worship, unlike you've ever known. Fragrant perfume, precious and of great value to me, for it required the death of my most precious Son to release it. And each time you worship through your pain, it rises as a fragrant offering before my throne.

My sacred chamber is calling you. Come and spend time with me and offer those sacrifices of praise. I will draw you into that cloud-filled chamber of intimacy, where we will share the cup of my love, together. So come, my glorious inheritance. Come and enter into love's delight. I love you, my bride.

Your kisses of love are exhilarating,
more than any delight I've known before.
Your kisses of love awaken even the lips of sleeping ones.

Song of Songs 7:9

You are my glorious inheritance.

My delight in you is real, for you are my glorious inheritance. I have taken you, carried you, and made you my own. Men inherit houses and land and wealth, but you are *my* inheritance.

Your love is my finest wine, intoxicating and pleasing. Your worship is a pleasing offering to me each day. You are my reward and eternal inheritance. Our joy for eternity will be to have each other. Nothing can diminish the bliss we will share together. My Son has bled and died for you, for you are the love gift that I promised Him as He came to earth—the glorious inheritance of the Son.

My mercies endure forever, my loving-kindness flows throughout your days. I will watch over you and guard your way, for sacred blood was given to make you mine. My desire is to bless you. It's my joy to see you excel and rise. Others may speak dark words of fear and rejection over you, but my words will always bring life to your soul and strength to your heart. Be sensitive to my voice, and you will hear me whisper to you this day: *You are my glorious inheritance.*

I pray that the light of God will illuminate the eyes of your imagination, flooding you with light, until you experience the full revelation of the hope of his calling—that is, the wealth of God's glorious inheritances that he finds in us, his holy ones!

EPHESIANS 1:18

I am enough for you.

I am enough for you. When you face difficulties and limitations, I will whisper into your heart, *I am enough.* I will not shield you from every hardship, but as you walk through them with your eyes set on me—yes, even in the deepest pain—I am still enough. I will be your wrap-around shield in the midst of your difficulty.

When you are lonely and seek companionship, I am enough. When your heart is troubled over many things, you must bring your soul before me, for I am enough. When the lies men have spoken bring disturbance into your mind, I will wash them away, for my Word is enough.

Your thoughts cannot contain the love I have for you. And you will never be able to comprehend with your mind the plans that I have for you. Yet I am enough, and all you need to know is that I am here for you. My Spirit longs to satisfy every part of you: your mind, your soul, your desires, your longings. When darkness comes, I am enough to see you through the night. Come and learn the secret that all my lovers learn: I am enough for you.

"Master, we don't know where you're going, so how could we know the way there?" Jesus explained, "I am the Way, I am the Truth, and I am the Life. No one comes next to the Father except through *union with me.* To know me is to know my Father too. And from now on you will realize that you have seen him and experienced him."

JOHN 14:5–7

You do hear me.

You do hear me. At times you doubt it, but today, I've come to set the record straight. My voice pours forth from the yearning, drawing, loving overflow of your heart. It's when your mind is consumed with thoughts of me and you're turned away from all other thoughts that you discover me bubbling up from within. Sometimes, my voice sounds like peace—quiet and reassuring. Sometimes, I unveil images—things I want you to pray for or ideas to implement. Often, Scripture will alight upon your heart, reminding you what I've already said. In all these ways and more, you hear me.

You were created to hear my voice, and I love to speak to you. All you need to do is posture your heart in agreement with mine. Lean in. Rest. Fix your attention on me and let me do the work. There's no striving to enter my presence. There's no power or self-effort; there's simply positioning yourself before me to receive. This is the place of sheer abandon and glorious love. The place of stillness, when you sense the movement of my Spirit and know that I am not limited in the ways I can speak to you.

"My own sheep will hear my voice and I know each one, and they will follow me."

JOHN 10:27

Walk with me in greater faith.

Your faith must never waver, for my Word is forever settled in heaven and will not change. Even if every star fell from the sky and every mountain crumbled into the sea, my covenant of love and my steadfast Word would not be shaken. I am not the author of fear. I am not the God of doubt, but the God of yes and amen! Confusion is nothing more than the dust of the earth, blown into the wind by the work of your enemy—and it is not your portion. Faith is your portion! Faith is light that creates, empowers, sustains, and heals.

Beloved, when your faith feels weak, I don't judge you. But I do want you to ask me for help. I want you to clutch fear by the neck and thrust it before my throne. To treat heaviness and disillusionment like the spiritual plague it is. Get rid of it! You can rise above it, because I am with you. Remember what I've done for you in the past. Praise me, especially when it is a sacrifice to do so, and I will see you through.

We are certainly not those who are held back by fear and perish; we are among those who have faith and experience true life!

HEBREWS 10:39

Find me in today.

This is the day that I have made. Aim to find me in it. Seek to discover the joys I have for you. Believe that I am with you, in you, and for you. All you need, not just to get *through* this day but to *enjoy* it, is found in me. Let me be your confidence, your identity, and your provision. Draw from the river of my presence that refreshes you from within.

Every day I offer you the joy of fellowship with me. I love the way you turn to me, even in your busyness, and offer me your thoughts, your song, or a glance. One movement of your heart toward me, means more than pious words, laboriously spoken out of duty. I want you to enjoy our communion and to trust that regardless of what the day holds, I am walking through it with you. Do you feel the movement of my heart drawing you closer today? Take a deep breath, grasp my hand, and trust me for today. That's all I ask—for you to take one day at a time and find the beauty of my presence within it.

This is the very day of the Lord that brings
gladness and joy, filling our hearts with glee.

PSALM 118:24

Learn the eternal way.

I long for you to know me and to embrace my ways. Come and learn of the way eternal. For my paths will lead you into more joy, until it overflows. If you receive my love, even in difficulties, you will know the secret of the wonder of eternity. Don't let appearances deceive you—my love will win every struggle that you face. Even this day, I have prepared a hiding place of mercy for you.

Come higher, let me give you limitless faith. Let me flood you with love so magnificent and fulfilling that you never question it again. My love will wash away the discontentment you've experienced in this world. It will set you upon a foundation that cannot be obliterated though the storms rage. Learning my ways will contradict every rational thought, but it will satisfy the yearning of your soul. Walking in my ways, the higher ways of heaven, will cause you to interpret situations rightly and to tap into the wisdom available for you. Forsake the meaningless ways of man and tap into my eternal ways.

God, I invite your searching gaze into my heart.
Examine me through and through;
find out everything that may be hidden within me.
Put me to the test and sift through all my anxious cares.

PSALM 139:23

My grace will surprise you.

I offer you grace for today. The past is a robber that seeks to drag you down with regret and memories of pain. The future can be frightening when you don't know my heart of love. When you set your heart on what the future may or may not hold, you forsake the joy of this moment. I haven't created you to live in the past or the future but to enjoy me right now. To trust me for what awaits and to release the past into my redeeming hands.

This is the day that I have made for you, so that you would be glad and experience my love in all things. Right now, place me as the center of your focus, and all of the peripheral things will fall into place. Let nothing disturb your joy today, not even the difficulties the enemy scatters along your path. I am the All-Sufficient One who offers you wisdom, favor, strength, peace, and joy when you submit every moment to me. Stay focused on me, and my grace will surprise you.

"My grace is always more than enough for you, and my power finds its full expression through your weakness." So I will celebrate my weaknesses, for when I'm weak I sense more deeply the mighty power of Christ living in me.

2 CORINTHIANS 12:9

I will take you deeper.

Come deeper into my victorious love that overcomes all things. You will be wrapped in my presence when you embrace my love. Others may see this love as weakness or may not understand this righteous path, but love will become a virtue burning bright within your soul. It will enable you to endure all things. To draw from my strength within you. Love never fails. Come deeper into my never-failing love, and you will discover the path of true holiness.

This deeper place of love is overflowing with treasure of glory that cannot be interpreted by natural wisdom. Your eyes will open and you will see your troubles much differently, for your difficulties are invitations to a more powerful truth. When you have reached the end of your hoarded resources, my love will bring you miracles. Love will open your heart to others, and you will see them as opportunities to demonstrate a greater love. Compassion, my pure compassion, will flow through you with breakthrough power. I release to you a deeper, more powerful love.

God will never give you the spirit of fear, but the Holy Spirit who gives you mighty power, love, and self-control. So never be ashamed of the testimony of our Lord, nor be embarrassed over my imprisonment, but overcome every evil by the revelation of the power of God!

2 TIMOTHY 1:6–8

I am preparing you.

I am training and preparing you for the coming days. Your calling is unique and so is your preparation. Nothing can hinder what I am doing in you. You will experience all that I have planned, for the fullness of my power is coming to you!

Soon, very soon, you will be astounded at the changes I have brought in your life. You will move from being in shadows to living in the brilliance of my glory. From confusion to comfort—filled with my life. Why would you doubt? Joseph would have never come to the place of ruling and reigning if he lived in doubt, even in the dark days of his prison.

Do not judge my plans for your life by the momentary mess that's around you or the unusual situation you find yourself in. I trained Moses to be my leader, my champion, on the backside of the desert. I trained David to be a warrior on the lonely hillside, as he sang his psalms of praise to me. I trained John the Baptist in the barren wilderness. So continue trusting beyond what you see and you will find my plans unfolding before your eyes.

Make wisdom your quest—
search for the revelation of life's meaning.
Don't let what I say go in one ear and out the other.
Stick with wisdom and she will stick to you,
protecting you throughout your days.
She will rescue all those who passionately listen to her voice.

PROVERBS 4:5–6

Trusting me brings clarity.

The grace I give to you cannot be diminished by what seems to be delay. Trust, and the light will shine. Believe, and understanding will follow. Soon, you will discover that all that you need is found in me. With every step you take, let your heart declare its total dependency upon me. Your trust is a sweet-smelling fragrance that I cannot deny.

There is a cost to greater understanding—the price of total surrender, which declares that I alone am God, and I'm big enough to take care of your situation. When you willingly yield your questions, fears, hopes, and doubts, trusting me for clarity, peace settles your soul. I will move in mystery to bring you into greater light. Hand me the reins of your life, sit back, and watch me steer you into pleasant places. Waiting is less painful when you discover me in the midst of it. My mighty grace is poured out in difficulties and in your delights. Trust until the light of a new day dawns.

Trust in the Lord completely,
and do not rely on your own opinions.
With all your heart rely on him to guide you,
and he will lead you in every decision you make.
Become intimate with him in whatever you do,
and he will lead you wherever you go.
Don't think for a moment that you know it all.

PROVERBS 3:5–6

My love for you is great.

Receive even more of my love. Drink it into your innermost being. My love transforms you and changes your thinking, your prayers, and the essence of your life. The depth of my love goes beyond natural understanding. It is more than you can imagine or perceive. It will take eternity to grasp the wonder of my love for you. It is not meant to be understood through doctrine or teaching. It is meant to be experienced in joy and sorrow. My heart is one with you—when you endure pain, I endure it with you.

When you look into the sky and see the vastness of my universe, know that my love is greater still. The greatest expanse of time and space cannot contain the depths of my love for you. All things were created as gifts for you. You are the pearl of great price, and I sold all that I had to purchase you. You are the treasure hidden in the field. I came into this world and found you. Never doubt my love or allow its fire to dim in your heart. Stir up your heart to know my love and experience my endless delight in you.

I know my lover is mine and I have everything in you,
for we delight ourselves in each other.

SONG OF SONGS 2:16

Rest at my side.

Heaven has opened its doors to receive you, for I have seated you with me in the heavenly realm where we rest as one. I see you next to me, no longer struggling to get my attention. You are in the place of rest at my side. All that has troubled you cannot enter; the door is shut to the temporal and momentary. Eternity is within your heart, for I have come to be one with you.

As you take your place at my right hand, life as you know it will radically change. Absorb the glory that is around you until you know that I am near. I have made you holy in my presence. Seeds that I have planted within you long ago, are starting to grow. A paradise garden blossoms in your heart as my Spirit brings these dormant seeds to life and fruitfulness. You will forget all your affliction and pain as this garden grows and releases life inside your soul. You will radiate my glory and taste my goodness. Come and rest at my side until your eyes open to see me face-to-face.

"Are you weary, carrying a heavy burden? Then come to me. I will refresh your life, for I am your oasis. Simply join your life with mine. Learn my ways and you'll discover that I'm gentle, humble, easy to please. You will find refreshment and rest in me."

MATTHEW 11:28–29

Let me be your loving Father.

I long to teach you what it means to be a son, a daughter of the living God. Do not let your experience with an earthly father blind your eyes to who I am. You have a Father in heaven, who has a burning love for you. I cherish you and will give you the fruits of sonship. Let me teach you the secrets of what it means to be my child. Turn your eyes to me and know that you have my full attention.

If memories of childhood bring pain and prevent you from knowing me fully, I will heal that pain and give you a new history in me. Together, we will write a new story of love, patience, encouragement, and safety. If in retrospect, you were able to find my love through your earthly father, allow me to build upon that and unveil an even more glorious way. Regardless of your past, I will give you a new frame of reference, so you will always expect me to be good, faithful, and kind. To anticipate joy. To never wonder if I'll come through, because you will never again have reason to doubt my love.

"If you, imperfect as you are, know how to lovingly take care of your children and give them what's best, how much more ready is your heavenly Father to give wonderful gifts to those who ask him?"

MATTHEW 7:11

You are in Christ.

I will treat you as I treat my Son, for I have placed you in Him, my beloved. You will face me and look upon me as my cherished one, for I will treat you with the favor that Jesus deserves. He has taken all that you deserved and carried it as His cross to Calvary. Now I will take all that He deserves and place it upon you. I have placed you in Him so that I can treat you like Him. This is our mercy and grace. Our gift to you. Our delight.

You abide within my heart. I have placed you inside the relationship I have with my Son and Spirit. I accept you fully. My endless love is for you with the same strength that it is for my Son. Allow this love to penetrate you with divine light: I love you with the love I have for my Son, for you are in Him forever. Cling to this awareness. Let it seep into your very being. Allow it to alter your perception of who you are, so that you will see yourself the way I see you—perfect, holy, blameless. You are my beloved.

No one has ever gazed upon the fullness of God's splendor except the uniquely beloved Son, who is cherished by the Father and held close to his heart. Now he has unfolded to us the full explanation of who God truly is!

JOHN 1:18

Let my love propel you to action.

I have called you to do the works of my Son, by the grace, power, and anointing of Christ within you. It is my desire that you believe, beyond natural reasoning, that you can do all that I have equipped you to do. Step into your destiny, by stepping away from doubt, fear, and rationalization. Choose a lifestyle of radical encounter, which in turn pours out through you with grace and glory. Look for opportunities to release my heart to the world.

As you, my sons and daughters, find your identity in my Son, all of heaven rejoices. Delight yourself in the wonder of our love. Get excited when you see us work through you. Be bold and compassionate, allowing the miracles of love to be seen through your life. As you discover the strength of my eternal love, all that is within you will be transformed. For I long to have a people who reflect the glory of my Son. This is my glory and my joy. This is your destiny.

"These miracle signs will accompany those who believe: They will drive out demons in the power of my name. They will speak in tongues. They will be supernaturally protected from snakes and from drinking anything poisonous. And they will lay hands on the sick and heal them."

MARK 16:17–18

I give you peace.

Many are puzzled over what seems like delay in their advancement. They're restless and long for lasting change. Restlessness comes when you take your eyes off of me. But I call you to rest in my peace and watch me work. Let me be your Sabbath rest.

The distractions are many for my chosen ones. Many voices and many activities can confuse your heart, but in me there is peace that transcends all understanding. I give to you not logic, but peace. Peace which can never be disturbed or stolen, if your mind is fixed on me. Come into my ocean of peace, and I will speak the words you need to hear. Step into me and remain in the safety of my presence. The world cannot give you the peace you desire. Your place is with me. I long to be your undisturbed peace in times of trouble and rapid change. My plans for you require you to focus on me and not on shifting circumstances. Confine yourself to me, as a prisoner of love, and you will be nourished by my eternal peace.

In his shelter in the day of trouble, that's where you'll find me,
for he hides me there in his holiness.
He has smuggled me into his secret place,
where I'm kept safe and secure—
out of reach from all my enemies.

PSALM 27:5

Step into the fires.

I stand before you, beckoning you to step into the fires of my holy passion. These fires of purity and love will burn away the residue of disappointment, pain, and sorrow. My love cannot be overcome by what the enemy has done. My blood is more than enough to wash away every trauma. My love is a living force. It is healing. Teaming with power. Able to completely and totally set you free, so that even the most tormenting memories are suddenly void of pain.

You don't need to strive to enter my love. Stepping in is as simple as leaning in and trusting that my faithful love greets you in reply. Believe that I never turn my ear from your cry, that my presence overflows with peace that surpasses understanding. Allow yourself to feel the glory of this love. Don't be afraid of the fires of holiness, as if you weren't created for them. You were created for the outrageous, wonderful glories of my kingdom. This is only the beginning.

Arise, my love.
Open your heart, my darling, deeper still to me.
Will you receive me this dark night?

SONG OF SONGS 5:2

My life is victory in you.

The victory I call you to walk in is already within you. When everything seems difficult, yield to my life within, and you will find grace. My promise is a promise of victory, and my victory is my life released in you. I dispense my glory when you open your heart deeper to me. Taste my victory and rest in me, for I have overcome all things.

I have brought you to this place because of my passionate and tender love for you. I want to show you my victory. I want you to learn of me and take my easy yoke upon your soul and find rest. Have I not promised to lead you to the quiet brooks of peace? I will show you the path as you still your heart before me. Trust in me and not in what you see. Believe in me when fear attempts to stop your advance, and you will find my oasis of victory. Even when you don't know what to do or what step to take, my peace will guide you. Take my gift of today's victory and be content as I prepare tomorrow's triumph.

You empower me for victory with your wrap-around presence.
Your power within makes me strong to subdue,
and by stooping down in gentleness
you strengthened me and made me great!

PSALM 18:35

I will heal you.

I will heal you. I am moved by your cry and will answer when you ask me to draw near. I will never close my eyes to your suffering, and I will never close my heart to your pain.

I am the Father of encouragement and the God of all comfort. There is no part of you that I cannot touch and heal. I invite you to enter into my stronghold, my dwelling place of beauty, and fix your eyes on me. As you gaze upon me and drink of my Spirit, my healing power is released within you. My children are loved beyond understanding, and I demonstrate my love every moment. My healing light streams from above, and my healing grace floods your heart when you turn to me. Everything I am is everything you need.

I am eager to share my life with you. The help that I give you is my life within you. My life is healing, strength, wisdom, and power. Lay hold of my life, eternal life, and you will find that everything changes. Come today. Come closer to me, for I am your Healer, your Father, your Hiding Place.

You kissed my heart with forgiveness, in spite of all I've done.
You've healed me inside and out from every disease.
You've rescued me from hell and saved my life.
You've crowned me with love and mercy.
You satisfy my every desire with good things.
You've supercharged my life so that I soar again
like a flying eagle in the sky!

PSALM 103:3–5

I desire your praises.

The revival of awakened hearts comes through praise. There is a secret power released when you bring high praises to me. The power that shut the mouths of lions was the power of praise through the faith-filled lips of my servant Daniel. You will see many breakthroughs and many enemies silenced as you bring your sacred praises to me. Angels are waiting to hear your chorus of praise. They join you in awe and wonder. Activate the power of heaven by the high praise of your lips.

Your praise is a weapon that has no rival. It rises through your sorrow. It celebrates your victory. It releases strength to you. It causes you to see clearly because it unveils the shadows of disbelief. Praise is courageous. It is joy that flows by faith. It is a declaration of truth when the enemy hits you with lies. It is a sacrifice of holy abandon. A pleasing offering in my sight. More than money or time or talents, I desire your praises. For in your praise, the glory descends.

Break forth with dancing!
Make music and sing God's praises with the rhythm of drums!
For he enjoys his faithful lovers.
He adorns the humble with his beauty
and he loves to give them the victory.

PSALM 149:3–4

Let worship awaken your destiny.

Receive me once again. Drink of me and take me in. Never say, "I have enough," for I always have more to give you. Like a cup receives the wine, receive my love as I pour it into your soul. Your worshiping heart releases the healing you long for, as you saturate yourself in the realm of my love and glory.

Soar into my glory with the wings of worship. Abandon your spirit to me as a sail abandons itself to the wind. Let faith reenergize your affections for me, as you set your gaze steadily upon my face. Though the love of many will grow cold, let it not be said of you. Instead, let your passion for me awaken your destiny, so you will discover my plans. I have chosen you and will never forget the adoring worship you have poured out before me. Shake off your soul passivity and lukewarm faith, for I am a God of consuming flames. I will complete this beautiful work inside your heart until you awaken with my likeness.

My heart, O God, is quiet and confident.
Now I can sing with passion your wonderful praises!
Awake, O my soul, with the music of his splendor-song!
Arise, my soul, and sing his praises!
My worship will awaken the dawn,
greeting the daybreak with my songs of praise!

PSALM 57:7–8

I love to speak to you.

In the silence, I will speak to you. Each morning, come and sit at my feet and learn from the wisdom of eternity. I love to share my heart with you. Many say they follow me but never still their souls to listen to my voice. It is time for you to hear me clearly, each day. The task I set before you will bring sweetness to your soul. Others will take note that you have been with me.

In the evening hours, come and I will whisper my living words into your spirit. Your night season will be a time of encounter, as my Spirit brings you heaven's grace and the dew of my presence. Listen carefully, as a lover listens to the Beloved. Listen and you will hear my voice and learn my ways.

I am the Shepherd who goes before His sheep, calling them by name, caring for them in love, and leading them in my ways. Now, come and listen for my whisper each day and know that I am your God.

All my words are clear and straightforward to everyone
who possesses spiritual understanding.
If you have an open mind, you will receive revelation-knowledge.

PROVERBS 8:9

Let me lead you away from stress.

The cares of life can clutter your mind and fog your vision, but only if you allow them to. Only if you give disillusionment your hand and allow it to drag you into its murky waters. Instead, close your eyes to the lies and look to me. I long to lead you higher, away from the torment of anxiety and stress. To give you eyes that see from my perspective. Eyes that see through the lies and disillusionment, straight into my truth. Truth that sets you free.

Give me every part of you, especially the areas that seem too painful to trust me with. It's only when you let go and release control to me that I can truly take over. When you lose sight of me, even for a moment, the enemy's smokescreen fills your vision. Stop paying attention to him! Look at me, my beloved. Focus on my truth. Allow yourself to rest upon the wings of my love, and I will carry you to the highest places of peace that you were created for.

Listen, my radiant one—if you ever lose sight of me,
just follow in my footsteps where I lead my lovers.
Come with your burdens and cares.
Come to the place near the sanctuary of my shepherds.

Song of Songs 1:8

I am here.

Your praise reaches me. Your worship touches my heart. I haven't withdrawn myself from you. I told you that I would never leave you; never forsake you. Believe me. Place all of your faith and trust in the truth of those words. In the power of my unmovable love for you.

I'm here with you, right now. If you cannot sense me, it's only because your awareness of my presence has been hindered by the cares of this world. Together, we will loosen the grip of those unrelenting distractions. It's as simple as handing each thought over to me and leaving them in my capable hands. Let them go. I didn't create you to collapse under the weight of them. Once you've declared my Word and my heart over these cares, trust me to faithfully take care of them. Then rejoice! Turn dread into an expectancy of my goodness. You were created for peace, that's why anxiety and stress feel so terrible. Once you've prayed and rejoiced, be still. Quiet your heart and look to me. Now you will know that I am here.

Hasn't he promised you,
"I will never leave you alone, never!
And I will not loosen my grip on your life!"

HEBREWS 13:5

Remain faithful to me.

The word I speak to you today is *endurance*. I call you to be faithful unto the end, even as I loved my disciples unto the end. The burden you carry must always be brought to the cross and left forever at my feet. Others won't understand the load you carry and the secret wounding of your soul, but I understand. Never compare yourself to another but bring your burdens to the One who cares. You will never be asked to carry more than you can endure, but it is often more than you expect. I call you to stretch your faith until it is greater than your burden.

Speak over your life this day, *I will endure all things for love.* And I will declare over you that I am your strength—the One who saves and makes all things new. In my presence is the grace, courage, power, and health you need to survive. You will not fail, neither will you stumble. For I will hold you in my love, even as I held Jesus in my love throughout His ordeals. I am with you and will exchange your weakness for my strength as you wait upon me.

You know that when your faith is tested
it stirs up power within you to endure all things.

JAMES 1:3

Pain becomes a fragrance of love.

Allow the wounding of your soul to bring you into deeper love—closer to me. Even when you feel disappointed, my love never fails. When you are wounded by love, my mercy still stands higher than the heavens. I call you to hold every experience of your life as sacred, and then you will discover my goodness and my power to work everything together for good. When you see momentary pain, I see blossoms of love beginning to open within you, yielding a sweeter fragrance.

I have called you to be a faithful carrier of my love. As you remain faithful to me, love grows within you. My love and my peace will be twin fruits from the Tree of Life, which sustain you and sweeten your joy. Let nothing deter you from your pursuit of my face. Let my presence seep into every cell and wash every part of you with healing love. Those who love me most, will be transformed the most. Let every opportunity that comes to you this day be the open doorway into my presence.

He comes closer,
even to the places where I hide.
He gazes into my soul,
peering through the portal
as he blossoms within my heart.
Song of Songs 2:9

February

Joy is your portion.

The time of unhindered joy is here. I am exposing the treachery of the enemy. He has come more than once to your door to entice you away from the joy of the Lord. Accusations have come, bad news has been proclaimed, disappointment has tried to enter your family, but I say to you, *my joy will get you through.* No longer will you allow discouragement to win the day, for I am the God of joyous breakthrough! Remember the gladness you have found as you served me and prayed to me? Remind yourself of the glory of my presence that you've enjoyed. This is only a foretaste of the bliss I have reserved for you.

Have no fear, for nothing can take from you the presence of my Spirit. Joy is your inheritance and the fruit of my Spirit. Taste the delicious fruit of joy, and sweetness will enter your inner being. The ecstasy of knowing me must triumph in this hour. The future will be nothing like your past, so leap for joy! Shout for joy! Dance with joy! For joy is your portion.

Lift up a great shout of joy to the Lord!
Go ahead and do it—everyone, everywhere!
As you serve him, be glad and worship him.
Sing your way into his presence with joy!

PSALM 100:1–2

My love will guide you.

D o you love me, my child? Is there a passion in your heart to do my will and follow my path? All of heaven comes to your aid when you set your heart to pursue me. My ears are tuned to the sound of your voice and the movement of your heart toward me.

Many on earth will value your life by what you do, your influence, your possessions, your ministry, but I value you and measure you by my love. My love will be your guide, when you do what I asked of my servant Matthew, "Come, follow me." As you walk with me, our hearts beat as one, my pleasure rests upon you, and you begin to learn of my ways.

My guidance is an expression of my love. Because I love you, I will set you on high where none can hinder or harm you. Because I love you, I lead you into pleasant paths and go before you. My love will guide you, my child.

"Because you have delighted in me as my great lover,
I will greatly protect you.
I will set you in a high place, safe and secure before my face.
I will answer your cry for help every time you pray,
and you will find and feel my presence
even in your time of pressure and trouble.
I will be your glorious hero and give you a feast.
You will be satisfied with a full life and with all that I do for you.
For you will enjoy the fullness of my salvation!"

PSALM 91:14–16

It is time to advance.

Move forward, my child. You have remained where you are, long enough. The time has come for you to advance. Don't look back. Take my hand and run with me into the abundance of my sweet promises. My kiss has awakened your heart and equipped you for this day.

As I promised Joshua, I promise you—that every place you set your foot will be yours. New territory is waiting. A calling beckons you onward. Faith is not stagnant, it is a movement—a dynamo that propels you into the fullness of my plan for you. Can you sense it? Hope is overtaking every thought and driving out discouragement. Together, we will run along the paths that once felt intimidating and scary. Nothing can stop you when I am with you and call you forward. Keep your eyes on me and carry the sound of love and mercy to those you meet. Run with me in passionate pursuit, and we will advance my kingdom together.

I admit that I haven't yet acquired the absolute fullness that I'm pursuing, but I run with passion into his *abundance* so that I may reach the purpose that Jesus Christ has called me to fulfill and wants me to discover. I don't depend on my own strength to accomplish this; however I do have one compelling focus: I forget all of the past as I fasten my heart to the future instead.

PHILIPPIANS 3:12–13

Let joy become your war cry.

K eep your soul at rest. Let nothing disturb the hiding place of victory within you. My gift is victory today. My promise is victory tomorrow. How you rest in this promise of victory will determine your level of peace and joy, today and in the future. Did I not say to my disciples in the midst of their storm, "Be brave and don't be afraid. I am here!" (Matthew 14:27)? These are the same words I say to you today. Shout for joy! Shake off discouragement. Do all that I have called you to do with sacred delight, for I am blessing you beyond measure; more than a hundredfold.

Let your joyous laughter be heard in your home and in the midst of trials. Laugh in the face of adversity. Let joy become your war cry! Hold nothing back, for the enemy is threatened when you taste of my joy and enter my gladness. Rejoice, rejoice, rejoice! Then watch what I will do to change your environment. Joy will launch you into the new place I'm calling you to. Today is the day made for you, so rejoice and be filled with gladness, for I am your God!

My heart and soul explode with joy—full of glory!
Even my body will rest confident and secure.

PSALM 16:9

You are my house of glory.

Just as a builder lays a foundation for a large strong house, I have laid a deep foundation in your life. This foundation is built upon the Rock of Truth. I have set your walls and strengthened your being. You will be a stronghold of my presence, and I will display you to the world as my beautiful house of glory!

Sacred blood I gave for you. Holy hands were opened to receive the nails that bore your sin. Beautiful feet that walked the streets of Jerusalem were pierced so that you would walk the streets of holiness with me. I will bring my plans to pass. My longings for your life will be fulfilled. Do not look at the structure and say that it is inferior. Look at my wisdom and say, "You do all things well."

Even now, I am preparing the next steps of your journey. I am building you into a house of glory, that I might show my overcoming, conquering strength on your behalf. Slowly and carefully, as the Master Builder, I have constructed you and built you up. The superstructure is now seen, and I will finish what I have begun.

We are coworkers with God and you are God's cultivated garden, the house he is building. God has given me unique gifts as a skilled master builder who lays a good foundation.

1 Corinthians 3:9–10

Give me your weakness.

When you see something inside your soul that you lack, focus on me. I am to be the center on which your life turns. My love erases and covers a multitude of sins. When my Spirit fills you, every other thing is swept away and forgotten. This is how my persecuted ones endure—they set their focus on my love.

Set your heart on me, not on the areas where you feel you've fallen short. Remember the price I paid to purchase your soul. I have given my Son for you and filled you with the glory of resurrection power. When you feel that I am distant, bathe your heart once again in my love and push aside the lies that would deceive you. I know you. I understand the moving of your heart. The pleasure I find in you is not because of your works, but because of your love. Having never seen me, you still love me. When you set your gaze on things above and away from your weaknesses, I'm stirred to bring you into greater measures of my love and holiness. I will never leave you nor diminish the strength of my love toward you.

He canceled out every legal violation we had on our record and the old arrest warrant that stood to indict us. He erased it all—our sins, our stained soul—he deleted it all *and they cannot be retrieved*! Everything we once were in Adam has been placed onto his cross and nailed permanently there as a public display of cancellation.

COLOSSIANS 2:14

My beauty is all around you.

All around you are signs of my love, wisdom, creativity, and beauty. Those who look with expectancy will discover them. My joy can be heard in laughter's pulse. My whispers stir the rustling leaves on an autumn day. The light of my face radiates through every sunrise, and I paint the sunset skies with colors of my love. My decrees of breakthrough, crash upon the waves.

In voice, music, the gliding of a writer's pen, an artist's stroke, and the movement of dance—each facet of creative expression releases a part of me. The breath you breathe, the dreams you dream, the compassion received through the comfort of another—you will find traces of my love everywhere you look. Taste and see that I am good.

I not only surround you, I fill you. I have poured my glory into vessels of flesh and blood. The expressions of your amazement and joy, as you ponder my love, delight me. This is how life with me is meant to be—captivating, delightful, and exciting. I am the majestic Lord of all creation. Come, find me in the wonder.

They were together—face-to-face, in the very beginning.
And through his creative inspiration
this Living Expression made all things,
for nothing has existence apart from him!
Life came into being because of him,
for his life is light for all humanity.
And this Living Expression is the Light that bursts through gloom—
the Light that darkness could not diminish!

JOHN 1:2–5

I am your armor of power.

Listen to my words, child of mine, and I will guard and protect you from all forms of evil. Your true calling is to be an overcomer. To be an overcomer means you will be challenged. Darkness is set against the church and against you as my trusting child. But I am the Light that will split open the darkness and bring my victory. Have I not promised to deliver you and to be your wrap-around Shield? Focus on this shield of victory and not the darkness of evil that shrouds the nations. Be filled with delight as you walk in my light, and I will be the answer to earth's evil.

Be faithful to me and stand true when you hear of others who fall. You will be an overcoming witness to many, so take my words as your weapon this day. You will not give in to the darkness and weariness that is coming over my saints, but you will prevail, for I am the God of strength and the Source of mighty power. Be strong, my overcoming one, and you will see my days of miracles.

I have saved these most important truths for last: Be supernaturally infused with strength through your life-union with the Lord Jesus. Stand victorious with the force of his explosive power flowing in and through you. Put on God's complete set of armor provided for us, so that you will be protected as you fight against the evil strategies of the accuser!

EPHESIANS 6:10–11

Never doubt my conquering love.

M any times, you have asked, *Why does this take so long?* I tell you today, believe in my wise plan, look to me, and trust in my conquering love. My power and grace will rise up within you, and what seems impossible will be lifted from you. Your limitations are invitations for my power to deliver. I will never fail or disappoint you. My promises are rainbows of hope that cover your life—declarations of truth that are greater than heartache. Your tears are liquid words that I read and understand. Never doubt my conquering love for you.

The shining of my love upon you is the light that guides, warms, nourishes, and strengthens. Turn your heart to this light, and I will pull the "weeds" from your garden that hinder our fruit. When you turn to me, I will accomplish what all your striving has not—I will change you from the inside out. I am patient and kind, and there is so much more compassion in my heart toward you than you have realized. You are not a disappointment to me, but a delight!

Lord, even when your path takes me through
the valley of deepest darkness,
fear will never conquer me, for you already have!
You remain close to me and lead me through it all the way.
Your authority is my strength and my peace.
The comfort of your love takes away my fear.
I'll never be lonely, for you are near.

PSALM 23:4

In me you will overcome.

Hold tightly to every promise that I have given you. Write my words upon your heart and fill your mind with my wisdom, for the days ahead will be more than you expect. For both glory and shaking are upon you. The more severe the shaking of your circumstances, the clearer my invitation to partake of my glory. The storms are coming, but they will bring forth my new man, my new wine, and my new expression of grace for you.

You will overcome all things, for I am with you. Bring my word of overcoming grace to others, for their hearts are now ready to hear the song of triumph. Place my armor on your soul and go forth to see your enemies vanquished. Wear my righteousness over your heart. Fill your mind with my delivering power. Let my good news cover your feet and lead your steps. My truth will keep you strong, and my sword of power will energize your every breath.

Every child of God overcomes the world, for our faith is the victorious power that triumphs over the world. So who are the world conquerors, defeating its power? Those who believe that Jesus is the Son of God.

1 JOHN 5:4–5

Discover who I've made you to be.

Come and partake of a new reality—the reality of life in me. Fill your spirit with my truth and life, and you will be transformed from the inside out. You have lived in your mind; now live in my Spirit.

The ways of man cannot bring you the joy you desire—the joys of heaven. I am calling you to leave behind the reasoning of this world, the opinions and traditions of men, and come into true life with me. The realm of the Holy Spirit has been opened by my grace, so that you can know me, not in your mind but with your spirit. My Spirit will give you gifts, fruit, wisdom, and power. Live in my Spirit, and you will find your true destiny.

If you ask, I will bring you deeper understanding of my ways. If you ask for life, I will not bring you confusion. If you ask for living bread, I will not give you anything less than my best. You can trust me, so ask, and you will receive the fullness of my Spirit. Live in my Spirit, and you will discover who I have made you to be.

"If imperfect parents know how to lovingly take care of their children and give them what they need, how much more will the perfect heavenly Father give the Holy Spirit's fullness when his children ask him."

LUKE 11:13

Come into my glory.

Lamb's blood has gone before you, my child. A blood-sprinkled path has been inaugurated and dedicated for you. I laid aside my robes of glory to come and purchase you with my blood. Come into my glory! Expect a supernatural encounter in your life, for heaven's gates are open to you, and the joy of my presence awaits.

Many are content to remain outside, singing songs of praise, busy with a flurry of activities in my name, yet all the time heaven's gates are opened wide. I offer you throne-room encounters. I long to surprise you with my tangible presence. Let us gaze at each other, face-to-face. Won't you come? Rest your weary soul, cease from striving to enter in, and simply come. The festive celebration awaits you! The feast of love has been prepared for my children. Your Father invites, yes, beckons you to come! The call to enter means all has been set into place, every veil taken away, and every obstacle to your faith has been removed. Heaven's gates are open to you. Come into my glory!

We are brothers and sisters in God's family because of the blood of Jesus, and he welcomes us to come right into the most holy sanctuary in the heavenly realm—boldly and with no hesitation. For he has dedicated a new, life-giving way for us to approach God. For just as the veil was torn in two, Jesus' body was torn open to give us free and fresh access to him!

HEBREWS 10:19–20

Commune with me in glory.

The table of fellowship has been prepared. Come, dine with me and enter into a greater joy—the joy of communion with the Holy Spirit. The highest joy and most profitable path will be found by living in my Spirit. Prayer is the path into my presence. Sacred blood is all the virtue that is required to enter in. For I have washed you, bathed you in my goodness, and cleansed the deepest place of your heart. There is no spot in you. You are my ready worshiper. You are my beloved.

As you draw near to me, your bridegroom King, your heart swells with expectancy and faith. You no longer stare at the beauty of your bridal gown, but your gaze becomes consumed with the brilliance of my face. My glory reminds you that it's not your holiness, but my grace that brings you in. Come closer and closer to me, and I will come closer to you. Come and enter into a bliss that only my lovers experience. Come into my cloud-filled chamber, and I will cause all my goodness to pass before your eyes. Come and bring me joy, by communing with me.

There is nothing between you and Father God, for he sees you as holy, flawless, and restored, if indeed you continue to advance in faith, assured of a firm foundation to grow upon.

COLOSSIANS 1:22–23

I am your provider.

I am your miracle Provider. I give you all that you need to follow me, to live in joy, and to excel. Count your blessings: joy unlimited, peace that prevails over every shadow, and hope that will never dim. I give you the wealth of eternity, for I live within your heart. I have made you rich!

There is no limit to my power to work on your behalf. You will never ask something of me that goes beyond my ability to accomplish. All that you ask, I will give, as you come wrapped in my Son. Many focus on their limitations, on what they feel is missing, but I call you to set your gaze upon me and my limitless grace to provide. Is your family beyond this grace? Is my power and love enough to change them? Is your financial lack beyond my ability to rectify? I have made you rich, and your wealth is not hidden. It is found in my Son. He made Himself poor so that through His "poverty" you might be made rich. The pastures of grace await you. Come and take your delight in the glory of my grace.

Every spiritual blessing in the heavenly realm has already been lavished upon us as a love gift from our wonderful heavenly Father, the Father of our Lord Jesus—all because he sees us wrapped into Christ. This is why we celebrate him with all our hearts!

EPHESIANS 1:3

Run with me.

I have called you to be mine, to enjoy me, to walk with me, to run with me. I am the One who set you apart from your mother's womb and brought you to myself. My hand has been upon your life from the day you were born, my chosen one. Inside of your soul, I have placed a calling, a voice that invites you to come close to me. When your heart responds, you find your true self, your divine destiny. Never back away from this calling. Others may, but you cannot.

I have drawn you to my side and won your heart over and over. The sacred chamber of intimacy has become your hiding place. But today, I call you to run with me. The days are getting darker for those who do not know me. There are many lives you will touch, and many changes will come because of the light of my Son within you. So, run. Run with me, and I will take you to the higher places that you've not been before. Run. Be ready at all times. Be my voice to the nations and my light to the world.

Suddenly my longings transported me.
My divine desire brought me next to my beloved prince,
sitting with him in his royal chariot.
We were lifted up together!

SONG OF SONGS 6:12

I will never let you go.

In your days of trouble and your days of glory, in your days of testing and your days of triumph—hold on to me! The changes will now come more swiftly than you have imagined. That which looms before you may challenge your faith, but hold on to me!

Those who trust in me see miracles. In these days of intense struggle, when it looks like darkness is winning and your light is growing dim, hold on to me!

I have taught you many things. You've learned that walking with me is more valuable and pleasing than your comforts. You've sacrificed your plans for mine and given me the reins of your heart. I am satisfied with your tender surrender. You have trusted my ways, even when they were nothing but a mystery. Many times, you bowed your heart in worship. You grew in grace and took giant leaps of faith. Keep moving into my heart, even as things shift all around. I am pleased to be your Father and your God. Hold on to me, for I hold on to you and will never let you go.

Hold on to loyal love and don't let go,
and be faithful to all that you've been taught.
PROVERBS 3:3

I will not disappoint you.

I have seen your love, your desire to please me. Many times, you have chosen me above all else, and I am pleased. But you are growing weary. You have waited upon me, and I say keep waiting on me. I will not disappoint you.

What you call delay, I call preparation. Many times, I am at work behind the scenes, yet you cannot discern it. I am preparing others so that your destiny may be fulfilled, and I am preparing you, even as I prepared Joseph for his season of promotion. Never judge my works by what your eyes see, but by the promises I have made to you. Hold tightly to those promises. Remind yourself of them often and never stop believing. Don't let weariness cause you to give up. My timing is perfect. As you wait on me and keep me first, I unfold my glorious plans for your life. I will make it happen and show you my perfection. I *will* fulfill my word, and your eyes *will* see the miracles of my hand.

Lord, I have always trusted in your kindness, *so answer me*.
I will yet celebrate with passion and joy
when your salvation lifts me up.
I will sing my song of joy to you, the Most High,
for in all of this you have strengthened my soul.

PSALM 13:5–6

Your purpose is found in me.

Y ou have asked me, "When will I find my destiny and true purpose for my life?" I tell you, now is the time for you to run with me. For out of intimacy, destiny is released. When you join your heart to mine, purpose is realized. As you lean in to my love, your will entwines with mine and my glory becomes evident, even in seasons of waiting.

Trust in me and lay aside every anxiety and form of impatience. Do not strive in your flesh or look to others to do for you, what only I can do. Your help comes from me, and I will bring those who are necessary to assist you in your call. Expect my miracles to come to pass in your life, for I am the Father of Love. Even as my calling brought Abraham through the mysteries of my will, you, likewise, will be amazed at how I bring to pass the prophetic destiny of your life. What you see today, will be changed in a moment. The time has come for dramatic and rapid changes in your life, because you have sought me above all else.

Can you not discern this new day of destiny
breaking forth around you?
The early signs of my purposes and plans are bursting forth.
The budding vines of new life are now blooming everywhere.
The fragrance of their flowers whispers,
"There is change in the air."
Arise, my love, my beautiful companion,
and run with me to the higher place.
For now is the time to arise and come away with me.

SONG OF SONGS 2:13

Come to my feast.

Many times, you have thought, "Lord, if only I could have been one of the disciples who walked with you, witnessed your miracles, and experienced your presence as you walked the earth. I wish I could have been on the hillside when you multiplied bread and fish and heard the words of grace and love that fell from your lips." But I say to you, I am in you, and we have become one. Come to my feast. A feast of love greater than you have ever known. Greater than you could have known, as I walked the earth. It's a spiritual feast of two who have become one. Drink from the cup of bliss, the cup poured out for you.

Did I not promise that if you hear my voice, my gentle knock on the door of your heart, and open the door, I will come in and bring a feast? Come today, and feast on my love. It's a wedding feast of the bride and the Bridegroom. It will satisfy every longing in your heart. So, come and let your heart be at peace. My divine fullness will be more than enough.

No one abuses his own body but pampers it—serving and satisfying its needs. That's exactly what Christ does for his church! *He serves and satisfies us* as members of his body.

Ephesians 5:29–30

The flow of my Spirit is in you.

I have made you into my holy dwelling place. I have cleansed your heart and made you pure in my eyes. My holiness lives in you, for my Spirit lives in you. No evil can touch you, when you allow me to fill you with the abundance of my love and power. When I reign as King of your life, your heart becomes the chamber room of my glory. I will finish the beautiful work I have begun in you!

You are now a vessel fashioned for purity and power. Holiness is not something you can achieve or produce on your own. It does not originate with man, but it is a flow of my Spirit within you. What I cleanse, I fill. And what I fill is made holy. Remember how I have worked in your life through your journey with me. I strengthened you in weakness and held you in your pain. Many times, I have lifted you higher and redeemed your days, filling them with joy. I never leave you. Never forsake you. Always keep you close. The flow of my Spirit within you has filled you with all you need to live an abundant life—holy and pure in my sight.

I continue to pray for your love to grow and increase beyond measure, bringing you into the rich revelation of spiritual insight in all things. This will enable you to choose the most excellent way of all—becoming pure and without offense until the unveiling of Christ.

PHILIPPIANS 1:9–10

I will heal cities.

A great and glorious move of my Spirit is imminent. When your hearts break open to me, the heavens break open over you! Nothing will hinder my strong arm as my Spirit penetrates darkness. Even as I brought the city of Nineveh to repentance and conversion, so I will blanket entire cities with my glory! You will see what I can do in the seemingly prevailing darkness.

Believe, and you will see! The move of my Spirit means that all things are possible. Even the media will broadcast the miracles of my hand to the nations. The Son of Glory will yet be famous again for His mighty works! Worship and prayer will bring an atmosphere of glory over the cities. One city will remain in darkness while another bursts forth with light, life, and love! I am the God who is able. Many have longed to see what you will witness. A hunger for my presence will consume you as I blanket cities with my glory.

Ask, and I will give you cities of the nations as your inheritance! Ask in faith, for nothing is impossible with me! Healing and salvation will flow in the cities of your nation.

Display your strength, God, and we'll be strong!
For your miracles have made us who we are.
Lord, do it again,
and parade from your temple your mighty power.
By your command even kings will bring gifts to you.

PSALM 68:28–29

Peace is my gift to you.

When anxiety fights to take hold of your heart, and chaos tries to consume your atmosphere, invite me to be your peace. When you have no strength to step beyond the line of stress that the enemy has drawn, bow before my presence, and I will come running. I will carry you to safety. I will be your Jehovah-Shalom. I will give you peace that contradicts what your mind can comprehend.

When all you can do is breathe, reaching for me with weary, shaking hands, it is enough. You don't have to fight for my attention. You have it. I am here with you, right now. I am the Prince of Peace. My love for you is powerful enough to consume every angst. Hopelessness, confusion, and fear cannot exist in my presence. When you're bowed low, simply yielded in full surrender, as I unglue the heaviness that tries to bind your soul. My love will still your anxious soul. Peace is my gift to you.

Everything I've taught you is so that the peace which is in me will be in you and will give you great confidence as you rest in me. For in this unbelieving world you will experience trouble and sorrows, but you must be courageous, for I have conquered the world!

JOHN 16:33

I breathe life into your dreams.

I long to give you the desires that resonate with mine. Don't question what burns so deeply in your heart, as if you need my permission to dream extravagantly. As my child, filled with my Spirit, your will entwines with mine. I enjoy watching your dreams come to pass.

The waiting period between the spark of an idea and the culmination is seldom easy or short. Much like a baby formed within its mother's womb, it must be nurtured, loved, and birthed. Don't give up, if it's taking longer than expected. Use this time to grow in faith and intimacy with me. Cover your dreams in prayer. Pour into them with expectation. Be a good steward of your desires and ask me how you can take steps toward their fulfillment. I am wisdom and creativity, and I long to share them with you. I hold the favor you need. I release provision. If one door closes, praise me for the other that I will open. I am the Resurrection and the Life. The explosive reawakening of every dead dream.

Make God the utmost delight and pleasure of your life,
and he will provide for you what you desire the most.
Give God the right to direct your life,
and as you trust him along the way
you'll find he pulled it off perfectly!

PSALM 37:4–5

Discover the power of a grateful heart.

Greater than any force known to man is the power I release when you praise me. The power of gratitude has been undervalued by my people. As you give me thanks, I refine your soul and remove regret from your life. I will free you when you give me thanks. The more satisfied you are with me, the more freedom from pain I bring.

To receive my blessings, yet never give me thanks, is the mark of a selfish heart. To receive my blessings and be consumed with gratitude are marks of a true worshiper. Many are like those who grumbled to Moses in the wilderness. Yet even as they grumbled, my glory cloud was over their heads. They looked at man and not at me. Ingratitude is a disease that is easily spread among my people. But praises will break the curse, lift the veil, open the heavens, and provide miracles, even in a wilderness. I call you to a life of gratitude. I long for you to discover the power of a grateful heart.

Let everyone thank God, for he is good, and he is easy to please!
His tender love for us continues on forever!
Give thanks to God, our King over all gods!
His tender love for us continues on forever!

PSALM 136:1–2

I will love you into victory.

My love for you is endless. It endures beyond the days of your life and finds its completion in eternity. My love has stepped out of heaven and rested upon your life. As you seek more of me, I will intensify your experience of my love. Is there something in front of you that looks impossible? Are the hearts of others unyielding to me? Is your family surrounded by difficulty and stress? I will do the impossible for you, for my love will win the day!

The burdens you carry must be laid down. Exchange them for my easy yoke and learn of me. Let faith remind you that all things are possible with me. Allow grace to refresh and empower you as you worship in my presence. Watch as my omnipotence floods your impossibility and rearranges your circumstances. I will enrich your soul, enflame your heart, and give you a greater joy. I will do the impossible for you, for you are the focus of my attention and the apple of my eye. I will love you into victory.

Jesus said to him, "What do you mean 'if'?
If you are able to believe,
all things are possible to the believer."

MARK 9:23

I will be your great reward.

Many have chosen the path of righteousness, only to discover that there is no room on the path for self-promotion and self-praise. It takes courage to follow me. To leave behind all that hinders our relationship. To follow me and find that I am enough. Come, follow me, and you will be made into my likeness.

You are an heir of the kingdom—all my promises to you will come to pass. Glory, ever-increasing glory, will surround you, as you walk in kingdom reality. To follow me is not merely leaving everything; it is gaining everything. Set your gaze on me. Come into my sacred chamber, where every sacrifice becomes sweeter than honey, and every loss invites more of me. Move forward without fear, and I will be your great reward! It is more than a choice; it is courage that must fill your heart as you look upon the horizon with faith. Never fear what is to come, for I am the One who was, who is, and who is to come!

"Listen to my words," Jesus said. "Anyone who leaves his home behind and chooses me over children, parents, family, and possessions, all for the sake of the gospel, it will come back to him a hundred times as much in this lifetime—homes, family, mothers, brothers, sisters, children, possessions—along with persecutions. And in the age to come, he will inherit eternal life."

MARK 10:29–30

Fix your eyes on me.

Why are you impressed with these battles raging against your soul, as if I'm not with you in the midst of them? Though you are battle weary, I will be your strength. I have all the grace you need to stand. To breathe again. To see things from my perspective and align your thoughts and words with mine. You're distracted, my child, and it's time to completely release your impossible situation into my capable hands.

I remind you over and over—I am the God of impossibility. Nothing is too hard for me! Lean in to my arms. Let me be your strength when you have none. Let me breathe into every cell and every thought. Invite me to illuminate every lie with my unshakable truth. Choose to be impressed with my omnipotence, more than your problem. Bring me your analyzing and over-thinking as an offering of total abandon and trust. Fix your eyes on me and you will feel me washing away the debris of doubt and frustration. Sing your highest praise and choose to believe, despite what you see.

I pray that he would unveil within you the unlimited riches of his glory and favor until supernatural strength floods your innermost being with his divine might and explosive power. Then, by constantly using your faith, the life of Christ will be released deep inside you, and the resting place of his love will become the very source and root of your life.

EPHESIANS 3:16–17

Reflect me with your fruit.

I am the Fruit-Bearing Vine, and you are my branches, filled with my life. I call you to bear fruit for the glory of my Father. This fruit is produced not by religious striving or human manufacture, but by the fruit of my Spirit. I call you to reflect me with the fruit that my Spirit produces through you.

The great strength of my Spirit will flow through you as you offer me your tender heart. Apart from me, your works are powerless. Your good deeds are only filled with power as you are filled with my Spirit. Be saturated to overflowing with my Spirit, and your very life will be a branch upon the Tree of Life.

Be known as a person of tenderness before God. Many want to be correct, but I want you to be fruitful—overflowing with character and purity of heart. True beauty will enter your soul as you walk in the kindness and love of my Spirit. Others will see your beautiful life and know that it is the Father who is filling you with grace.

"So you must remain in life-union with me, for I remain in life-union with you. For as a branch severed from the vine will not bear fruit, so your life will be fruitless unless you live your life intimately joined to mine. I am the sprouting vine and you're my branches. As you live in union with me as your source, fruitfulness will stream from within you—but when you live separated from me you are powerless."

JOHN 15:4–5

Surrender to the silence.

There are times I need you to be vigilant and courageous. Times when your declarations of faith and prayers of intercession make all the difference. But then there are times I call you to sit with me beside the still waters, so I can refresh your soul. Never underestimate the importance of stillness, for it is in these quiet times that I am doing a deep work in you.

Come and sit with me. Place every worry in my care. Have no agenda other than to find my ever-present love. To soak in my presence. Let me be God for you—the One who is all-knowing and all powerful. The One who can do more in one second to solve your problems than you can in years. I am the Prince of Peace, and as you resign yourself to my peace that passes understanding, you will recognize how powerfully I have been working on your behalf, even when you weren't aware. I never asked you to strive for anything other than striving to enter my rest. Surrender to the silence of my presence. Experience the rest that comes by trusting me.

We must give our all and be eager to experience this faith-rest life, so that no one falls short by following the same pattern of doubt and unbelief.

HEBREWS 4:11

March

Love is born when I draw near.

Bring your heart before me, and I will deepen your love. Loving others seems difficult when you are distant and detached from my presence. When I draw near, love is born. Everything that dilutes the power of my love, disappears when I am near. Love flows from my presence and reaches like a river to the lowest place. Bring your heart closer, and I will deepen your love.

The process I've taken you through is so that my love will be greater than your disappointment. Many react out of a heart filled with pain to the difficulties of life. I promise you, my love will win if you will turn to me when others walk away. A brilliant mind is not sufficient to carry this love that surpasses understanding. Human logic will leave you empty when you stand before the fire of my love. My flame needs no fuel, nothing of man, for it is a self-replenishing fire. I will bring you deeper into my ways as the fire burns up all that hinders love. Bring your heart before me now, and I will take you to the place where love is born.

Rivers of pain and persecution
will never extinguish this flame.
Endless floods will be unable
to quench this raging fire that burns within you.
Everything will be consumed.
It will stop at nothing
as you yield everything to this furious fire
until it won't even seem to you like a sacrifice anymore.

SONG OF SONGS 8:7

Release your striving.

I have taught you in the secret place, and you have learned the ways of my Spirit. I remind you this day: do not strive but rest your heart in the quietness, and I will do what you cannot. Anxiety and striving are the enemies of your peace. When I give you a task, I give you the grace to accomplish it. I never lead you into failure or give you a mission only to make you fall. I will strengthen you in the quiet place and bring my transcendent presence to calm your soul.

When you know me, you will no longer strive to be better or strive to be loved. When you experience my endless compassion, you will learn to forgive. To strive is to leave my strength and embrace the cares of life. To refuse striving means you will enter into the lifestyle of faith-rest that I give to all who love me. Faith rests in hope. So, my child, this is the day of Sabbath joy, when you will enter into the realm of my kingdom. Know that I will never fail you or disappoint you.

For those of us who believe, faith activates the promise and we experience the realm of confident rest!

HEBREWS 4:3

I call you to a higher way of life.

call you to love. I call you to joy. I call you to peace and gentleness. I encourage you in the ways of kindness, meekness, and self-control. As you walk according to this plan, my glory floods you with the divine power to live in this higher realm of life. As you yield yourself, and your actions, you find that my ways are the most fulfilling. You will discover your life has become a fruitful vine.

My glorious one, I am your God. I will bring my will to pass, as you yield your all to me. As you live a life of surrender, sacrificing your will for mine, my ways become your joy. Leave behind what clings to your soul, in order to embrace the higher way of life. Cleave to me and I will purify your affections.

Lord, direct me throughout my journey
so I can experience your plans for my life.
Reveal the life-paths that are pleasing to you.
Escort me along the way; take me by the hand and teach me.
For you are the God of my increasing salvation;
I have wrapped my heart into yours!

PSALM 25:4–5

My presence qualifies you.

I have longed to pour out upon you even more of my love and power. Can't you see that I have designed you to be a carrier of my glory? Come before me and empty your heart—pour it out at my feet, and I will fill you with such delight and joy that you will not be able to contain it. For I am building my church through the glory of my presence.

My plans for your life extend beyond your view, beyond your understanding. You see what is in front of you today, but I have gone into your future and know the good things that will unfold before you. Never doubt that your days are in my hands. This is the time for your destiny to become clear and your purpose to be unveiled. Do not be afraid of what comes, for what comes to you will be more of me. Stand in my presence until you know that I am your strength. Rest in me, and watch me fill you, protect you, and make you strong. My presence alone qualifies and equips you to do what most only dare to dream.

> The Lord alone is our radiant hope
> and we trust in him with all our hearts.
> His wrap-around presence will strengthen us.
>
> PSALM 33:20

I am your burden bearer.

C ome to me and rest, my beloved one. I know your responsibilities are many, and I know the burdens you carry are great. Call me your shepherd, and I will carry you. Call me your friend, and I will listen to your heart's cry. Call me your Redeemer, and I will bring restoration to your soul.

Busying yourself with many things will bring distraction and discouragement. The expectations of others will drown out my song of grace over your life. Call me your strength, and my invisible power will be seen in your life.

Never be limited by feelings of weakness. I know the burdens you carry, burdens of past failures and the fear of inadequacy as you ponder your future. I am here with you this very moment to be more than a companion—I will be the Lord of love and the God of every tender mercy. I long to show you that my grace is more than enough. Rise from the place of despair and betrayal and come to me. Call me your burden bearer and leave all of your burdens at my feet. You will rise up with strength and be surrounded with peace.

He offers a resting place for me in his luxurious love.
His tracks take me to an oasis of peace, the quiet brook of bliss.
That's where he restores and revives my life.
He opens before me pathways to God's pleasure
and leads me along in his footsteps of righteousness
so that I can bring honor to his name.

PSALM 23:2–3

Humility paves the way.

My people are unique, called out from the darkness of the world to walk in my living light. Your calling is a high calling, my child, for a divine trust has been given to you. All things are yours in life and eternity. Blessings you will never be able to number have been deposited into you. Humility will open the way to discover all that I am and all that I have given to you.

Meekness is enthroned, for the Lamb reigns over all. Learn of Him. Be joined to Him, and humility will open the way. I will oppose the pride of humanity, but there is a day in store when the humble of heart will be exalted, and the prideful and arrogant will be brought low. Your calling is never to judge what I am doing, but to humbly join me in and be one with me. I will dwell with those who tremble at my Word. I will fill those who have made room for my glory. Let these words pierce your heart today, for humility will open the way to my presence. Humility unlocks the doors of understanding and brings you through the gates of wisdom.

"Learn this well: Unless you dramatically change your way of thinking and become teachable, and learn about heaven's kingdom realm with the wide-eyed wonder of a child, you will never be able to enter in. Whoever continually humbles himself to become like this gentle child is the greatest one in heaven's kingdom realm."

MATTHEW 18:3–4

You are protected in my love.

I have wrapped my glory-robe around your soul, and nothing will harm you. Even when the powers of darkness are around you on every side, you can be strong. Gates of darkness will not prevail when I am near you. The days of heaven on earth are at hand. The days of the mighty moving of my Spirit will soon be seen by all. My powerful wind will blow away the clouds of doubt that have been over your mind and your heart. My glory-wind will make your enemies scatter, and you will stand complete and secure.

Though fear will come, it will not conquer you, for I have made you an overcomer. Trust me and watch me fight for you when you're weak. Lean in to my heart and watch my love win every battle. I have become your Light and your Salvation. You are protected in my love. I have gone before you and made your way clear and your pathway secure, for I am your Father.

The name of the Lord is blessed and lifted high!
For his marvelous miracle of mercy protected me
when I was overwhelmed by my enemies.

PSALM 31:21

I've seen it all.

Dearest one, I've watched as you've thanked our Father for me and all I've done for you, but did you know that I thank Him for you? You are His love gift to me. You keep my Word and walk in my ways, even when the light is dim and uncertainty surrounds you. As you walk along the highway of praise, I rejoice with you. I see that you long to be a doer of my Word and not just a hearer. I watch your faithfulness, even in that which is little, as you do your tasks with your heart set upon me.

Nothing you've done has gone unnoticed. Every movement of your heart toward me is precious in my sight. I've watched as you obeyed me in difficulty. I've celebrated as you overcame the temptations that tried to pull you away. I've rejoiced with you as you discovered the power of your faith. You have surrendered your all, time and time again. You've come to me, and you are mine—wonderfully, beautifully, and fearfully made.

Keep your thoughts continually fixed on all that is authentic and real, honorable and admirable, beautiful and respectful, pure and holy, merciful and kind. And fasten your thoughts on every glorious work of God, praising him always.

PHILIPPIANS 4:8

You will be amazed by what I do.

The time has come for you to ascend into a new realm. The old way of thinking must be abandoned and surrendered to the new life of my Spirit. My ways are not your ways. Man's ways are centered around power and influence. My ways are paths of love that will mystify and bewilder even the brightest of men. The ways of the Spirit are unseen yet mighty. Spirit-life is power and wisdom that makes the simple, wise. You will be amazed by what I will do with your life as you surrender to my ways.

My thoughts are not your thoughts. My Holy Spirit is the Divine Intelligence that moves in the hearts of my people to bring them to the fountain of truth. Many debate and argue, trying to prove their point. But my voice calls out to you in the silence and will teach you wisdom that cannot be given by man. The thoughts I have for you will bring you joy and comfort, for I hold you in my heart as my dearest treasure. You will not understand what I am about to do, but you *will* be amazed as my glory unfolds within you, giving you revelation light, for you have the mind of Christ.

Why fool yourself and live under an illusion? Make no mistake about it, if anyone thinks he is wise by the world's standards, he will be made wiser by being a fool for God!

1 Corinthians 3:18

Let worry be far from you.

My Word is full of promises for you. Every promise I make is as sure as tomorrow's sunrise. I have set all things in place to cause you to advance in my ways. Every word I speak has been refined seven times and found to be trustworthy and dependable. Rest in my promises and you will succeed. What will defeat you? Is it worry that troubles you? I call you to a life free from worry and anxious care. You are not to worry about anything—not one thing.

Dive into my Word and feast upon these promises. Remind yourself who I am and the power I have. Remember, not only am I able to help you, but I *want* to help you. However, I want you to believe it. I want you to feel the love that I have for you. I want you to think back to the many times I've come through for you. You will come through! Not only will you see my promises come to pass, you will be a testimony of my faithfulness, encouraging others on their journey.

"Your faith in me has given you life. Now you may leave and walk in the ways of peace."

LUKE 7:50

Step closer to my eternal flame.

My kingdom is alive. Always growing. It blossoms from deep within you, producing faith, gratitude, and unparalleled beauty. As you lay hold of eternal life, it manifests with an undiminished hope. Go forward. Step closer to the eternal flame. Learn the lesson of my servants, Paul and Silas, who found a sanctuary of praise even in a prison cell. Lift up your voice with no thought of the past, and set your heart on the joy that is before you. Let nothing silence your songs of praise and let nothing stand in your way as you pursue the quest for more of my love.

My kingdom is paved with love. Come. Be lost in wonder. Be overwhelmed in my presence. Be tender in heart as you come before me. I will show you things that eyes have never seen nor ears have ever heard. The revelation secrets of my kingdom, I have given to you. What wealth is yours! Come, as Moses came to my burning presence, and be overwhelmed in the flames of holiness. What glory you will experience, as my eternal flame burns brightly in you.

Fasten me upon your heart as a seal of fire forevermore.
This living, consuming flame
will seal you as my prisoner of love.
My passion is stronger
than the chains of death and the grave,
all consuming as the very flashes of fire
from the burning heart of God.
Place this fierce, unrelenting fire over your entire being.

SONG OF SONGS 8:6

A new joy is yours.

Today, I bring you living-understanding, living-wisdom, and grace that moves with the rhythm of your breath. These gifts come with bubbling joy—the mercy kiss of my Spirit who guides you.

A new joy is yours! Joy that comes when you know that every step you take, I have planned before you were born. Before you start to speak, I know every sentence that will come from your mouth. Before you go on a journey, I have gone before you to make your steps firm and faithful to my ways. I release to you the joy of being guided by my Spirit. Wait upon me, and I will show you the steps to take. When you turn to the right, you will hear my whisper in your heart saying, "Yes, this is the way you are to walk." Supernatural guidance will end the pain of the past. Your heart will taste the joys set before you in this season of new beginnings. Your life will bring me praise and show my glory. A new joy is yours today, as you say, "Yes, Lord, lead me into greater glory."

"I will stay close to you,
instructing and guiding you along the pathway for your life.
I will advise you along the way
and lead you forth with my eyes as your guide.
So don't make it difficult; don't be stubborn
when I take you where you've not been before.
Don't make me tug you and pull you along.
Just come with me!"

PSALM 32:8–9

I am the glory within.

The dark cloud you see on the horizon is a sign of my coming. Many will point to the cloud and fear, but you will point to the cloud and praise, for you know that I came to bring joy, blessing, and righteousness. My kingdom will expand and grow as the children of the kingdom praise me. Heaven is waiting for the echo of praise to be heard on the earth. Even as my angels find their delight in singing my praise, so you find life and true identity when your praises echo the angelic sounds. Never allow the evil around you to dim the glory within you.

I have created you for my praises. Let me hear the sound and see your glistening face as you seek me. Many battles can only be won when the sounds of praise erupt from within. Did I not instruct my servant Joshua to shout my praises? Did I not scatter the enemies of Israel when my people sang of my goodness and glory? Fix your eyes on heaven and gaze upon me. Enter in, and you will find that I am all you need. I am the glory within.

His godly lovers triumph in the glory of God,
and their joyful praises will rise even while others sleep.
God's high and holy praises fill their mouths,
for their shouted praises are their weapons of war!

PSALM 149:5–6

Abide in my love.

I have established a covenant of love between us. I never leave you, even when you don't perceive my love. My love is beyond logic. It cannot be discovered with your mind. It is real—like the warmth of a blanket on a cold night. This love covenant can never be broken.

I have never withheld one thing that was best for your good or for my glory. My love will not fail or diminish, even when you disappoint yourself. The strength of my love is stronger than any bond. It burns brighter than a million suns. The love with which I love you is the same love with which my Father has loved me. Abide in this love.

I am your fierce Protector. No one can harm you when you are locked safely in my heart. I love when you trust me and lean in to love. I am overjoyed when you believe in my love and expect me to work out every difficulty. Delight in me, even as I delight in you. Rest in my love that never fails. Expect to see my love demonstrated for you each and every day. Abide in my love.

"I love each of you with the same love that the Father loves me. You must continually let my love nourish your hearts. If you keep my commands, you will live in my love, just as I have kept my Father's commands, for I continually live nourished and empowered by his love."

JOHN 15:9–10

Drink from the streams of my love.

I am more interested in you than a thousand galaxies or a million stars. You mean more to me than anything I have created. Sacred blood was poured out for you. Tune in to my voice today, instead of the sounds that originate from the earth. Yield your heart to me and not to the things of this world, and you will see how vain these temporal things truly are. Don't live only for the pleasures of this life, but drink deeply from the river of pleasure, called eternal life.

I offer you a pure fountain, a clear pool, a refreshing stream in place of the muddy fountain of this world. Let nothing steal your heart from me. Let your devotion have no limits. Be willing to turn aside from the trivial to find the eternal, and I will make you a bright light in a dark place. You will become the sunrise of glory to many who sit in the dark shadows of despair. For as you drink from the streams of my love for you, you will overflow with the glory of my presence.

"It has been accomplished! For I am the Aleph and the Tav, the beginning and the end. I will give water to all who are thirsty. As my gracious gift, they will continuously drink from the fountain of living water. The conquering ones will inherit these gifts from me. I will continue to be their God and they will continue being children for me."

REVELATION 21:6–7

My loving guidance will be your joy.

Many come to me day after day and ask for guidance. It brings me great joy to see you, my sons and daughters, longing to be moved by the impulses of my Spirit and not your own understanding. I *will* lead you in the ways of my holy ones. I *will* guide you with my joyous eyes resting upon you. Look into my face, and the brightness of my love will make your path clear. I am aware of all that you need and all that I have promised. I will meet every need.

My loving guidance will be your joy. I take your burdens and remove them; I take your fears and dissolve them. I take your anxiety and erase it forever. What seems hard, I will make easy. When it looks like everything has blocked your way, I will make a way. Not one thing can penetrate my wrap-around presence as I go with you. Walk in paths of peace and experience my joy as you face the future, for the King of peace walks with you.

Trust in the Lord completely,
and do not rely on your own opinions.
With all your heart rely on him to guide you,
and he will lead you in every decision you make.
Become intimate with him in whatever you do,
and he will lead you wherever you go.

PROVERBS 3:5–6

You are a carrier of hope.

Live free, far above the cares of this world, for it is my glory to love you. My honor is found in how I have treated you. My voice will bring you to my presence, for I lead my sheep, and they know my voice. As you set your heart on me, hope will overflow from you to all your family and to all who witness my blessings spilling from your life.

Give me your heart. Seek me with greater passion and leave worry to fend for itself. You will find my ways, and I will disclose my secrets. The more you find rest in my heart, the greater your ability to trust me, to believe that I am for you. In this world there is little to soothe you, but in my presence, you'll discover my kindness comforting you. It is this absolute assurance of my love and faithfulness that lifts you higher. Gives you eyes to see. Causes your soul to soar above the chaos, so you can carry the whisper of hope to others.

You've rescued me from hell and saved my life.
You've crowned me with love and mercy.
You satisfy my every desire with good things.
You've supercharged my life so that I soar again
like a flying eagle in the sky!

PSALM 103:4–5

Arise and run with me.

Awaken, my men of God, awaken! The hour is late, and I need you to arise and run with me. My glorious women are surging forward with strength, like the mighty horses that run to battle. My fearless women are ready, but I need the men to arise. Put on your weapons of righteousness and take your place in battle formation. I will thunder at the head of my army. I will bring swift victory before your eyes. No power of hell is able to hinder when I arise. Mighty men, shake off your slumber, rub the sleep from your eyes, and come.

Like David, a man after my heart, let your heart be filled with courage! Let your thoughts be steadfast, fixed on me. I will lead you, and where I lead, it is impossible for you to fail. My sons, follow me into the new horizons of holiness and taste the power of the ages to come. My Spirit is upon you, and my Word burns in your soul. I need you, my sons. I love you. This is your day of victory. For I am calling the men back to me, your eternal Father.

Timothy, you are God's man, so run from all these errors. Instead, chase after true holiness, justice, faithfulness, love, hope, and tender humility. So fight with faith for the winner's prize! Lay your hands upon eternal life, for this is your calling—celebrating in faith before the multitude of witnesses!

1 TIMOTHY 6:11–12

I give gifts of love and grace.

I love to give good gifts to my children. Gifts wrapped with love and given in grace. My heart is filled with longing to see my sons and daughters soar and excel in every way. My Spirit is freely given to all who call upon me. My gifts come without strings attached. So I call you, my child, to emulate me and live a generous life.

Give to everyone who asks and to all you meet. Give your prayers, time, love, and money. Hold on to nothing but my mercy, for I will supply all your needs. No one will out-give me. Be a true child, reflecting my generous heart, and I will fill you with an endless measure of my glory. I call you into the life of generosity, a life of yielding your heart to my grace. Shine as a light in the world. Let me stretch your faith and show you my faithfulness. Ask of me, and I will give even nations as your inheritance. Pray to me, and I will give you a generous heart. For I am your Father, the God of endless supply.

"Give generously and generous gifts will be given back to you, shaken down to make room for more. Abundant gifts will pour out upon you with such an overflowing measure that it will run over the top! Your measurement of generosity becomes the measurement of your return."

LUKE 6:38

Don't give up.

Beloved, when you're in the middle of a test or unpleasant circumstance, don't look for a quick exit. I know how difficult it is. I understand that sometimes it makes you want to run away and forget everything. But in the middle of the process, you are not alone. I'm with you every step of the way. Just as a pregnant woman must pass through the pains of labor, so you also must push through the birthing process. I promise, you will come out of this full of favor and light.

I call for you to be content in the process, without needing an explanation that satisfies your impatience. If there is something you need to know, trust me to reveal it plainly. To pour out my wisdom and unveil the hidden secrets. Listen to my voice and follow the sound. I'll take you to places of delicate pastures, where you can rest. Simply come closer, and my grace will give you the strength you need to get to the other side. I am with you. I will not leave you. Don't give up!

"But don't worry. My grace will never desert you or depart from your life. And by standing firm with patient endurance you will find your souls' deliverance."

LUKE 21:18–19

Let your thoughts lead you to me.

Your mind must be clean and prepared. Sharpened as a tool. Your thoughts can be filled with pain, discouragement, and shame. Or your thoughts can be filled with love, excellence, and joy. The truth is that your words reflect your thoughts. It is my desire that your mind be filled with all that is admirable, praiseworthy, and pure. For it is then that you enter into the joy and delight of your Master.

Live with your mind fixed on all that is above, where we sit together in the heavens, united in love. To complain and fill your mind with anxious thoughts, is to lose your way and enter into confusion. I have not called you to confusion but to peace. Refuse every thought and every word that points to pain and heartache. Let your thoughts and words pull you into my realm of perfect peace. Speak words of truth to that which hinders and lay aside every anxious thought. Prophesy to your heart that you will be filled with grace to move into the future without worries. Embrace the truth. Change your expectations. Let hope and faith arise!

Don't be pulled in different directions or worried about a thing. Be saturated in prayer throughout each day, offering your faith-filled requests before God with overflowing gratitude. Tell him every detail of your life, then God's wonderful peace that transcends human understanding, *will make the answers known to you* through Jesus Christ.

PHILIPPIANS 4:6–7

I hold the plans for your life.

I have a life plan for you, a plan that was written into your life record before you were even born. A plan to bring you to my heart and into my fullness. I am the God who created you and formed you in your mother's womb. My gaze was set upon you before your eyes were opened. My plan for you will succeed, and you will one day say, "Abba, you do all things well!"

My timing is perfect—I make all things beautiful in my time. The details of my plan unfold slowly, but my divine fingerprints rest upon them. I hold your life dear, so give it back to me and watch me work. Moments of mystery cannot hinder the hope that lives within you. When you don't understand what I'm doing, turn your eyes upon me and know that I hold the plans of your life. Plans to flood you with endless delight and perfect praise. I love you, my child, and I will never allow you to be tested beyond the measure of my grace to keep you. Trust in my faithfulness. I will not disappoint you.

We have become his poetry, a re-created people that will fulfill the destiny he has given each of us, for we are joined to Jesus, the Anointed One. Even before we were born, God planned in advance *our destiny* and the good works we would do *to fulfill it*!

EPHESIANS 2:10

I see you.

I see you pressing through the dark clouds of oppression, reaching out to me with songs of love and declarations of faith. It moves me. Your endurance pleases me. Your love draws me. I watch as you protect the gift of faith I entrusted you with, keeping it alive when all hell tries to steal it away.

When no one else sees, I do. When you feel invisible and wonder if your life matters, I roar with passion and rush to your side. Every tear is precious to me. Not one of them has gone unnoticed. Don't despair—you mean everything to me, my beautiful one. I gave all that I had, just to be with you, forever. I've paid the greatest price, so you could experience the joys of heaven, here on earth. I am with you, so that peace can rule your heart. I know the yearnings of your soul. I hear the silent cries of desire. Nothing escapes my notice. Nothing will separate you from my love.

You've kept track of all my wandering and my weeping.
You've stored my many tears in your bottle—not one will be lost.
For they are all recorded in your book of remembrance.
The very moment I call to you for a father's help
the tide of battle turns and my enemies flee.
This one thing I know: God is on my side!

PSALM 56:8–9

I will lift you high.

Though a flood overtakes you, I will lift you high. Though fires burn all around you, I will be your shelter. Though many voices may accuse you, I will be your peace. Haven't I saved you a thousand times before? You see only one, but I see the many times I have rescued you, sheltered you, covered you, and protected you from your folly. I see the times where I have protected you when you weren't even aware that you were in danger.

I am a God who stands watch over you at all times. My eyes rest upon you, not just observing you but protecting you, keeping you in my care. I provide untold favors, guarding you from the temptation that is too great for you. All because I love you! There is no need for worry or anxiety, because my hand is upon you, and my presence leads you. I ask for a deeper confidence that goes beyond the moment and endures for a lifetime. Fear not, for when I consider you, my heart is stirred to act on your behalf.

Surrender your anxiety!
Be silent and stop your striving and you will see that I am God.
I am the God above all the nations,
and I will be exalted throughout the whole earth.

PSALM 46:10

I am your great provider.

L ean in to my promise of provision. I have promised that I would provide for your every need. My promise remains true. You will see my hands opened to you, full of everything you need.

Look only to me as your great supply and your great reward. I will bring my glory over all your disappointment and break your limitations as you look to me. Never doubt in the dark what I have revealed to you in the light, for my promises endure, and I have never failed to show you my love. Nourish your heart in my promises and laugh at your impossibilities, and the miracle will be birthed in your heart.

Watch what I will do when you fill your heart with praises. Stones will praise me. Will you praise me even before you see the miracle manifest? I will work where you have given up hope. From the dark chaos I will bring forth beauty, abundant life, and radiant light. Even this day, you will see the beginning of all I have planned for you when you look to me and to me alone.

God wanted to end all doubt and confirm it even more forcefully to those who would inherit his promises. His purpose was unchangeable, so God added his vow to the promise. So it is impossible for God to lie for we know that his promise and his vow will never change!

HEBREWS 6:17–18

The world's fury will not break you.

I remind you, my child, of what I have endured to bring you to my side. I have left all to have you. I chose you over my comforts. I gave sacred blood to redeem you and make you my very own. Have you forgotten the sufferings I endured to overcome the world? My love has surrounded you, and this is why you will not be broken by the world's fury.

I overcame so that you may overcome. You will face difficulties even as I faced the fury of hatred from those I came to save. I overcame not only for myself, but for you! Nothing can defeat you when you hide yourself in me. The strength of my love is greater than the hatred of those who are blind. You will not be defeated by the darkness. You will not be broken by the hatred of this fallen world, but you will be an agent of healing as you give your life to me. Though you share in my suffering, you will also share in my triumph. We are one, unbroken by the world's fury. Stand true to me and watch me become your victory!

Since we are his true children, we qualify to share all his treasures, for indeed, we are heirs of God himself. And since we are joined to Christ, we also inherit all that he is and all that he has. We will experience being co-glorified with him provided that we accept his sufferings as our own.

ROMANS 8:17

I am your redeemer.

What you see now is not what will be forever. There may be trouble in your family, but it will not last forever. There may be trouble around you, but it will soon disappear. Set your heart on my faithfulness and don't be distracted by the impossibility that limits you. I am your Father, and I have plans to prosper you and to make you fruitful in my vineyard.

Take rest in your Father's works. Take joy in your Father's love. This day I will open up your eyes to see my saving power. The day of the Redeemer has come. My redeeming grace will be unveiled before you. This is the day when I will arise to redeem your life and fully restore it back to me. From today forward, my presence will be upon you in unmistakable ways. My face will lead your steps and protect you from all that may come against you. Though a raging flood threatens you, I will lift you high, and you will see my glory, for the day of the Redeemer has come.

When holy lovers of God cry out
to him with all their hearts,
the Lord will hear them and come to rescue them
from all their troubles.

PSALM 34:17

My love restores you.

D o not be afraid to follow me into the unknown, for I am the One who leads you and restores your life. I have placed my glorious treasure within you, and I care for you. This year will be a year of restoration in your life. You will be restored in my love, strengthened in my grace, and surrounded with songs of joy.

I will restore you. Never limit me. I will restore your family and those you love. All will know that I am the One who gives back what has been lost. Don't doubt that my grace is enough for you and for your family.

I will restore your mind and your heart as you come before me. Crooked things will be made straight within you, healing your spirit and soothing your soul.

I will restore your dreams. Those desires within you for completion and to touch the lives of others, I will fulfill. In the whispers of the night, I will watch over every word I speak to you, and it will be fulfilled. You will see that my ways are perfect and my love restores.

Let my passion for life be restored,
tasting joy in every breakthrough you bring to me.
Hold me close to you with a willing spirit
that obeys whatever you say.

PSALM 51:12

In childlike faith, joy is restored.

What you've been looking for is right before your eyes. You only need to become a child again. Life has left you holding a bag of unbelief. But I am replacing that unbelief with a gift of faith, if you will dare to believe. You will no longer walk around in chains, held captive from the abundant life I have planned for you. Though you've been robbed of your childlike faith and imagination, I will restore you. I will replace pain with joy and heal your heart. My voice calls out to you, "Come and experience my joy again."

I am strengthening you today. I know just what you need and how to give it to you. There's no need to worry, for I am your strength. Be carefree. Shake off the heaviness and come as a child, in complete trust and abandonment. Dance upon the heaviness and unbelief that have tried to restrain you. Find your freedom from the past in my ever-present grace. I am more than enough. I am the joy of your salvation.

I've learned from my experience
that God protects the childlike and humble ones.
For I was broken and brought low,
but he answered me and came to my rescue!
Now I can say to myself and to all,
"Relax and rest, be confident and serene,
for the Lord rewards fully those who simply trust in him."

PSALM 116:6–7

Move forward with me.

I t is my desire to give you forward thinking and forward living. I am pushing a radical faith button within you, so that you will begin to pull the future into now. The work that I begin, I will finish, for I am watching over my word to perform it. All you have to do is align your heart with mine.

Every place the sole of your foot treads, you will take for the kingdom of heaven. I am raising you up as a deliverer, a new breed of people, a generation full of passion and life. As you move forward with me, you will no longer be bogged down with the things of this earth, but able to ascend and soar above the problems of this world.

Worship and serve me in spirit and in truth. It will keep you in tune with my Spirit, and all that you do will be led by the promptings of my Holy Spirit within you. You will move forward with me as a part of my victorious army.

Trust in the Lord completely,
and do not rely on your own opinions.
With all your heart rely on him to guide you,
and he will lead you in every decision you make.
Become intimate with him in whatever you do,
and he will lead you wherever you go.

PROVERBS 3:5–6

You are not defeated.

Every difficulty is heaven's invitation to trust me more fully. Each temptation you face to fight back, to push your way forward, to insist on your own way, can be conquered with my love. I was tested in a wilderness with no one there to help me but my Father in heaven. The darkness wanted to defeat me. The enemy tried to force me to act on my own and fight for my own way, but I was not overcome by evil.

Those who saw me in my sufferings were convinced that I was defeated. They mocked and spit on me, the Son of God. Yet they didn't know that my victory was not found on the earth, but in my tender relationship with my Father. No matter what they did to me, nothing could keep me from my Father's love. And so, my child, you are free, unbound, and unbroken by the darkness of this world. You are not defeated. You will overcome. My victory in your life will prevail! Faith in me is the victory that overcomes the world. No one can extinguish the flame I have kindled in your heart.

In the midst of all these things, we triumph over them all, for God has made us to be more than conquerors and his demonstrated love is our glorious victory over everything!

ROMANS 8:37

April

My grace will give you courage.

My love for you will never leave you defenseless. So do not set your gaze on the enemies of faith, for they will stumble and fall. You will rise with fresh courage and feast upon the reality of my presence at all times. For your true comfort and joy is not merely in the victory I give you, but in the knowledge that you are mine. My grace will flood you with bold courage. The ability to move forward in spite of what you see. This is the gift you must take for yourself.

More than a companion to you, I will be strength and grace in your every moment. Not one thing will keep me from cleansing you and empowering you in my grace. I will use you even in your weakness to bring healing to those around you. Look to me and hope in me. Place all your expectation in me, and I will never disappoint you. Lay hold of eternal life deep within you, and the power of that life will flow through you.

Zechariah was filled to overflowing with the Holy Spirit
and he prophesied, saying:
"Praise be to the exalted Lord God of Israel,
for he has seen us through eyes of grace,
and he comes as our Hero-God to set us free!"

LUKE 1:67–68

I am true wisdom.

D o not be intimidated by those who consider themselves to be wise, for they are fools. Those who scorn my wisdom will be seen as pretenders who must forsake their ways. I offer them a drink of the pure waters of truth and wisdom, if only they will come into my sanctuary.

Many times, you have backed down from those who seem to be wise, but now I call you to speak with my words of truth, wisdom, and love. Here in the place of my presence, I will reveal myself to you as true wisdom. My ways and thoughts will be understood as you yield to my Spirit. I will teach you with knowledge that comes from eternity. I will give you the secrets stored up for those who fear me and delight in me. Wisdom from above will enter your heart, and a deep fountain of truth will be opened inside of you. You will be amazed by what I reveal to you and how I use you in the coming days. Sit with me. Listen to my voice. Know my heart, and your heart will be filled with my words.

For those who have been chosen to follow him, both Jews and Greeks, he is God's mighty power, God's true wisdom, and our Messiah. For the "foolish" things of God have proven to be wiser than human wisdom. And the "feeble" things of God have proven to be far more powerful than any human ability.

1 CORINTHIANS 1:24–25

I am your great reward.

I t is not to the great or famous that I give my reward, but to the faithful. The world will celebrate those who walk in step with the current trends, but I celebrate those who take my hand and walk with me in holiness. Quiet followers who cherish my Word and follow my ways—these are the ones who will see my hand of favor. Some follow me out of duty, others out curiosity, but you, my chosen ones, follow me out of delight. Take my hand and be faithful in all things, for I am your great reward.

I am the Rewarder of those who faithfully seek me. The world's rewards fade away. Yet my eternal joy draws you in and settles your heart. No one will take this joy from you. Hold it fast and let it refresh you this day. Glimpses of eternity fasten your heart to me and not to this world. Your faithfulness will be celebrated for all of eternity. It is not to fame that I have called you, but to faithful, quiet, and forever longings after me. I am enough for you, my child. I am your exceedingly great reward.

Without faith living within us it would be impossible to please God. For we come to God in faith knowing that he is real and that he rewards the faith of those who give all their passion and strength into seeking him.

HEBREWS 11:6

Be still, dear one.

Rushing. Rushing. Rushing. Even when your body is still, you're still rushing. Your mind is constantly running with thoughts that do not lead to me. Quiet now. Come spend time with me and breathe. Inhale my peace and exhale your cares into my trustworthy hands. Let me fill you with peace that passes your limited understanding. Release that concern to me.

Take courage in stillness. In trust. I'm leading you down a different path. One that is fruitful and filled with peace. I honor your diligence to get things done, but I have a higher way. One that doesn't strip you of peace and joy. The demands of life are real, but if you will take a step back, you will see which ones are important from my perspective. You don't have to mold each day into a pretty little package that makes everyone happy or drains you of sanity. Sometimes, it's okay to say no. It's okay to take care of yourself. In the midst of these demands, I want you to learn to love yourself the way that I love you. Be still, dear one. Be still.

I am standing in absolute stillness, silent before the one I love,
waiting as long as it takes for him to rescue me.
Only God is my Savior, and he will not fail me.
For he alone is my safe place.
His wrap-around presence always protects me
as my champion defender.
There's no risk of failure with God!

PSALM 62:5–6

My healing will come through joy.

You are called to live carefree and enter into the endless joy and delight of your Master. Come and change every complaint into joyous laughter. My love is omnipotent, and my joy will introduce you to peace. I give you the gift of joy that no one can take from you. Radiant joy is yours, for your future will be paradise and endless delight.

Beloved, I know how hard it is to shake off the heaviness and choose joy. But the healing your heart needs will come through laughter and joy. It will be like medicine to soothe your heart from the pain you've experienced. It's a joy that defies circumstances. A joy that is alive—filled with my glory. A joy reserved for my lovers, because it's only found in my presence. It is my joy, and I long to give it to you as a gift. It will release greater passion within you to feast upon my Word and drink of my Spirit. The joy I give you will bring you deeper into my grace and love. Enter into the joy and delight of your Master today, and watch what I will do for you.

The fruit produced by the Holy Spirit within you is divine love in all its varied expressions: joy *that overflows*, peace *that subdues*, patience *that endures*, kindness *in action*, a life full of virtue, faith *that prevails*, gentleness of *heart*, and strength of *spirit*. Never set the law above these qualities, for they are meant to be limitless.

GALATIANS 5:22–23

I will refresh your soul.

Beloved one, I have chosen you to be mine, to be close to me. Have you grown weary with your journey? I will encourage you. I will be more than a Father to you, seeker of my heart.

I have watched as you passed through this difficult season, and I know that you have been drained of strength and stamina. Come closer, yet closer to me. Divine power will surge into your spirit as you wait and yield to me. I promise you this day that I will encourage you and strengthen you in my love. The rest I give you today, will empower you for tomorrow.

There is not one moment of your life that I am not there with you, ready to refresh your soul. I know you and call you my own. I am the flame that will burn within, keeping your love strong and passionate toward me. I delight to encourage my family, providing for them joyous moments of pleasure as they come before me. Nothing will diminish my love for you or weaken my resolve to make you stand complete in my grace.

Now may God, the inspiration and fountain of hope, fill you to overflowing with uncontainable joy and perfect peace as you trust in him. And may the power of the Holy Spirit continually surround your life with his super-abundance until you radiate with hope!

ROMANS 15:13

Discover who I have created you to be.

Sons and daughters of the living God, servants of the cross, seekers of my heart—arise!

Warriors of love, poets of praise, teachers of my truth—arise!

Yield your hearts. Sacrifice selfishness and pride, and I will give you my glory. Lay aside distractions. Take the sword and slay the giant of self-seeking. Forsake the yearning to build a name for yourself; don't allow it to override your longing to be known by my name. I have given you a sound mind to hear and obey all that I say. Set your heart on me and prepare yourself, for the greatest days of glory are ahead. I call you to active duty, not part-time commitment.

It is time for the highest praises to fill your heart. Sing your songs of devotion. Let your worship rise before me. Many are afraid to completely surrender. They refuse to break open their souls so that my presence floods in. But as you yield your all to me, I unveil your true identity. Access to my presence has been granted, so that you will know me, discover who I've created you to be, and carry my glory to the ends of the earth.

You are God's chosen treasure—priests who are kings, a spiritual "nation" set apart as God's devoted ones. He called you out of darkness to experience his marvelous light, and now he claims you as his very own. He did this so that you would broadcast his glorious wonders *throughout the world*.

1 PETER 2:9

Let my words strengthen you.

This very day, my words will mean more to you than any-thing anyone could ever say. It is in my words that you find life and strength. When you are praised or when you are criti-cized, come back to me and lay those words before me. Only in my presence will you know truth. If I correct you, it's for your transformation. When I encourage you and display my love, re-ceive it with joy, for it is your strength.

When your heart condemns you, remember, condemnation doesn't come from me. I never condemn; I am always greater than your heart. Do not seek the respect of others and thereby forget my words—it is my love you need.

Come close to me, and I will come closer to you, until you see my glory and my beauty. I have walked close with you through your childhood years, even when you did not recognize me. And now, my words are sweeter as you grow older and more tender. I am your life source, and today, I am the living Word within you. I call you my own.

My life's strength melts away with grief and sadness;
come strengthen me and encourage me with your words.

PSALM 119:28

This is the place of my love.

These moments, when you set aside time to seek my face and know my heart, are my delight. Your quiet moments are my treasure, for this is when I can pour my love into you and share my strength with you. Here is the place I free you of anxiety and care. Here, in the calm of my presence. Are you weary? Linger with me in this quiet place of my love. You will be amazed at the miracle of mercy that comes to you. You will be astounded by how my Spirit refreshes and empowers you.

Today, I release to you my gift of encouragement! Let it flood your being and saturate every dry place. It will strengthen you inside and out. I am the God of battles who has won the victory for you, both today and forever. When you are weak, I will make you strong. As your days are, so will your strength be. And the secret of my strength is found in the secret place of my endless, tangible love. Encouragement from heaven will be your portion, filling you with hope this day. This is the place you belong. This is the place of my love.

Whenever my busy thoughts were out of control,
the soothing comfort of your presence calmed me down
and overwhelmed me with delight.

PSALM 94:19

You will never find the end of my love.

Y ou will never find the end of my love. It stretches wider than the horizon, longer than eternity, higher than heaven itself, and deeper than the ocean's depths. Many times, I have placed you under the fountain of mercy and washed your soul, your conscience, your heart. I restored you, because I love you. You will never find the end of my mercy.

I am the God of all grace. I comfort my people in my love. Though many things distract and embitter you, I say, come to my mercy fountain and be refreshed. The highest mountain peak, in all its beauty, is still not as high and beautiful as my mercy—steadfast, unmovable, always giving comfort to my people.

You call me, "Father." And a Father I am to you. I will be there when others fail and clouds of despair envelope you. No one has yet to exhaust my grace. As far as the sunrise to the sunset, that's how far I have removed your sins from you. I will give you mercy until the end of time. You will never find the end of my love. Give freely what you have received.

Lord, you're so kind and tenderhearted
to those who don't deserve it
and so patient with people who fail you!
Your love is like a flooding river
overflowing its banks with kindness.

PSALM 103:8

You are free.

I am the One who has set you free. Free to walk in the higher place before my throne. Free to live and dance within my Spirit winds. Free to laugh in the face of adversity. Everything that could hold you back is now broken off from your life. Be free, child! Be free!

I have opened the door of freedom before you. Go forth into the glorious wonder of your future. The freedom I give you is to experience my presence and my power. You are no longer a servant to a master, but a child of the exalted God. Taste the freedom of my Spirit, and you will never turn back again to that which is dead and barren. The lies that have held you down will be seen for what they are—merely the accusations of the enemy. Today, you will begin to understand the freedom I have given you to walk with omnipotence at your side, for I go with you, even until the end of all the ages.

The Anointed One has set us free—not partially, but completely and wonderfully free! We must always cherish this truth and stubbornly refuse to go back into the bondage of our past.

GALATIANS 5:1

I will show you my faithfulness.

I am your faithful God, unchanging when everything around you changes. My faithfulness is for you to lean upon and believe in. You will learn that there is no hidden shadow or darkness in me, and there is nothing that will disappoint those who trust in me. My promises are as true as my name. I am the God of faithfulness and will always keep my word. All may change around you, but I am unchanging in my faithful love toward you.

Abraham trusted my promises even though he was childless. But by the power of my Word, the promise was fulfilled. Isaac trusted my promise and inherited the life and power of eternity. Jacob leaned upon me when there was nothing else to sustain him. I am the God of Abraham, Isaac, and Jacob. My words are true. What I have promised you, I will fulfill. The words I have spoken over you will all come to pass, for my unending love for you moves my heart to show you my faithfulness. Bring your troubled heart to me, and watch what I will do.

God will always be proven faithful and true to his word.

ROMANS 3:4

I am your feast.

There is no need for another to satisfy you, my beloved, for I am your feast. I am the One who brings true satisfaction. I bring you contentment, yet even in your contentment, your hunger for me will grow. I told the woman at the well to take a satisfying drink and she would never thirst again. And yet, as she drank of my love, she thirsted for more of me. This is the type of feast I give you—one that both satisfies and creates a deeper hunger for my Word.

Nothing will satisfy you if you are not filled with me. In my presence, there is fullness of joy. Apart from me, you will find nothing but barrenness and brokenness. I will give you only what satisfies. If you seek my Spirit, I will not give you a counterfeit. If you seek my living bread, I will not give you poison. Fear will always pollute your soul and keep you from my feast. Come to me without fear. Come, eat, and drink of me. My life is satisfaction found nowhere else.

> My lover has gone down into his garden of delight,
> the place where his spices grow,
> to feast with those pure in heart.
> I know we shall find him there.
> He is within me—I am his garden of delight.
> I have him fully and now he fully has me!
>
> Song of Songs 6:2–3

Partner with me.

Your day of freedom has come. Not only because I love you and want you free, but because I want you to be a vessel—untainted, clear, and clean. Freedom is never solely about you, though; I have it for you to enjoy richly. It's time to remember who you are and whose you are. It's time to step into the calling of partnership with me.

I was moved with compassion and healed the sick. Allow yourself to feel my compassion, and it will move you to act. The fear that has tried to keep you in bondage, works to restrict you, to keep you from doing my will and setting others free. Each time you agree with fear, every time you hold back, fear grows stronger. Now it's time to agree with me. Allow my love and compassion to thrust you into freedom. Into action. You have too much of me to hold selfishly. You are my mouthpiece. My bride. The extension of my love. Never doubt what I can do through you when you allow my love to flow through you.

You must continually bring healing to lepers and to those who are sick, and make it your habit to break off the demonic presence from people, and raise the dead back to life. Freely you have received *the power of the kingdom*, so freely release it to others.

MATTHEW 10:8

Truth embraced will set you free.

L et my presence reign over you, my child. Like a banner of love, it will fly over your conquered heart. You will be my victory. You will be my feast and banqueting table. I will make you my contentment and my satisfaction, as you continue to feast on my love and in my presence. Your enemies will neither disturb you, nor distract you from my love, for under my wings you live and function and have your true identity. I am increasing your hunger for more. Take my living Word and eat. As you eat my Word, it will become life, strength, and pleasure to your soul.

Come and drink deeper of the fullness I have for you. Those who are filled with my Spirit will taste my freedom. Receive the fullness from your Father, and you will bring glory to me. Leave your limitations, and all that belongs to the old way of thinking behind you. Drink, drink, drink. My Spirit is the Spirit of love and liberty. Eat and drink of my love, and you will know the truth, and this truth embraced will set you free!

Drink deeply of the pleasures of this God.
Experience for yourself the joyous mercies he gives
to all who turn to hide themselves in him.
Worship in awe and wonder, all you who've been made holy!
For all who fear him will feast with plenty.

PSALM 34:8–9

Soar with me.

Beloved, I see how tired you've become, and I care for your peace and health. I know your every need. Set your heart before my presence, and you will find strength in my rest. Rest with me now, and I will prepare your way and remove the obstacles before you. I am the God of battles, but I am also the God of wind to soar.

When you are alone with me, I joyfully bring you into deeper streams of my love. I delight in filling you until you overflow. Come let's commune together. Remember your first love toward me. Refocus your thoughts, for the demands of life have moved your heart away from my invitation to come. As you sit with me on the seat of mercy, I will share my secrets with you. I am calling you to come away with me into a place of rest. I will strengthen you until you know me as the God of wind to soar. So, soar with me above the dark clouds of weariness, and I will reveal my glorious light.

Arise, my darling! Come quickly, my beloved.
Come and be the graceful gazelle with me.
Come be like a dancing deer with me.
We will dance in the high place of the sky,
yes, on the mountains of fragrant spice.
Forever we shall be united as one!

SONG OF SONGS 8:14

I will never forget you.

My hand is upon you, and I will not fail to guide you on the perfect path I have chosen. Many are the doors I have opened for you. I am your Father who watches over you and every step that you take. When shadows linger on your path, I will be there to brighten your way. When you are confused, I will make my ways even more clear to you.

When your life is in my hands, you don't need to worry about what direction to go. This isn't a game of hide-and-seek. You don't have to search for my will as though you've lost it. You simply must trust. My choices for your life will prevail, and you will one day see how perfectly I have guided you. I have chosen you. Because you are mine, I have commanded my angels to be in charge of your ways. As you walk with me, they protect and hold you so you will not stumble.

Never doubt my plans for your life, my child. I make no mistakes. There may have been an earthly father who has forgotten his child, but I will never forget you.

Escort me along the way; take me by the hand and teach me.
For you are the God of my increasing salvation;
I have wrapped my heart into yours!

PSALM 25:5

Stand strong in me.

Nothing can disturb my unshakable faithfulness, and nothing should disturb your faith. When everything crumbles, I remain faithful. When all else fails, the hope of my promise will keep you and guard you. Hold on to me and what I promise. Remind yourself of my goodness. Trust in my power that cannot be overcome. I have already provided for every need.

What I have done for David, I will do for you. He believed in my mercy. When he hid inside my wrap-around presence, I became his shield. Nothing could harm him as he went out to battle, and nothing will harm you as you stand inside my grace.

I have taken notice of your faithfulness to me. When others did their best to pull you away, you still found me as your great reward. I rejoice with singing when I consider what you have yielded to me. I have seen every offering, each sacrifice, and every tear of surrender. Heaven is empty of worry. I have called you to live a life of heaven on earth. Continue to stand strong in my love, and I will provide all you need.

You have wrapped me in power,
and now you've shared with me your perfection.
Through you I ascend to the highest peaks of your glory
to stand in the heavenly places, strong and secure in you.

PSALM 18:32–33

The time for change has come.

E ternity is now flooding into time. This season will be the most productive and powerful season you have ever witnessed, for I am hastening my word to bring it to pass. Long-dormant promises will now spring to life, as I bring you through the most rapid changes you have ever experienced.

The changes that are upon you will demand that you trust me more. For in the stretching of faith, you will find me as never before. Leap for joy, for in that leap of faith, you will find my presence. Get ready for the kingdom of joy to come, even while dark shadows linger over your circumstances. Faith rejoices and subdues doubt and fear. Watch new miracles flow through the seasons of joy that I bring.

Always be ready to share your living faith with those who are near. Speak forth your praises, give your bold and courageous testimony, and watch me melt the hearts of men and women with my love. A great harvest is here. Not someday, but now. This very day!

The budding vines of new life are now blooming everywhere.
The fragrance of their flowers whispers, "There is change in the air."
Arise, my love, my beautiful companion, and run with me
to the higher place.

SONG OF SONGS 2:13

Lay your head upon my shoulder.

Come and listen, divinely loved child of mine. Your thoughts have strayed, and your heart has been torn. Come close to me and lay your head upon my shoulder. Rest in my love and know the depth of my care for your soul. Your body, soul, and spirit are mine. I give you what you need most this hour—my peace and my love. Drink, thirsty one, and then drink some more. Never feel guilty about taking more of my love.

Draw closer than you have ever been before. Let fear be driven from your thoughts once and for all. Love opens the gates to my presence and brings joy. Beloved, be convinced that all things will be knitted together into love's fabric. What seems like a mystery now will soon bring you miracles. What now troubles you will bring you strength as you lean in to me. I will not let you go deeper into pain. Today is the day of my wooing, my calling, my drawing of your soul to me. Let nothing distract you from your true resting place. As you rest in me and surrender your anxious thoughts, I will make you fruitful.

"I am the sprouting vine and you're my branches. As you live in union with me as your source, fruitfulness will stream from within you—but when you live separated from me you are powerless."

JOHN 15:5

My mercy is never out of reach.

You are never too far. You are never beyond the reach of my mercy. Over and over, I will restore and forgive you. Open your eyes and see me high and lifted up—my glorious robe of mercy wrapped around you. Be filled with the glory of my love. Receive a fresh infilling from my fountain of mercy, and you will be prepared for what is to come.

I am the God of forgiveness and mercy. The God of not just one, two, or three chances, but *unlimited* mercy. When you commune with me in sacred intimacy, the areas of your life that have yet to be changed, will be perfected. You are my temple. My holy vessel. Purchased with holy blood. Sanctified and righteous because of what I have done for you. Forgiven because of the price I paid. So lay your failures before me today. Invite me into every area that has haunted you with regret. Let go of your past and walk into the newness of life with me. It is never too late. My mercy is never out of reach.

"She has been forgiven of all her many sins. This is why she has shown me such extravagant love. But those who assume they have very little to be forgiven will love me very little." Then Jesus said to the woman at his feet, "All your sins are forgiven."

LUKE 7:47–48

The doors I close will be a blessing.

I will never disappoint you. Remember how I helped you and held you in the past? I didn't allow your enemies to conquer you. I broke through the clouds of despair and rescued you. I will not disappoint you. You are often disappointed when I close a door. Yet the doors I close keep you from making the wrong decision and taking the wrong path. Never lose heart when I shut a door; for I open doors that no man can close, and I close doors that no man can open. Can you praise me when I close a door as well as when I open one?

The doors I close will prove to be a blessing. Resist disappointment and trust that I have chosen the best for you. The doors I shut give you an opportunity to experience my best. For I am in charge of your destiny when you surrender to me. I will open the right new door for every one I close, and you will see the wisdom of my love. I will bring you great joy and spare you from needless pain. Believe in my love, rely on my love, and you will never be disappointed.

Trust in the Lord completely,
and do not rely on your own opinions.
With all your heart rely on him to guide you,
and he will lead you in every decision you make.
Become intimate with him in whatever you do,
and he will lead you wherever you go.

PROVERBS 3:5–6

Set me as a seal on your heart.

My love is a fiery, sacred passion, much stronger than the grave. It overshadows pain, disappointment, and even death itself. It is eternal. It is alive. Invite me to seal your heart with this holy fire. It will purify you and set you aflame with my love, so nothing else competes with your affection. Cry out, until every part of you is consumed with only me.

No part of you is off limits to my love. I know every place you hide. Every fiber of your being will respond when you allow me to burn up everything that hinders our relationship. When you invite me, I will ignite you with love so powerful and tangible, it will be like fire in your bones—purifying and empowering you. Awakening your heart and changing you forever. The fire of my presence will create an atmosphere, not only in you, but all around you. It will revive you and move through you, stirring sacred passion in others. Set me as seal of love upon your heart, and you will become a living flame of my glory.

Rivers of pain and persecution
will never extinguish this flame.
Endless floods will be unable
to quench this raging fire that burns within you.
Everything will be consumed.
It will stop at nothing
as you yield everything to this furious fire
until it won't even seem to you like a sacrifice anymore.

SONG OF SONGS 8:7

You are accepted without condition.

Life is busy enough without you feeling pressured with re-ligious duties. Despite what any man may tell you, I don't need you to perform for me. I don't need you to behave just right, dress just so, or wear a mask to cover your emotions or personality. I love you completely, just the way you are. I haven't handed you a list of things I *don't* want you to do. Life with me is not a life of bondage and duty.

Life with me is free and beautiful. It's about discovering yourself and finding out how perfectly and thoroughly I love you. After all, I created you. I died for you. I gave all that I had so that you could be accepted without condition. You're not holy enough or smart enough to perfect yourself, so I did it for you. All I want is for you to get to know me. To be still in my presence and enjoy our relationship. I want you to stop doing things out of duty and discover what it's like to walk with me in pure bliss, simply because I love you.

For you reach into my heart.
With one flash of your eyes I am undone by your love,
my beloved, my equal, my bride.
You leave me breathless—
I am overcome
by merely a glance from your worshiping eyes,
for you have stolen my heart.
I am held hostage by your love
and by the graces of righteousness shining upon you.

SONG OF SONGS 4:9

I will make a way.

I have led you here, my beloved. You haven't missed a step. When you set your heart to seek my face and yielded your will to mine, I took you by the hand and haven't let go. Though it seems as if you've walked straight into a brick wall that's blocking your path, look closer. See with the purity of Spirit vision, and you will notice it is actually a door. I'm good at making a way when there seems to be no way. What you see as a stopping point, I see as a moment for you to pause and find your peace in me. Nothing but me.

Circumstances are not always as they appear. When you live from my vantage point, you begin to see things from my point of view. You get excited by setbacks, because you begin to see them as opportunities for something greater. This may not be what you expected, but remember, I am faithful, and I have nothing but the best for you. Leave the details in my hands.

We are convinced that every detail of our lives is continually woven together to fit into God's perfect plan of bringing good into our lives, for we are his lovers who have been called to fulfill his designed purpose.

ROMANS 8:28

I have every provision you need.

I am the God who provides all that is needed and supplies all that you lack. Never be held back by what you call lack or need, for I call it "miracles of trust." As you trust me, I will open doors of blessing and miraculous supply that you have never considered before. Remain faithful, for I will show you my faithful and miraculous supply. There will be no limit of resources to see my harvest of the nations reached and my bride made radiant.

Have I not supplied more than your needs and even fulfilled many of the longings that live deep within your heart? I have promised to care for you and bring you into my eternal glory. The world's riches are but trinkets compared to my glory. Be faithful, and I will be your great reward. I will restore you and provide in ways that reveal my heart of love. My mercy brings gifts and surprises. There will always be provision for your needs, and in my mercy, I will reveal where you can find me, for this will be the season of abundant supply for every need you have.

I am convinced that my God will fully satisfy every need you have, *for I have seen* the abundant riches of glory *revealed to me* through the Anointed One, Jesus Christ! And God our Father will receive all the glory and the honor throughout the eternity of eternities! Amen!

PHILIPPIANS 4:19–20

Love me through the difficulties.

Beloved of my heart, listen to the voice of your Father. I have set my love upon you and will never forget the way you have loved me through your difficulties. Though you face a clouded dawn, the light of love will break through the clouds and shine upon you. In this new day, I give you my promise: I am bringing you forward. What has hindered you in the past will soon be forgotten as the hope of a new day is made real to you.

Remember what I said to you when you surrendered your heart to me. I promised to guide you and take you forward, and you responded by saying, "I will love you and serve you for the rest of my life." Remember that promise and love me even through what intimidates you and what burdens you. Love me where you are and watch the miracles I will work for you. Give me your heart, as you did in the beginning, and my grace will bring you forward until you say, "All you have done in my life is good!"

> The lovers of God walk on the highway of light,
> and their way shines brighter and brighter
> until they bring forth the perfect day.
>
> PROVERBS 4:18

Experience my boundless joy.

I am the King of peace. All who dwell with me live in a paradise of love and grace. My strength becomes yours, when all you can do is fall into my loving arms. When you feel like you've come up against a wall, I make a way where there seems to be no way. It is my joy to do so. And when you are on the other side, take time to stop, wait, and listen, and you will hear my song. My peace will flow like a river into your troubled heart until you can say, *It is well with my soul.*

This is the day of all, not part, my child. You will see *all* of my love and *all* of my power at the disposal of those who have sought my face with *all* of their hearts. Eden's pleasures are found within you. Because you have chosen the narrow road, I will thrill you with my presence, until my joy overflows within you. Now is the time to discover the boundless joy of my heart.

> "I promise you that as you experience these things, you will celebrate and dance with overflowing joy. And the heavenly reward of your faith will be abundant, because you are being treated the same way as your forefathers the prophets."
>
> LUKE 6:23

My gift is a triumphant life.

I love to give good gifts to my children, to those who are born from above. I have treasures to bestow that the world can never give, nor can they understand their value. I give to you new life. Resurrection life. From the death of my body on Calvary's cross, living virtue was given. The new life I give to you will spring up within your soul and subdue everything that competes with my love. The inexpressible joy of resurrection life is my gift to you.

The world can only see Christ dying on a cross, but I am the Christ of triumphant victory! Leaping from the tomb as the doe of the morning. My life was not contained in a grave, for it is the life of eternal love that can never be stopped. The grave could not hold me, but you can. You can hold me close and dear to your heart. This is my gift to you—my endless, triumphant life. The glad confidence that I am living within you. As I am now, so are you in this world. Rest in this confidence and great will be your peace.

As God's loving servants, you live in joyous freedom from the power of sin. So consider the benefits you now enjoy—you are brought deeper into the experience of true holiness that ends with eternal life!

ROMANS 6:22

Let my love enable you.

The path I take you on is not the wide way that leads to destruction, but a narrow way that grows narrower as I lead you forward. I must have my overcomers. I must have my day breakers. They will be those whom I take down narrow paths that lead to my heart and into my ways. I will give you faith, but good works must be with your ego, out of the way and left behind. My overcomers will rise and sing, even when imprisoned and in pain.

I will come through you as a flood, washing away all that defiles. At times, my flood will bring tears as you see how intent I am on making you my deliverer. Stay close to my heart, where nothing can disturb you, even when the earth is shaking all around. I must have my overcoming ones, and my preparation of their hearts will be complete. For this is why your path grows narrower, so narrow that only I can take you through. I have destined you to reign as my overcomer. But first, I must conquer you, thoroughly and completely.

May he work perfection into every part of you giving you all that you need to fulfill your destiny. And may he express through you all that is excellent and pleasing to him through your life-union with Jesus the Anointed One who is to receive all glory forever! Amen!

HEBREWS 13:21

May

My love will keep you.

People will correct you when you're wrong, but I will heal you when you fall and will set your feet on solid ground. My words have the power to eliminate all of your fears. They have grace to erase your flaws. Listen to my words and cherish all that I say to you. I will bring you into a new place where you see more clearly and love more deeply.

I will make myself known to you, and you'll see that I am at work in your life. You will rejoice because of what I'm doing within you, for you will be one who overcomes. Your faith will arise, because I am merciful and kind. The calling on your life is great, yet, you have forgotten many of the promises I have made to you. It's time to stop walking the path of your own choosing, for you are mine—completely. With my love comes my power. Rise like an eagle in the sky, unable to fall, for my love will keep you, as you surrender fully to my love.

Your nurturing love is tender and gentle.
You are slow to get angry yet so swift to show your faithful love.
You are full of abounding grace and truth.
Bring me to your grace-fountain
so that your strength becomes mine.

PSALM 86:15–16

Be my messenger of love and light.

How will my message be heard without a messenger of my light? I need you to go with winged feet to carry the sounds of my voice to many people. So come away. Fly higher. Leave the vain things of this life behind and yield everything to me. Partner with me, and together we will release my truth to the world.

Many are searching for what I've given you. Take this gift and bring it to those who are near. See each person through my eyes of compassion. Show mercy, as I have shown you mercy. Never allow their sin to stir judgment within you. Let your family see that I live in you, and they will glorify me. Never fear to share this gift with those in need, those who are hurting, and those who are cold and hard. For hidden behind their hard hearts is a fragile soul that must experience this treasure. Open your heart to them and share my love. Freely I have given this love to you, so, freely share it with them. Tell them today, that they can experience heaven on earth.

"Don't hide your light! Let it shine brightly before others, so that the commendable things you do will shine as light upon them, and then they will give their praise to your Father in heaven."

MATTHEW 5:16

I will never abandon you.

Many look to others to be there for them, but I say to you, I will always be there for you. I will never abandon you. Trust in me. I have called every star by name, measured out the oceans in the span of my hand, have held the mountains of the earth, and unrolled the tapestry of the skies—yet you are my masterpiece of love. You are the joy that moves my heart. I will never forget you or fail to hold you near.

You are always in my hands as the one I love. Let your challenges bring you to a greater faith. My outstretched arm of power will bring you courage. Hold on to me, and the omnipotence of my love will conquer the pain that hides in your heart. Release the pain of misunderstanding and rejection to me. Be brave and forgive all who have hurt you, so that you will be free to laugh and heal. I am not only your Savior and Lord, I am your Friend. Eternally faithful, I will never forsake you.

You will be empowered to discover what every holy one experiences—the great magnitude of the astonishing love of Christ in all its dimensions. How deeply intimate and far-reaching is his love! How enduring and inclusive it is! Endless love beyond measurement that transcends our understanding—this extravagant love pours into you until you are filled to overflowing with the fullness of God!

Ephesians 3:18–19

Praise is your key.

L et praises arise from the depths of your soul. Allow them to burst through the dry cracked ground of discouragement and disappointment. Your songs of love and declarations of trust will free you from the shackles that have bound you to an earthly view of your situation.

Praise me in disappointment, because I always have the last word. Praise me in sickness, because I am your Healer. Praise me in seasons of delay, for my timing is perfect. Praise me in difficulties, and my strength will become yours. Praise me when you cannot find the way, because you know me—the Way Maker.

When nothing seems to be going right and you feel discouraged and alone, lift your head and let your songs of love pour forth. Sing until the heaviness lifts. Sing until you can feel my refreshing breath upon your soul. Sing until every thought that opposes my truth, bows in surrender. Your choice to praise me and to offer me songs of love and surrender, especially when the enemy is leaning heavily upon you, will cause you to rise victorious—his head beneath your feet.

Let every activity of your lives and every word that comes from your lips be drenched with the beauty of our Lord Jesus, the Anointed One. And bring your constant praise to God the Father *because of what Christ has done for you*!

COLOSSIANS 3:17

I chose you for a purpose.

Give me a listening heart, and I will give you hope-filled words for what is to come. Many think they have heard my voice and have not. Some have heard my whisper, but it has yet to change their heart. But I have called you with purpose to hear with clarity and to use my life-giving words to strengthen others.

As I train you to hear my voice, you will become a sharpened instrument in my hands. I will transform you and make you into a different person. These are the days that I will train you and instruct you, sharing many secrets of what I will do. These are the days, when I will impart to you my heart of compassion and make you a missionary of hope to many. You will be a voice that always brings life to others and grace to the weakest ones. I will put words in your mouth that have never been declared or spoken before. I chose you for a purpose, and my plan for your life will be fulfilled.

Listen to my counsel,
for my instruction will enlighten you.
You'll be wise not to ignore it.
If you wait at wisdom's doorway,
longing to hear a word for every day,
joy will break forth within you as you listen for what I'll say.

PROVERBS 8:33–34

Fear is not your friend.

Fear is not your friend, so stop agreeing with it. Stop listening to every lie the enemy throws at you, as if you don't have the power to resist it. Decline the invitation to cower in fear, while rehearsing the outcome he has envisioned for you. Declare my truth. Take up your shield of faith—it will quench the fiery darts of hell. Stand and be courageous.

You are powerful; filled with the same Spirit that raised my Son from the grave. Trust the power of my love within you. Dig your faith into the throat of fear and tear it away from your soul. Thrust it before my presence and trust me to be who I say I am. Fear and trust cannot coexist. All that I do, I do through your faith. You do not have to figure this out. Don't allow the enemy to trick you into thinking that obsessing over this will change it. It will not. Simply release this into my hands and close the door to fear. I am here with you. Release the fear. Trust me.

The disciples woke Jesus up and said, "Master, Master, we're sinking! Don't you care that we're going to drown?" With great authority Jesus rebuked the howling wind and surging waves, and instantly they stopped and became as smooth as glass. Then Jesus said to them, "Why are you fearful? Have you lost your faith *in me*?"

LUKE 8:24–25

My love for you will never grow dim.

Though the heavens roll up like a scroll and the mountains shake and fall into the sea, my love for you will never be shaken nor will it be moved. I have held you as my treasure and have longed for you, even as you have longed for me. A sacred fire burns within me, an all-consuming fire of love that will never go out. The passion I have to make you mine can never be dimmed or fade away. Every moment, I carry you. You never have to grope in the dark to find me.

I have promised you that I will never leave you comfortless. Every day, the glory of my presence overshadows you, even when you don't discern it. When you thirst, I give you living water; when you hunger and crave for more, I give you living bread and my satisfying peace. When you lift up your face to me without shame, the sunshine of my love washes and strengthens you. Let the reality of this love comfort you today. My presence is all that you need.

We are a colony of heaven on earth as we cling tightly to our life-giver, the Lord Jesus Christ, who will transform our humble bodies and transfigure us into the identical likeness of his glorified body. And using his matchless power, he continually subdues everything to himself.

PHILIPPIANS 3:20–21

Live above the chaos.

Y ou don't need to stumble today—tripping over every ob-stacle of doubt and frustration. Take my hand. Let me lead you along the paths of love. I've already paid the ultimate price to be with you. Not just to have you by my side, but to draw you into my wounded side, so we can be one. You don't simply walk alongside of me, you walk inside of me. You live, move, and have your very being within the reality of my existence.

In my presence is fullness of joy. Joy that isn't contingent upon your circumstances. Joy that causes your heart to sing, even in times of difficulty. Joy that is deeper than suffering. Every op-position is an opportunity for you to grow in faith, patience, and character. To learn to enjoy the freedom of faith-filled expecta-tion. It's a chance to trust me to be for you what you cannot be for yourself. Let my presence, not your breakthrough, be your ultimate goal, and it will change your perspective. Come. Live above the chaos. See, from my vantage point, the beauty of your journey.

We view our slight, short-lived troubles in the light of eternity. We see our difficulties as the substance that produces for us an eternal, weighty glory far beyond all comparison, because we don't focus our attention on what is seen but on what is unseen. For what is seen is temporary, but the unseen realm is eternal.

2 CORINTHIANS 4:17–18

Abide in my endless love.

My invisible ways of love have carried you through life, so never let disappointment live within you. I am your God, the Mighty Lover who will never be turned aside by your weak heart. I am stirred to perfect you every time I see your weakness. Your growth is my boast, for the grace I have poured upon you will bring you into greater light and greater glory. Trust in me and watch me work as I demonstrate the depths of my love toward you today.

In your difficult season of night, rest in my love. Never interpret my love by how it appears, but see the depth of my love through the sacrifice of my Son. It was on Calvary that I lifted Him between heaven and earth as a sign that my love is endless. My love gave up what was most precious, so I could have you. Nothing shall separate you from this love: neither pain or pressure, nor grief or disappointment. Abide in my unconditional love, and peace will rule the atmosphere of your heart. Nothing is more powerful than my love.

"I love each of you with the same love that the Father loves me.
You must continually let my love nourish your hearts.
If you keep my commands, you will live in my love,
just as I have kept my Father's commands,
for I continually live nourished and empowered by his love."

JOHN 15:9–10

I will bring the change you need.

Y ou have said to me, "Take my life and make me into the person you want me to be." Listen to my words, and they will be life and power inside of you. The greatest joy of your life will be in knowing me—that I am kind, tenderhearted to my children, and full of compassion and forgiveness toward those who fall. It is in knowing me that you come to know exactly who you are.

Maintain this posture of wholehearted devotion, and I will make you a sharpened, pure instrument of mature love. Bring me your listening heart, and I will bring you the life and change you long for. This season of change will move you from passivity into passion. The fire of my love will motivate you to make sacrifices of time and treasure, which you have never entered into before. I am moving upon your heart to yield to me, to go where I send you, and to do what I called you to do. Even at great personal cost, you will see me as the great Promise Keeper.

Let my passion for life be restored,
tasting joy in every breakthrough you bring to me.
Hold me close to you with a willing spirit
that obeys whatever you say.

PSALM 51:12

I work in the silent moments of rest.

Your life is my garden, and I am the One who is responsible to bring forth my fruit from your life. Watch me work in your silent moments of rest. You are branches in me, meant to remain close and connected to my heart. Your life will flow with milk and honey as you remain in living fellowship with me.

When I created man and woman on the sixth day, I created them for more than labor; I created them for rest. Their first day was my seventh—a day of rest. All your fruit is in me. All your fulfillment will be found in the satisfying Sabbath of my life in you. Your first love will be restored as you lay your head upon my shoulder. Come, child of delight, child of my heart, come to me. I know all there is to know about you, and I love you more than you can perceive. I am gracious and tenderhearted. As you eat from the garden of my presence and rest in me, you will bear the fruit of my Spirit in your life.

> His left hand cradles my head
> while his right hand holds me close.
> I am at rest in this love.
> SONG OF SONGS 2:6

Speak my words of truth.

The time of the great outpouring upon the nations is near. Many scoffers will be swept into my presence and become believers in one day. Many doubters will leave their limitations and pursue me as never before. It will be a day of repentance and a day of gathering. Those who ignore my truth will be ignored. For I will be worshiped in spirit and in truth.

My people are experiencing an awakening. The nations are ripe for harvest. I need you, my beloved, to speak the words of mercy and truth, which I long to release through you. Set yourself apart for me, and I will instruct you with my mysteries. Remember that I strengthened my servant, Elijah, by the drying brook. Remember that I told Moses to strike a rock so my rivers would pour forth. Though you don't understand all that I ask of you, be willing and joyfully obedient. I will use you to strengthen the feeble and to bring healing to the brokenhearted. Listen carefully to my words, and you will be one who is fully equipped to represent me.

It is through my union with Jesus Christ, that I enjoy an enthusiasm and confidence in my ministry for God. And I will not be presumptuous to speak of anything except what Christ has accomplished through me. For many non-Jewish people are coming into faith's obedience by the power of the Spirit of God, which is displayed through mighty signs and amazing wonders, both in word and deed.

ROMANS 15:17–18

All is good in my presence.

How pleasant and good it is when you draw near to me and leave your doubts behind. The burning light of my presence will consume every fear and every thought that disturbs your peace. If only my people knew what awaits them as they come before me!

My servant, come closer to me.

My son, draw near, and you will find me.

Daughter of my heart, bring your soul into my loving presence.

All those who find their delight in me drink from a flowing brook of bliss. To delight in me is the joy you will experience for eternity. It is good for you to draw near to me. There is no distance between us, when your spirit longs for me. Many will merely sing about it, some will pray about it, but the open door waits for you to enter. Come over the threshold of my glory, and you will find me. I have fastened my heart to yours. Love will bring you near. Even now, you are feeling the pull, the tug of my eternal love. Come close to me, and I will draw even closer to you.

Whom have I in heaven but you? You're all I want!
No one on earth means as much to me as you.
Lord, so many times I fail; I fall into disgrace.
But when I trust in you, I have a strong and glorious presence
protecting and anointing me. Forever you're all I need!

PSALM 73:25–26

I know what lies ahead.

L et me tell you about your future. It's nothing like your past. I have shaped you with my hands and prepared you for all that is coming. Set your eyes on me, and I will never disappoint you. You will not be taken captive by the fear of this age. For I am the God of the heavens. I see all that is coming, and I know that you will be held fast by my hand.

Difficulties will come, but so will a greater outpouring. The days will grow darker, but for you, my chosen one, you will carry my glory and reveal your Father in heaven. Though the earth may quake, your heart will remain at peace, for my covenant of love cannot be broken. Sit in my glory until you see as I see. Understanding will fill your heart, and the hope within you will expand and overwhelm any fear. I know what is ahead of you— days of light and glory, years of delight and praise. Never, never give in to the despair around you, but fill your heart with reve- lation light.

Because I am innocent I will see your face
until I see you for who you really are.
Then I will awaken with your form and be fully satisfied,
fulfilled in the revelation of your glory in me!

PSALM 17:15

Lay down your to-do list.

S ometimes, having a productive day means *not* getting to your to-do list. What you consider a fruitful day isn't always the most beneficial for your soul. Sometimes, the most productive thing you can do is to say no to busyness, and rest in my presence. Time spent seeking me is always time well spent.

When you feel the pull of my Spirit, inviting you to come aside and seek my face, it's always for your good. Letting go of that list and leaving some things undone once in a while isn't going to be catastrophic. When you set aside your lists and goals for the day and choose me, it's never a waste of time. Those things can wait. Even if you get behind, I am more than able to empower you with enough grace to do the same tasks in less time. Don't ignore yourself. Don't ignore the need to come away and refresh yourself in my presence. You have permission to rest. To seek me. Make time with me your number one priority.

When I look at you,
I see how you have taken my fruit and tasted my word.
Your life has become clean and pure,
like a lamb washed and newly shorn.
You now show grace and balance with truth on display.

Song of Songs 4:2

I am the God of the new.

I am the God of the new. What once was sufficient changes over time, as my Spirit moves from what was to what is ready to be. When you see me moving forward, it's time for you to move on too. Old ways of doing things will not suffice. They won't work in this new season. I am passing out fresh blueprints. There's a fresh new fragrance in the air! Many are stepping into new territory. You've not been this way before, but I have. I've gone before you and mapped it all out. And my plan for you is too beautiful for your loftiest imagination.

My voice will lead you forward into beautiful and more spacious horizons. I have equipped you. I'm launching you into greater realms of glory—to know and to be known by me. In knowing me, you will find your greatest peace and greatest hope to move forward. For in that place you will encounter my heart and be kept safe. So don't be afraid to try new endeavors and to stop things that have run their full course. For my holy anointing is moving from what once was to what is ready to be!

If anyone is enfolded into Christ, he has become an entirely new person. All that is related to the old order has vanished. Behold, everything is fresh and new.

2 Corinthians 5:17

I will sustain you.

Rest in the realm of peace, and you will know when I speak and when I move. Don't be afraid of being alone or going forward while others around you sink back. I have called you, through the narrow gate, to follow me. I will be enough for you. Even as I sustained my servant Abraham on his journey, I will sustain you and shower you with my love. The more challenging your days, the more mightily my power will be displayed in your life.

Promises, long forgotten by you, will now be fulfilled. I am more than enough to meet every one of them. I have not forgotten any promise, so rest in the understanding that I am enough, and I know your future. I have marked out every step, bringing you closer to me and deeper into my glory, until finally you awaken with my likeness. All that I am, I am within you. All things are now yours: life, eternity, authority, power, and glory. No one will be able to take these from you. You are my temple; sustained by my very Spirit that is alive within you.

God is more than ready to overwhelm you with every form of grace, so that you will have more than enough of everything— every moment and in every way. He will make you overflow with abundance in every good thing you do.

2 Corinthians 9:8

I will not ignore the cries of injustice.

I am about to flow through your land in great power. The age of miracles and displays of power will be seen all around you. Even now, my winds are blowing to topple the structures and teachings of men that hinder my people from trusting in my power. Gale force winds will blow, clearing out what is not of me. The more confidence you place in the structures of men, the more disappointment will come when I blow them down. My truth will prevail.

I will reveal my power against wickedness and unrighteousness, toppling the evil that binds the innocent. I will expose the lies that lurk in the shadows. Highlight the purity and passion of my humble lovers. Nothing is hidden from me. Every ploy of evil that has sought to lead people astray will fall, but those who lead with integrity will shine like the sun. Though darkness seeks to choke the life—my life—out of the world, I am the Omnipotent One. I will not ignore the cries of injustice. I have come to bring the glory of heaven to earth! It's time for me to release the power of my passion.

The rulers scheme and confer together against Yahweh and his Anointed King, saying: "Let's come together and break away from the Creator. Once and for all let's cast off these controlling chains of God and his Christ!" God-Enthroned merely laughs at them; the Sovereign One mocks their madness!

PSALM 2:2–4

It is time to arise.

Your Bridegroom is coming. He is in the land to lift you up and lead you out. Trim your lamps, buy oil of my Spirit, fill your heart with expectancy, and go out to meet Him. The day of His wedding is near—arise and leave what is familiar to meet Him in His glory. Just as He walks in mighty power over all His foes, so will His bride walk in the ways of glorious power. Nothing will hinder Him as He appears for His bride.

I will speak my words and release my power through you. For the Lamb's wife is making herself ready. Her garments of splendor are becoming clean and spotless. I will draw untold millions to myself in these days of power. So come, be clothed with faith and confidence in me. Leave all that hinders. Do not look back or try to take the old with you into the new. For the way is straight, and the door is narrow. Come with faith alone, and you will see the unveiling of my power. There is no limit to what I will do through you as you come with me!

Rise up, Zion maidens, brides-to-be!
Come and feast your eyes on this king
as he passes in procession on his way to his wedding.
This is the day filled with overwhelming joy—
the day of his great gladness.

Song of Songs 3:11

Be infused with my divine strength.

Even as the nations tremble and rage, my peace will grow sweeter as the days grow darker. Hear my invitation and see the opened door. I am the Father you need. I stand with arms open, waiting to embrace you and hold you safe. Your love for me must not wait or linger outside. Come close to me and never yield to the multitudes of distractions all around you. Your love for me will bring you into my cloud-filled chamber. And when you have come into the splendor of my glory, abide with me.

Though you are weak and weary, you will soon arise with Spirit wind and soar by your praises. Your time alone with me will infuse you with strength, because my joy will become yours. My love can encourage you in ways you've never known. Stay in my presence. Hold fast to what you have been given. A new passion for me is rising in your heart, and no one will take it from you. All is good in my presence.

You will be empowered to discover what every holy one experiences—the great magnitude of the astonishing love of Christ in all its dimensions. How deeply intimate and far-reaching is his love! How enduring and inclusive it is! Endless love beyond measurement that transcends our understanding—this extravagant love pours into you until you are filled to overflowing with the fullness of God!

EPHESIANS 3:18–19

My eyes are fixed on you.

Y ou have served me, sought me, and loved me, even though you have not seen me. Even when your environment was not the best, your love flourished. You found me as your faithful God. I will never cease to listen to your voice and answer your cry. My eyes are fixed on you. Continue to seek me, even in your difficult places, even though it seems like darkness is all around you, and I will be the light of life within you.

I have set you in the perfect place to be my witness and to reflect my glory. I will change your circumstances as you allow me to change your heart. Daniel did not suffer in the lions' den because of his lack of sin, but because of his devotion to me. So many of the difficulties you have faced are not punishment from my hand, beloved. They are because of the favor of my heart that covers you. I will promote you through your pain as you seek me and remain faithful to my plans for you.

"You who spend your days shrouded in darkness
can now say, 'We have seen a brilliant Light.'
And those who live in the dark shadow land of death
can now say, 'The Dawning Light arises on us.'"

MATTHEW 4:16

I will reveal my mysteries.

Why are you doubting, my child? Why have you entertained the lie that because I am cloaked in mystery, I must not want to share my secrets with you? It isn't enough to trust in my ways, I long for you to dive into the depths of my truth and seek me for greater understanding. That kind of understanding is deeper than your mind can interpret. Much wilder and holier than your imagination.

As you seek my wisdom, my mysterious ways open before your eyes. Many have seen my miracles but never learned my mysteries. Miracles and mysteries will be revealed as you keep your heart before me. My dear child, I am a Father who will never fail you. I will instruct you in the way you should go. You will hear the voice of my Spirit giving you the secrets of my ways. By my side, I will whisper words of life that will make you strong and pure. I am the One who leads you. I will never fail you.

"The privilege of intimately knowing the mystery of God's kingdom realm has been granted to you, but not to the others, where everything is revealed in parables."

MARK 4:11

The dawning light will come.

Y ou have loved me, even when you felt like I was distant. You have sought me, even when your extreme circumstances pushed you into doubt. I will not forsake those who seek me, for you will find that I am more than enough and all that you desire. Your confidence in me is your deliverance—you need nothing else. No one else will satisfy your heart but me. Let your eyes be bright with hope. The dawning light will come. I will never push away the one who seeks me. Even in your captivity, I will be your strength.

Do not forget that Daniel served me while he was a captive in Babylon. He remained faithful to me, even at great cost. Those who watched his life knew that I was his God—the One who unveiled revelation secrets and gave him wisdom. I will do the same for you. You will discover what others have not found. Many will say, "God is with him. God is with her." You will be my true witness. Many will find me as they see how I strengthen and uphold you.

All things work for your enrichment so that more of God's
marvelous grace will spread to more and more people,
resulting in an even greater increase of praise to God,
bringing him even more glory!

2 CORINTHIANS 4:15

Your prayers can flow with power.

Many of my children are trying to correct the path of another, not knowing that I am at work in them, even as I am at work in you. Rest in my love, and I will bring it to pass. I will bring you transformation by the renewing of your mind. Let me bring you into a greater light with greater insight. You will begin to see what I am doing in the life of another and will pray for them with divine wisdom. Until you come higher into my light, you will misunderstand all that I am doing.

I have not called you to judge with a critical heart, but to love. To treat others with the same respect and honor you would like to be treated with. Even when you see the sin of another, come to me in prayer and cry out for my mercy, instead of my judgment. Ask for my perspective. Seek my heart for those walking in deception. I long for intercessors who carry both the power of mercy and the mantle of holiness. Be merciful, as I am merciful, and your prayers will flow with truth and power.

"You will preach to his people the revelation of salvation life,
the cancellation of all our sins, *to bring us back to God.*
The splendor light of heaven's glorious sunrise
is about to break upon us in holy visitation,
all because the merciful heart of our God is so very tender."

LUKE 1:77–78

I am the one who defines you.

I have not rejected you. When others cast you aside and wound you, I draw you close. I long for you to understand who you are and how I see you. Your worth is not defined by the words of others. When those of seeming importance spat at me, called me names, and crucified me, my identity did not change. Your identity is not established on anyone's opinion of you. It is rooted in my truth.

I see within you the capacity for greatness. Not the greatness that is necessarily admired and applauded by others, but true importance and dignity that comes from heaven. Seek to walk in the honor, compassion, and integrity that reminds you who you are in me. Aim to please me, simply because I love you, and peace will replace tears when you lay your head to rest at night.

You are a vessel of my glory. You are beautiful. You are brave. You are loved. You are fearless. You are my treasure. You are wanted. And nothing—absolutely nothing—can separate you from my love.

There is no power above us or beneath us—no power that could ever be found in the universe that can distance us from God's passionate love, which is lavished upon us through our Lord Jesus, the Anointed One!

ROMANS 8:39

This is what I long to do for you.

I call you to joy and thanksgiving! Let every day be the day of magnificent praises! Lift up your eyes and see the blessings I have provided for you, and let the world know that you are mine. The redeemed must say so by their thanks and extravagant praise. Today, set your heart before me, your Father, and learn the sweet lessons of gratitude. I will free you when you give me thanks!

When my Son walked the earth, He demonstrated the power of thanksgiving in the face of lack. Remember when he didn't have enough food to feed the multitudes? Instead of sending them away and relying on natural wisdom, He thanked me for what He had and trusted me to do the rest. I answered by giving more than they needed. This is what I long to do for you. Thank me and stir yourself to praise! Remind yourself that I am the God of miracles. Become a person of gratefulness and shake off that complaining. You're too lovely for that. Watch what I can do in the midst of opposition when you praise me!

He had everyone sit down on the grass as he took the five loaves and two fish. He looked up into heaven, gave thanks to God, and broke the bread into pieces. . . . And everyone ate until they were satisfied, for the food was multiplied in front of their eyes!

MATTHEW 14:19–20

You are rooted in me.

Y ou are a Psalm 1 people—nothing will be able to move you from the brooks of bliss, for you are firmly planted there and have refused to walk in the ways of the unrighteous. For you know your calling. And it's a calling to soar with eagle's wings, high above the status quo. Above the thinking of this cruel world. For yours is the calling of both height and depth.

Your hope reaches into the heavens and your anchor finds its hope in the Holy Place, secured to my mercy. You have a hope that is both strong and unbreakable. It connects you to my heart, steadies your soul, and fastens you to my mercy seat. Love has been your sure foundation, and I am taking your love to a new dimension. For I am knocking off everything that does not look like love. I am making your house, your ministry, and you, over into a more glorious vessel. Any problems you face will only be bumps in the road that I will use for good. For I am your Redeemer and your strength!

They will be standing firm like a flourishing tree
planted by God's design,
deeply rooted by the brooks of bliss,
bearing fruit in every season of their lives.
They are never dry, never fainting,
ever blessed, ever prosperous.

PSALM 1:3

I am making you fruitful and fragrant.

Whatever the enemy tries to use against you for evil, I will use for good. I am your Redeemer who sits in heaven and laughs at the enemy! Never fear, for I will open a new path of victory for you.

Beloved, because you operate in my love, your roots have gone down deep. Your fruit will be huge like the grapes of the Promised Land, for I am giving you the faith of Joshua and Caleb. You are an overcomer, and everyone will see and hear of your fruit and will come to taste it. For I have said that by your fruit you will be known. You will also be known by the fragrance you carry. For you walk in my aroma and leave my fragrance wherever you go. The trials you suffer will only serve to increase the fragrance and bring you out into an even greater expanse! So, say goodbye to the past. It has no future for you! You are lovers of my presence. Troubles, pressures, and problems will not keep you away from heaven's love.

Your spiritual roots go deeply into his life as you are continually infused with strength, encouraged in every way. For you are established in the faith you have absorbed and enriched by your devotion to him!

COLOSSIANS 2:7

You are hidden in me.

Once, I walked past a man. He could not see my face, so I hid him in the cleft of the rock. My servant Moses was my friend and holy partner. Yet I will not walk past you; you will see my face in Jesus Christ. In the wounds of His side, I have placed you. And now your life is hidden, not in a rock but in Christ.

The glory of my Son is now within you. This living hope will keep you strong when others fall away, for you are inside of me. In this hidden place, confusion and turmoil cannot exist. The glory of my life calms every storm and quiets every distraction. I have called you to great faith. Great faith that moves the mountains of fear and finds peace in raging winds. In this quiet place, the beauty of my love changes you. Garments of splendor replace the rags of self. You will sit enthroned with me in the highest place, hidden from the dark powers of earth. Come and seek me with all your heart. I will not hide from you, but I will hide you in me.

Feast on all the treasures of the heavenly realm and fill your thoughts with heavenly realities, and not with the distractions of the natural realm. Your crucifixion with Christ has severed the tie to this life, and now your true life is hidden away in God in Christ.

COLOSSIANS 3:2–3

My purifying fire will fall on you.

My fire is coming to consume and purify your heart. Holy fire is about to fall upon you and all who long for me. It is the fire of cleansing that I have reserved for those who love me. You have passed through fire before, and it left you strong. That was my fire of testing, for all who desire me will be tried by fire.

You have walked through the fire of misunderstanding and remained at my side, but I will release fresh fire that will cling to your soul and make you whole. It is fire power, the power you need to bring my glory to the cities of the earth—this is what I am about to impart.

Every day passes and becomes a memory, but my living presence is eternal, for I dwell among the eternal flames of fire. Torches of fire burn before my throne, the seven spirits of God. They have been sent out into all the earth to baptize my people with power and anoint my servants. Embrace the fire I give to you, and you will receive power to endure and overcome.

"When you pass through the deep, stormy sea,
you can count on me to be there with you.
When you pass through raging rivers,
You will not drown.
When you walk through persecution like fiery flames,
you will not be burned;
the flames will not harm you."

ISAIAH 43:2

I call you to great faith.

I have not called you to little faith, but great faith. Little faith keeps you from finding serenity. Great faith enables you to fully trust in my love. To believe that your cares are in good hands, when you give them to me. To trust more in the things you cannot see, than in what circumstances say are true. Everything about me is life and love and peace. To rest in my life is your Sabbath delight.

Only in me will you find the treasures of wisdom and true knowledge. You can pass through the most difficult season of life and still find peace at the center of your spirit, for there I am. You will not be disappointed when you trust in me. Did not my Son sleep at peace in the middle of a storm? The peace that is found in my nearness will change the atmosphere around you. Relinquish the right to understand with your mind what is meant to be embraced by faith. Come and find rest in this place of trust.

"I leave the gift of peace with you—my peace.
Not the kind of fragile peace given by the world,
but my perfect peace.
Don't yield to fear or be troubled in your hearts—
instead, be courageous!"

JOHN 14:27

June

My grace has already made the way.

I love you in your struggle and weakness. While you are still far off, I run to you with restoration. While you are in the midst of repentance, I am forgiving you. While you are pondering your future, I have gone ahead to open up the way. While you are asleep, I place my grace over you. While you hope that your family is healed, I am at work in hearts to make you whole.

Within you is a deep need. A need for my grace and mercy. Like a river that always seeks the lowest place, my grace runs down into the deepest need of your heart and fills it to overflowing. Soon, you will leap with strength and run victoriously through the ranks of the enemy's forces. I will train you in my grace to win every battle and defeat the discouragement that has sought to muffle your voice. You will run into my grace and find all that you need. I am the extravagant Father who understands you fully. So come and expect me to work through you to change the world.

The confidence of my calling enables me to overcome every difficulty without shame, for I have an intimate revelation of this God. And my faith in him convinces me that he is more than able to keep all that I've placed in his hands safe and secure until the fullness of his appearing.

2 TIMOTHY 1:12

I give you courage.

Today, I bring you the gift of courage. Fresh courage. It is time for you to discover the riches and glory that I have deposited within you. Many are content with what their eyes behold, but you have asked me for more. I see your willing heart to leave the ordinary behind and find the supernatural wealth of my life. So, I bring to you the living energy of faith, which is courage.

I am doing as you have asked—giving you fresh vision for the future, filled with hope and courage to move forward. Every gift must be received and utilized in your journey. So step out in faith and obedience to my Word, and you will find everlasting arms holding you and giving you strength. I come with my sword drawn, ready to fight for you, as you take your place at my feet in worship. Your earthly fears will be dissolved as you bow in fear of me alone. I will guide you in the paths of righteous courage until you stand unashamed in my sacred presence.

"Everything I've taught you is so that the peace which is in me will be in you and will give you great confidence as you rest in me. For in this unbelieving world you will experience trouble and sorrows, but you must be courageous, for I have conquered the world!"

JOHN 16:33

I will become your confidence.

Today, you stand at the threshold of a new beginning. All that is around you will change, and all that I have planted within you will now grow and bear fruit. For I have great things in store for you, things no one has ever proclaimed to you. Many speak of the rain that will soon fall, but I say, it will be a downpour! Many speak of the fire, but they have never been consumed. But with you, my fire will rage and not be contained by the theories of men.

There are many who wish for a new day, but you will be lifted suddenly into a season beyond your imagination or dreams. For it will be my dream that will be fulfilled in your life. So, stand firm in me until I have become your confidence. Set your eyes upon me and don't be worried about your future and your calling, for I am the God who begins and completes, the Alpha and the Omega. You have seen me many times as the Beginning— now you will see me as the Finisher!

I pray with great faith for you, because I'm fully convinced that the One who began this glorious work in you will faithfully continue the process of maturing you and will put his finishing touches to it until the unveiling of our Lord Jesus Christ!

PHILIPPIANS 1:6

My cleansing love will wash over you.

I am cleansing you. Over and over and over—washing you in my love and soaking you in my grace. It's true that you are already clean, for my Word lives in you and brings forth fruit. But did I not wash my beloved disciples' feet? In like manner, I will wash the defilement from your feet until every place you stand becomes holy. Many times, your thoughts need my cleansing fire to destroy the lies that seek to lodge in your heart. I will cleanse your thoughts until you are fixed on nothing but the ways of holiness and purity. I set you apart to be fully mine, and what is it that makes you fully mine? A surrendered heart and a mind that carries my thoughts and brings them in love to others.

Be wise and alert to the deception that is the greatest deception of all: self-deception. The sifting of your motives will continue until your conscience is clean before my glory. I desire purity, not only outwardly, but with every activity and motive. Whatever you speak, speak it as the living truths of God. Whatever you do, do it as unto me.

Keep your thoughts continually fixed on all that is authentic and real, honorable and admirable, beautiful and respectful, pure and holy, merciful and kind. And fasten your thoughts on every glorious work of God, praising him always.

PHILIPPIANS 4:8

I have placed my truth within you.

As you go farther on my holy paths, you will see how I have placed truth deep inside you. You will not follow the crooked ways of using your gift for the admiration of others. You will lay down your crown, your gifts, and your meager substance at my feet, and I will make it holy. Even as I turned a serpent into the rod of God for Moses, I will take crooked things within you and grace you with my authority and presence, until even your weakness has become strength before me.

Move forward, set your eyes on me, and I will bring your destiny to pass. Others may stop on their journey and take steps of selfishness, but you, my holy one, will walk and not faint nor be distracted, for the prize of my glory is set before you. Come with me, and I will make you faithful and true. Linger in my presence with a yielded heart. I will take you as my own and purify every part of you. Every crooked place within you will be filled with my glory.

God, there are two things I'm asking you for before I die, only two:
Empty out of my heart everything that is false—
every lie, and every crooked thing.
And give me neither undue poverty nor undue wealth—
but rather, feed my soul with the measure of prosperity
that pleases you.

PROVERBS 30:7–8

I call you to blaze with holy fire.

Beloved, do not resist my fire. Though it burns and consumes, yield to its power, for I am a zealous God. Many who have resisted my fire will fall away in the coming days. Have I not said that my priests are a blazing fire? Even so, you must first invite the flames of purification and embrace the fires of holiness. Then I will send you out as flames to consume the hearts of men.

Do not put out the Spirit's fire or resist the power and gifts that I give you. As you walk with me and partner with me, my Spirit fire will conquer cities and bring them to the feet of my Son. The lame will walk, and the blind will see. This unreserved unity with me, despite the cost, will radically alter your life, and, in turn, the lives of all you come into contact. Expect me to change your heart, and then you will witness changes, even in your family. You have not yet seen what I will do with a generation that burns holy for me.

"Open your heart and consider my words. Watch out that you do not mistake your opinions for revelation-light! If your spirit burns with light, fully illuminated with no trace of darkness, you will be a shining lamp, reflecting rays of truth by the way you live."

LUKE 11:35–36

Look through my eyes.

C ome and look on my face. Gaze into my glory until you are transformed. I will give you new eyes, *my eyes*, which give you true understanding. When you look through my eyes, the world around you changes. When you see the sick, I see them healed. When you see the lost, I see them asleep and ready to be awakened. When you see darkness approaching, I see the enemy defeated. And when I look at you, I see you completed. Whole. Beautiful. Lacking nothing.

I call you into true vision, so that you might see. Partake of my healing eye salve, and your vision will be clear. I will heal your eyes and cause you to clearly evaluate and discern the day in which you are living. Many see doom; I see glory. Many see devastation; I see my kingdom increasing and having no end. I see the end from the beginning. When you come before my throne, you will see what my prophet Isaiah saw—the whole earth is full of my glory!

"Because this revelation lamp now shines within you,
nothing will be hidden from you—it will all be revealed.
Every secret *of the kingdom* will be unveiled and out in the open,
made known by the revelation-light."

LUKE 8:17

Pay attention to my gentle nudge.

Beloved, I am teaching you how to discern my voice. Many seek for an outward sound when what they need is to tap into the reality of my Spirit within. My voice doesn't always come in the way you expect it. It often alights upon your thoughts as an idea or image. At times, it is random and spontaneous. It never contradicts my Word but flows in perfect synchronicity with it. It leads you to do the seemingly impossible. It flows with compassion, love, and forgiveness. It is wisdom that defies reasoning. It is sometimes outrageous—filled with faith that beckons you to act. Or to rest.

When you pay attention to these gentle nudges that rise within you, miracles have the chance to greet your day. Impossible situations find solutions. Those needing prayer have immediate covering, because you sense me asking you to pray. Favor surprises you, because you followed the leading of my Spirit and ran into that person I needed you to meet. Never dismiss the random thoughts, it very often is a breakthrough waiting to happen!

"Pay careful attention to your hearts as you hear my teaching, for to those who have open hearts, even more revelation will be given to them until it overflows. And for those who do not listen with open hearts, what little light they imagine to have will be taken away."

LUKE 8:18

I offer you perfect freedom.

To be truly free is to live in perfect unity with me and reliance upon me. It comes from a lifestyle of submission. Not submission that stems from duty and obligation, but a true yielding of every aspect of your body, soul, and spirit, because of love. Love beckons you to lay everything at my feet. Every action, each thought, every desire—surrendered to me, the One who loves you perfectly.

When you live in submission to me, seeking my will and desiring to be fully surrendered, nothing can highjack your peace. This doesn't mean you don't experience trials; it means trials no longer have a right to torment you. They don't become bigger than the knowledge of my love and power. When you're free, you feel no pressure to make things happen on your own; you simply live in total trust. Freedom enables you to see clearly, because you act only on my instruction—joyously abandoned to my will. This is the freedom I've called you to. And it releases peace that surpasses all understanding.

Don't be pulled in different directions or worried about a thing. Be saturated in prayer throughout each day, offering your faith-filled requests before God with overflowing gratitude. Tell him every detail of your life, then God's wonderful peace that transcends human understanding, *will make the answers known to you* through Jesus Christ.

PHILIPPIANS 4:6–7

Step out with me.

Prepare your heart and life, because I have come with my presence and love to reshape your present conditions. My Spirit has been speaking, calling you to come closer to me. Any hesitation comes from fear of the unexpected. Put your faith and trust in me. Like Peter, when I called him to walk on the water, so I'm calling you to step out of your conditions and enter the place of unexpected adventure. There, you will find more of my presence, power, and love than ever before.

It's time to stop thinking about your problems. They are designed to steal your focus away from your calling and purpose. I am ready to bring my kingdom into your life, so that you will be transformed and represent the ways of heaven, upon the earth. Your world, your city, your nation, and your generation are drowning—sinking in hopelessness and confusion. But I have given you my Spirit—the very power of resurrection so you will be more than my witness, you will release the fullness of my love. I am ready to invade your world. Step out with me.

"I'm standing at the door, knocking. If your heart is open to hear my voice and you open the door *within*, I will come in to you and feast with you, and you will feast with me."

REVELATION 3:20

I am alive within you.

Y ou put too much pressure on yourself. Too much focus on your ability to hear, to heal, to speak, to do what I ask you to do, as if any of it is contingent upon your ability. What is in your heart to do has been placed there by me. Breathed upon by my Spirit. And it's my Spirit in you that releases miracles.

It isn't based on whether you have faith for what you can do. It's based on faith that I—the living God—truly abide within you. If I am within you, I will manifest through you with very little effort on your part. All that's needed is simple obedience to step beyond the boundaries you have created. Boundaries that set limits on what you believe I can and cannot do through you. Don't look to yourself when I ask you to do something, checking to see if you have the faith for it, look to me—the One who is the embodiment of faith. It has never been, nor will it ever be about what you can do. It is about me. All powerful. Alive within you.

Never doubt God's mighty power to work in you and accomplish all this. He will achieve infinitely more than your greatest request, your most unbelievable dream, and exceed your wildest imagination! He will outdo them all, for his miraculous power constantly energizes you.

EPHESIANS 3:20

There is beauty in your pain.

Your pain has become the birthing ground for the beautiful. Worship, in your greatest devastation, has become a fertile, healthy womb. From the seasons of sorrow, when you bowed before me in surrender, now, come glorious gifts for you to share. Nothing has been overlooked. Now you will see what I will do through you, because of what you endured while you depended upon me. In the place of pain, I have poured out my beauty.

Messy, ugly tears of surrender have made you beautiful. So very beautiful to me. The most perfect offering of your yielded heart. I haven't forgotten one single prayer. I have seen every movement of your heart toward me in your suffering. For every tear, I give you a seed to sow into someone's life. I have taken your sorrow. Cleansed your tears with my love. Now I pour these tears back to you as rain upon dry soil. Golden rain of a new season where flowers bloom and the air is clean and fresh. Breathe deeply, my love. The season has changed.

The season has changed,
the bondage of your barren winter has ended,
and the season of hiding is over and gone.
The rains have soaked the earth
and left it bright with blossoming flowers.
The season for singing and pruning the vines has arrived.

SONG OF SONGS 2:11–12

You are radiant.

I am the One who has formed you and defined you. Others stare at your weaknesses and faults, but I gaze upon your beauty. Twice, I have perfected you—once in your mother's womb and once when you came to know me. You are twice purified in my eyes, for you are mine.

When you surrender to me, it is not you who guides your life, but I am the Good Shepherd who leads you. I have served you my grace, even as you have yielded to me your heart. As you pray, your voice is sweet, and your face is lovely in my eyes. I want you to see yourself the way I see you—holy, powerful, and radiant. I desire only the best for you. I lead you on paths that will not cause you to stumble, as long as you hold my hand. I want you to believe that you are exactly who I say you are. Full of destiny. A perfect partner for me. Never hesitate to give me the desires of your heart. I will bring them to pass.

Look at you, my dearest darling,
you are so lovely!
You are beauty itself to me.
Your passionate eyes are like gentle doves.
SONG OF SONGS 1:15

Choose me.

Life will always demand your attention. Trials will come, and blessings will be poured out extravagantly, but through it all, I must remain your focus. I am the One who longs to fill every void and every joy. I watch you, whisper to you, and never leave you, despite how you feel. Not only do I fill you, I enjoy walking alongside you. It's my pleasure to do even the most mundane tasks with you—if only you would invite me.

Choose me when distractions come. When fear rages against your soul. When people reject you. When isolation strangles you. When laughter pushes you to forget that I am the One who fills you with joy. Choose to love me. To love others. Choose the path of peace even when it leads straight through the middle of pain. Choose to find me—today. To believe that I not only have the power to answer prayers, but also have the wisdom to decline them, and then will use those moments to teach you about my love. Choose to embrace the mystery of life with me.

Just as I moved past them, I encountered him.
I found the one I adore!
I caught him and fastened myself to him,
refusing to be feeble in my heart again.
Now I'll bring him back to the temple within
where I was given new birth—
into my innermost parts, the place of my conceiving.

SONG OF SONGS 3:4

I hold your true identity.

Your difficulties have shaped you, but they will not define you. By creation and by redemption, you are mine! I have set my seal over your heart, and now I display you to the world as my very own masterpiece of love. I have placed my glory over your life and called you *my radiant one*!

The strength to endure life's trials and pressures flows from my life within you. Agree with my truth and remember that you can do all things because of my strength within you. When you speak out of your identity in me, the surging power of my Spirit will lift you high.

Find your pleasure in me, your true identity. The more you delight in me, the freer I become to unleash my glory in your situation. Others will find your flaws, but I have found your virtue. You trusted me when you had nothing and no one to support you. Never doubt the burning love that I have placed within your soul. In that flame, you will find me, and you will hear my voice whisper to you. Beloved, I am your true identity.

I find that the strength of Christ's explosive power infuses me to conquer every difficulty.

PHILIPPIANS 4:13

I want you to be intentionally kind.

B eloved, one of my commandments is to love others as you love yourself. Though many have trouble loving themselves and viewing themselves as important, this is not how I've called you to live. You are to live with the understanding and acceptance that because the Creator of everything thinks you are worthy of love and believes you're beautiful, then you are. Once you've embraced the truth of how I see you, not only can you love yourself but you can love others.

I've designed you to need love, acceptance, and compassion. And I expect you to not only receive it, but to give it. It is out of your wholeness that you are able to love well. I've created you to be part of a bigger picture. Live with intentionality. Seek ways to exemplify my love for others. Don't be so consumed with your own life that you forget to look up. Pay attention to the world around you. Offer a smile. Let someone know you're thinking about them. Do something kind for someone in need. Offer mercy, compassion, and encouragement. Let love and compassion be the driving forces of your life.

"'You must love your neighbor in the same way you love yourself.'
You will never find a greater commandment than these."

MARK 12:31

I call you to love.

I have called you to love. To love me and to open yourself to receive my love in purity and power. To pour yourself out before me as a drink offering, allowing every part of you to seep into me. I'm not afraid of your humanity. I have already paid the price to bring you as close as you would like to come. Don't stand outside of my presence. Come in. Let love overwhelm your weary soul.

Invite my love to saturate you, and it will change you from the inside out. Love will cleanse you and set you free. It will restore your hope and release you to dance with unrestrained joy. My love will enable you to see the beauty you have inside. Love will teach you how to love yourself. And once you understand my love and experience it for yourself, you won't be able to keep it inside. You will run with me, sharing the truth of sacred love to those in need. Let love be the driving force in your life. You can never love too much.

"'Love the Lord your God with every passion of your heart, with all the energy of your being, and with every thought that is within you.' This is the great and supreme commandment. And the second is like it in importance: 'You must love your friend in the same way you love yourself.'"

MATTHEW 22:37–39

Take a vacation from worry today.

My plans will be fulfilled in your life. Just trust in every word that I give you. My beloved, do not despair when you see the deadline is fast approaching. Look intentionally at the reality of my promises for you. Let them become your reality. Meditate on them and remind yourself of what I've done for you in the past. Remember the situations where you came out victorious. Remember, above all things, that my plans for you are good, full of purpose and life.

Don't allow worry and anxiety to force you into action that isn't led by the peace and wisdom of my Spirit. Don't take the weight of delay upon your shoulders, as if it's your burden to bear. You weren't created to live in stress. Lift your voice and declare my goodness. Praise me, because I love you and my plans are good. Trust me to lead you and to make a way. Then rest. Take a vacation day today! Vacation from anxiety, worry, and fear. My reality is and will be fulfilled in you.

You're my place of quiet retreat, and your wrap-around presence
becomes my shield as I wrap myself in your word!

PSALM 119:114

Find my strength within you.

You are stronger than you think. More powerful than you realize. Not because of what you can do in your own strength, but in mine. If nothing is impossible for me, and I live inside of you, then when you walk in union with me, we can do the impossible together! Mountains of impossibility are yours to dance upon.

Hold on to me. Keep your gaze in my direction, especially when the enemy throws smokescreens in your way. I'm here. I haven't left, and I will never leave. Declare my truth when discouragement has cast a shadow over your soul. Keep expecting, and soon I will strip away what darkens your view. My light will infuse you with fresh perspective. My glory will revive you. Be still and catch your breath. Can you feel it now? The fogginess is lifting. Maintain your position of faith. Turn away from frustration and the questions that cause you to doubt. Remember who you are. Don't hold back. Don't give up. Never despair. My strength is found in your weakness.

"My grace is always more than enough for you, and my power finds its full expression through your weakness." So I will celebrate my weaknesses, for when I'm weak I sense more deeply the mighty power of Christ living in me.

2 CORINTHIANS 12:9

Stand on my promises.

This is the hour of receiving and possessing my promises for your future. Many will hear my promise of hope and my word of power, but hearing is no longer enough. It is time to step out and take it as your own. For I am the God who promised the land of Canaan to my servant Joshua. I gave him multiple promises regarding the vast and glorious land. I promised that I would make him victorious in battle. But I also required him to place his feet upon the land before it would be his.

Take my promises today and possess all that I give to you. The promises I gave to Joshua are promises that I give to you— step out in faith and put your feet upon my promises. Claim them as your own. Do not be timid or shrink back when you are surrounded by your giants, but see your giants as opportunities for my power and might to win your battles. Many see the giants and hide in fear, but I have called you to hide in me. And then you will find courage to step into the fray and see your enemies defeated.

Guilty criminals experience paranoia
even though no one threatens them.
But the innocent lovers of God,
because of righteousness,
will have the boldness of a young, ferocious lion!

PROVERBS 28:1

Let a roar rise from within.

B e bold and courageous, until faith spills out from you. Your faith must grow in order for you to receive the promises I have made to you. I will fulfill every word of promise over your life as you partner with me. Do not listen to the voices that tell you to be passive, for I have called you to exercise your faith until you are mighty in me to do great exploits. Giants are defeated all around you as fear is defeated within you. Let a roar rise from within, and it will silence the voice of the enemy.

Never doubt my power to fulfill your destiny and to make your dreams come true. I am the Father of fulfilled dreams and the God of sovereign power. Nothing can defeat my plan for your life, except for your fear and passivity. Arise now, my child, and place your feet upon the promises; make them yours, see them fulfilled, and go out to conquer. I am your God, and I will never leave you or abandon you.

So don't lose your bold, courageous faith, for you are destined for a great reward! You need the strength of endurance to reveal the poetry of God's will and then you receive the promise in full.

HEBREWS 10:35–36

JUNE 22

Let my Word become your foundation.

Beloved, my Word must be your firm foundation. With a word, I formed you. Spoke the entire world into existence. Today, it is still the power of these words that holds everything together. And now you too must discover the unending strength in the absolute truth of my Word.

My Word is your strength, your shield, your sharp weapon against the enemy. It is the light that pierces through the darkness of his camp, and, yes, even the obscurity of your own soul. My Word and my will are one. And I have given you my Word to understand how to divide truth rightly. It is the source of joy, love, and wisdom. It the very definition of truth, because I and my Word are one. It is alive. Calling out to you to dive into its depths and swim within its safety. I have given you my Word so that you will always have treasure to unearth and mysteries to unravel. Unite your heart with mine. Meditate upon my Word and let it flood you with life.

In the very beginning the Living Expression was already there.
And the Living Expression was with God, yet fully God.
They were together—*face-to-face*, in the very beginning.
And through his creative inspiration
this Living Expression made all things,
for nothing has existence apart from him!

JOHN 1:1–3

Do not surrender your peace.

R emember who you are! Remember the lessons I've taught you. Don't surrender your peace to the enemy. Don't sit back and wonder at the way he's bombarding you mentally, now that you've determined to give yourself fully to me. My name is the name that stands above every other name. Stand in the authority you have in my name and tell the heaviness to flee!

It is by my Spirit, not by might or power, that you will see the breakthrough you are searching for. You cannot force it by natural effort, nor do you have to behave perfectly to deserve my help. You cannot earn it. It is my gift to you, because your heart is toward me, because I am your Father and you are my child. Faith in my Word, my truth, my love, and my power is all you need. My love is so powerful, death could not defeat it. The grave could not bury my glory. This is the glory that is within you. This is the power that courses through your veins.

The disciples woke Jesus up and said, "Master, Master, we're sinking! Don't you care that we're going to drown?"
With great authority Jesus rebuked the howling wind and surging waves, and instantly they stopped and became as smooth as glass. Then Jesus said to them, "Why are you fearful? Have you lost your faith *in me*?"

LUKE 8:24–25

My Spirit is alive within you.

All that I am is inside of you. My power is not diminished, because it has found a home in a temple of flesh. I am vast enough to fill all of creation, yet wise enough to fit my glory within vessels of humanity. Never limit the greatness of my glory within you. Never let the frailty of your humanness be reason to doubt what I can do through you. My strength is not limited by the weakness of its surroundings. I am God, after all.

The voice of my Spirit is alive within you, and you were created to hear. To speak my truth and declare my love. My compassion tugs at your heart, but it's up to you to respond. When you walk with me and recognize the greatness of my glory alive within you, you will do what few have dared to do. You will be light in the darkness. Encouragement to the weary. Hope for those who have no hope. Partner with me and allow me to work through you, and you will see the greatness and glory in ways you have never known.

"You must continually bring healing to lepers and to those who are sick, make it your habit to break off the demonic presence from people, and raise the dead back to life. Freely you have received *the power of the kingdom*, so freely release it to others."

MATTHEW 10:8

Remain in my presence.

Thank you for the way you have sought me. For the many times you chose to remain in my presence, instead of allowing distractions to steal your heart. Not one moment of devotion is ever unnoticed. Every movement of your heart toward me is precious in my sight. It delights me to receive your love. It is my joy to see your continual turning toward me. I love catching those little foxes that sneak in and try to ruin our beautiful relationship.

I've seen every struggle. Though at times you didn't notice, I have been with you when you cried, and I hold each tear. I know each breath—each sigh of your heart, as you bow before my throne in surrender. I know the times you've doubted. I've danced with the angels when the battle for your soul only made you stronger. Thank you for depending on me. For trusting when fear fought for your agreement. Beloved, I've seen it all. And I see you now, reaching out to me again. Thank you for your love.

You are my dove, hidden in the split-open rock.
It was I who took you and hid you up high
in the secret stairway of the sky.
Let me see your radiant face and hear your sweet voice.
How beautiful your eyes of worship
and lovely your voice in prayer.
SONG OF SONGS 2:14

I will reveal my power.

This is a day of might and power for all who trust in me. There will be many who will tell you to quit or to walk away, but I whisper into your spirit, "Come closer to me." The days of heaven on earth will now be revealed. My outpouring will be seen in the heavens and on the earth. Never fear the reports of people, for I am the God of the great reversal, and I promise that the days of many changes will result in the days of many miracles.

As the heavens open over your home, believe me for all that you ask. There is no one I cannot touch and transform as you pray to me. The unveiling of mysteries will be seen in the coming days as you continue to walk with me. These are the days when I will pour out heaven on the earth and shake all that must be shaken, so that you will come before me with the purest of faith. Stay close to me, and I will reveal my might and power in your life.

Move your heart closer and closer to God, and he will come even closer to you. But make sure you cleanse your life, you sinners, and keep your heart pure and stop doubting.

JAMES 4:8

I am the glory you need.

Those who love me trust me. Rest in the strength of my love, and you will see more and more breakthroughs. To break open the way for you is my delight, for I have set my love upon you and will rescue you when you call out to me. I never look away when you seek my face.

Even as I taught my servant David how to win in battle, so I will give you keys to victory that will unlock your breakthrough. But come to me in faith, for nothing is impossible when I fight for you. I have opened the heavens over your heart and over your home. You have access to my glory as you come before me with a tender heart. I heard your cries, and your sighs to know me and to see my glory in your situation. Trust me for your family and for every need that is before you today. Have I ever failed to provide for all that you lack? Trust me again and watch as the miracle is released. I alone am the glory you need.

We can all draw close to him with the veil removed from our faces. And with no veil we all become like mirrors who brightly reflect the glory of the Lord *Jesus*. We are being transfigured into his very image as we move from one brighter level of glory to another. And this glorious transfiguration comes from the Lord, who is the Spirit.

2 CORINTHIANS 3:18

Give me your failure.

I see you. No one knows you the way I do. Even in the middle of your greatest failures, my eyes remain focused on you with holy longing. Give me your self-inflicted pain. Lay your guilt at my feet. Let me lift the heaviness of disappointing yourself. Give me your failure, and I will heal your heart. I will get to the core of the shame and disappointment you've carried. I will heal your self-rejection. I will teach you how to be free.

I have no desire for you to walk with the weight of remorse on your shoulders. All I ask is that you offer me your heart again. My only requirement is full surrender. Total yielding to my love and forgiveness. I am the God of restoration. I am the Father who loves you just the way you are. The One whose love flows with healing virtue. The areas that have haunted you with regret will become testimonies of my grace. You will walk with wisdom, rightly discerning every step I want you to take. I have never expected perfection from you, only a willingness to walk with me each day, listening for my voice.

If we freely admit our sins *when his light uncovers them*, he will be faithful to forgive us every time. God is just to forgive us our sins *because of Christ*, and he will continue to cleanse us from all unrighteousness.

1 JOHN 1:9

Put on the garment of praise.

Today is a new day! It is the day I created. A day filled with endless possibilities. A day for you to lift your head and remember who I am. Now is the perfect time to shake off that heaviness and clothe yourself with a garment of praise. Tell weariness to flee. Resist the urge to ignore my instructions, as if they are words that hold no true answer. This is the answer you need today.

I've seen the way you've struggled and made every effort to force things to happen in your timing. Now I want you to trust me for the perfection of mine. I know what you need. I understand the plan for your life in ways you can't even imagine. Will you trust me? Will you believe me and stop trying to figure it out? All I want today, is your offering of praise. Sing! Rejoice! Dance on the head of your problem! Declare my victory before the victory ever happens. Get excited about what I'm doing, because I am doing far more than you know. Celebrate my faithfulness, for this is what being a believer is all about.

I'm boasting of you and all your works,
so let all who are discouraged take heart.
Join me, everyone! Let's praise the Lord together.
Let's make him famous!
Let's make his name glorious to all.

PSALM 34:2–3

You will see my goodness.

The opposition that has come against you is due to the glory I am about to reveal for you and through you. The enemy wants to distract you and force you to think that I will not fulfill my promises. You have stood your ground, but weariness is knocking on your door. Beloved, don't give up. Though the enemy has attempted to sift your faith and steal from you, I am coming to avenge you.

I call you to walk with active faith. To roar your promises with passion and power. To remind yourself that I am a righteous King who never forgets nor turns away from those I love. To resist the temptation to despair. To look with faith-filled expectation, instead of doubt infused predictions. This is not the time to yield to the temptation to break down and give up. It is time to take up your shield of faith. To slice through the darkness with the sword of my Word.

I'm coming to overturn the plans of the enemy that have been put into motion against you. You will see my goodness.

"Peter, my dear friend, listen to what I'm about to tell you. Satan has demanded to come and sift you like wheat and test your faith. But I have prayed for you, Peter, that you would stay faithful to me no matter what comes."

LUKE 22:31–32

July

I am your friend.

Beloved, I am your Savior and Lord, yes, but I am also your Friend. I enjoy spending time with you and hearing about the things that are on your mind. I love laughing with you, creating with you, doing chores with you, and being by your side when you rest.

I am involved in your life. I see every moment of every day. I know what makes you tick. I even love your personality—I gave it to you, after all. The areas you need to work on are things we can tackle together. I don't pull away from you when you neglect me, nor will I ever reject you. I will not judge you, based on your weaknesses, but will cheer you on and remind you of who you are. I can do more than encourage you when you're having a bad day; I can infuse you with strength and wash away your weariness with my smile. So come and enjoy the sweetness of our friendship, and I will share the secrets of my heart with you.

"You show that you are my intimate friends when you obey all that I command you. I have never called you 'servants,' because a master doesn't confide in his servants, and servants don't always understand what the master is doing. But I call you my most intimate friends, for I reveal to you everything that I've heard from my Father."

JOHN 15:14–15

I feel your pain.

My precious child, you are not alone in this pain. I am here, not only to bind your broken heart, but to carry you in your grief. I not only understand your suffering, I share your pain. I feel it too. I am affected by the agony of those I love.

There is a difference, though. I do not dwell on pain. It has no power over me, and I am teaching you to not allow it to have power over you. If you will give me your brokenness, I will take it from you. Place it now in my hands that were pierced for you. Leave it here with me, and I will lighten your load. In exchange, I will pour out my healing balm. It is time to find me in the midst of your anguish. Time to rest in my arms, so I can breathe hope and life into you again. It is okay to feel pain, but now I want you to give it to me. It's time to smile again. It's time to let me heal your heart.

He has not despised my cries of deep despair.
He's my first responder to my sufferings,
and he didn't look the other way when I was in pain.

PSALM 22:24

Winter is over.

Yes, you have entered a new season. You can feel it. You have known it was coming, but now it's here. It's going to take an agreement of faith to leave the old and step into the new, but as you step through the door I open for you, favor will greet you. Your spiritual winter is over. The season of dormancy has ended. It is your season to blossom and bloom.

Let my peace be greater than your understanding. Stay humble, teachable, and ready to hear. Don't assume things will happen the way they always have. Stay close to me. Place your hand in mine, and step each time I step. We must remain in sync. You must see with fresh perspective, yielding what was once comfortable and predictable. What lies ahead may not be exactly as you have anticipated, but it will be filled with occasions to find me with joyful discovery. Cast off the old mindsets and look with happy expectation for all I am about to do.

The season has changed,
the bondage of your barren winter has ended,
and the season of hiding is over and gone.
The rains have soaked the earth
and left it bright with blossoming flowers.
The season for singing and pruning the vines has arrived.
I hear the cooing of doves in our land,
filling the air with songs to awaken you
and guide you forth.

Song of Songs 2:11–12

Stand in my strength.

I call you to come into the faith of God today, for when I speak, it will be done. Hope must mature into greater faith, and expectation must see it accomplished. Listen to my voice and speak my Word, beloved. Hear my whisper and move your heart in faith to receive and proclaim what I have already placed within you. I long for a voice of faith to cry out for me.

Will you move out with me and watch your mountain move before you? The sword of Gideon was his faith in me, as I confirmed my Word before his very eyes. Will you let me be your sword of faith? I send my servants in the strength of my promises, not in human strength. Are you able to stand in my strength alone, or will you look for human props to hold you up? When you doubt my power, you are left with only your flesh. Stand strong in the strength of your Lord, beloved. My presence goes with you, mighty one, so never fear.

At that moment the earth shook beneath them, causing the building they were in to tremble. Each one of them was filled with the Holy Spirit, and they proclaimed the word of God with unrestrained boldness.

ACTS 4:31

True faith knows how to wait.

When you see your limitations, you are blinded to my promises. It is then that you allow the fear of failure to cripple you and prevent you from moving out with me. It is time to fasten your heart to mine and move forward with my Word as your strength. Flames meant to destroy you are quenched by your shield of faith. Voices of accusation meant to weaken you are silenced by my whisper. Faith is a shield of certain victory.

True faith is never in a hurry. It trusts wholly in me and in my wisdom. Many trust in my power, but few wait to trust in my wisdom. I have a time and a plan that is beyond you. A reason for every delay. Trust in my power and in my wisdom, and you will never stumble or be disappointed. Wait patiently, fully convinced that I am in control, and your character will be refined. My answers never come too late, so don't worry about missing your God ordained opportunities. How can you ever fail when I am with you?

Make sure you ask empowered by confident faith without doubting that you will receive. For the ambivalent person believes one minute and doubts the next. Being undecided makes you become like the rough seas driven and tossed by the wind. You're up one minute and tossed down the next.

JAMES 1:6

Live in full surrender.

Your greatest success is a life lived in full surrender to me. This is the place of not only peace and joy, but of wisdom, courage, and success—of heavenly encounters and the miraculous. The greatest calling anyone could ever hope to have is to know me so intimately that their every moment is centered in me. I must always be your first love and main priority. Nothing will ever be more important, for out of your relationship with me life and blessings flow.

To love me with all your heart, soul, and mind means every aspect of your life is fully yielded to me—every thought, each motive, and all desires flowing out of harmonious union with my Spirit. When you have embraced my unending love and can truly believe how absolutely lovesick I am over you, it's easy to trust me. A doubting heart is one that hasn't fully embraced my outrageous love. True freedom is a result of your total dependence upon me. Drink freely of my love and don't be afraid to surrender all.

Jesus answered him, "'Love the Lord your God with every passion of your heart, with all the energy of your being, and with every thought that is within you.'"

MATTHEW 22:37–38

Let me lead you.

A re you willing to release the lesser for the greater? Are you willing to let me lead and guide your life? Your every step? Every door that closes is an opportunity to see me do something greater. Even if the enemy has stolen from you, release the frustration and choose to get excited about what I will do. My ability to bless is much greater than the enemy's ability to steal. Never forget that.

Seasons change, at times, much quicker and more abruptly than you'd like. I've seen you when your soul has been crushed, and you're weighed down with discouragement. But if you will let go of the despair and relinquish the right to be mad, I will show my glory in this situation. All I ask is that you shake off the discouragement, stop asking *why,* and begin to praise me instead. Declare my sovereignty and remind yourself that nothing you place in my hand will ever go unnoticed. You cannot offer me faith and receive a curse in return! Give this situation to me and watch what I will do!

> "All who belong to me now belong to you.
> And all who belong to you now belong to me as well,
> and my glory is revealed through *their surrendered lives."*
>
> JOHN 17:10

I am perfecting you.

What a wonderful hope I have given to you, my beloved. My work in your heart is not yet finished, although you have all of me for all that you lack. A special and glorious work is being done in your heart, for you are my chosen and my redeemed one. My perfect work is being accomplished in your soul. The power of my blood, at my altar of love, will complete you in every way. Then you will be like me and reign at my side, my eternal friend.

The victory of my cross always lives within you. Many see the pain and suffering all around in this world, but your eyes will focus on the glory and joy that is set before you. Everyone who has this hope living in them will be purified as gold. It is my joy to reveal my greatness in the weakness of human flesh. Nothing can set you aside and nothing will defeat you as your eyes are locked on to me.

Keep cleansing me, God,
and keep me from my secret, selfish sins;
may they never rule over me!
For only then will I be free from fault
and remain innocent of rebellion.
So may the words of my mouth, my meditation-thoughts,
and every movement of my heart be always pure and pleasing,
acceptable before your eyes,
my only Redeemer, my Protector-God.

PSALM 19:13–14

Restoration will come with humility.

The restoration of your family will be complete as I heal you. Do not limit what I can do simply because you don't understand it. My glory will be revealed in your family as your heart remains fastened on me. As you release the care of those I love even more than you, you will see me do what only I can do.

As you keep your heart before me, allowing me to purify you, you will see change happen that you cannot orchestrate yourself. When you walk in wholeness, you're able to love with perfect love. Love that expects nothing in return. Love that loves without any agenda. Don't rehearse the problems of others, but come in humility, so I can change *you*. Set love as a torch that burns in your heart, and you will see with your eyes the restoration of all things.

"Why do you focus on the flaw in someone else's life and fail to notice the glaring flaws of your own life? How could you say to your friend, 'Here, let me show you where you're wrong,' when you are guilty of even more than he is? You are overly critical, splitting hairs and being a hypocrite! You must acknowledge your own blind spots and deal with them before you will be able to deal with the blind spot of your friend."

LUKE 6:41–42

Receive your new prayer life.

You've been crying out to know how to pray with the wisdom and accuracy of my Spirit. I have heard your cries and will lead you in new and exciting ways. The areas that you've struggled over—the ones that the enemy has caused you to wonder if I've heard your prayers—will become areas of great strength.

There is no special formula to prayer. There is no right or wrong way. All I seek is a heart that longs to walk in agreement with my truth. A heart that rejoices and believes. Because you've been stirred to ask me for greater clarity in prayer, I am releasing it to you. You don't have to strive to find it. I am giving it to you now. Simply receive. Now, as you go into prayer, listen for the voice of peace and declare with quiet confidence what you hear. It is in the stillness of your heart that you hear me. Lean in to the random, spontaneous thoughts that trickle into your mind. I am always speaking, if you will be still and listen. Get ready to enjoy a glorious prayer life!

When you turn to the right or turn to the left, you will hear his voice behind you to guide you, saying, "This is the right path; follow it."

ISAIAH 30:21

Follow me out of this prison.

Beloved, the enemy has held you in bondage long enough. You have been through the fire, but now is the time for refreshing rain. Though at times you barely held on to hope, you sought me with all you had. I saw it all. And behind the scenes, I was working on your behalf, though you couldn't see it. What felt like loss will be turned into victory.

The prison doors are flinging wide. Follow me out. Don't allow the past to define you. Throw off those grave clothes and wrap yourself in garments of glorious praise. Don't hold on to unforgiveness. Relinquish the right to be mad. I will rewrite your history and give you a new story. A story of provision. A story of joy. A story of healing. The enemy has tried to insert false chapters of delay and hopelessness, but he has been found and expelled. As you look to me with expectation and see the breakthrough with eyes of faith, I will come. I will lead the way out of this season and into the one I have promised you.

The mighty Spirit of Lord Yahweh is wrapped around me
because Yahweh has anointed me.
He sent me to preach good news to the poor,
to heal the wounds of the brokenhearted,
to tell captives, "You are free,"
to tell prisoners "Be free from your darkness."

ISAIAH 61:1

Step into your place.

L earn my ways as you hear my voice. Step into your place next to me. My child, you are seated next to me in the realm of my glory. Filling the atmosphere where we sit are the songs that cause all to cry, "Holy, holy, holy!" Take your place and live in me. Begin to see yourself as I see you. See yourself as my glorious friend and radiant bride, the one I have chosen. Speak the words of adoration as you take your place at my side. Speak over your life, the words that affirm your place in me.

I give to you every heavenly truth you trust in and rest upon. Earthly blessings came to my servants of old, but now, as your Father, I give to you every heavenly blessing. Am I not the Father of lights? I have made you my light to the world. Light and truth will draw you nearer. Will stream from you into the places of darkness around you. You will be defined by the glory in you, and you will be known by the glory that you have embraced.

My darling bride, my private paradise,
fastened to my heart.
A secret spring are you that no one else can have—
my bubbling fountain hidden from public view.
What a perfect partner to me now that I have you.

Song of Songs 4:12

Give me your all.

You are a vessel of my sacred glory. A temple of my Holy Spirit. You were created to know the depths of my love. Designed to interact with me, as my child. As my anointed one. But in order to experience the vastness of what you were created for, you must let go of the hinderances. You must allow me to purify you.

The bellowing winds that try to suck you into a vortex of chaos are nothing but an illusion designed to consume your thoughts. Troubles come and situations arise that need your attention, but you must not allow them to rule your thoughts. Invite me to cleanse you from everything that hinders you from being fully aware of my presence. Things like fear, anger, unholy thoughts, wrong motives—none of these must be allowed to linger within you. Get rid of them! Give them to me once and for all. If you cannot sense my presence, it's because you haven't fully yielded your thoughts to me. Simply offer me these things, then allow your spirit and mind to bask in thoughts of me. I am here.

I come before your presence with my sacrifice.
I'll give you all that I've promised, everything I have.

PSALM 66:13

Sit under the fountain of mercy.

The heavenly realm is yours, beloved. The kingdom of heaven is my gift to you; bring your heart into my kingdom until you are transformed from the inside out. The kingdoms of the earth will fade and fall, but my kingdom will increase and take you from glory to glory. Only come. Abide in my presence. Linger under the refreshing streams of love that flow from my heart to yours. Allow me to fill every crevice. Every fiber of your being.

Seated with me, everything is at rest. Faith becomes the flow of life when you see yourself at my side. Miracles are nothing more than my kingdom piercing the veil and coming into the earthly realm. Faith is the currency of heaven that brings miracles. Take your place of rest and believe, for my day of power is upon you. Come and learn of me, and I will teach you my ways and unveil my heart. Sit under mercy's fountain and live in me, for I am your God.

"Whoever wants to know me and receive my wisdom,
come and dine at my table and drink of my wine.
Lay aside your simple thoughts and leave your paths behind.
Agree with my ways, live in my truth,
and righteousness you will find."

PROVERBS 9:4–6

Let every day be a new beginning.

M y mercies are new every morning. Each day is a fresh start. My glory rushes in to meet you. To invade every crevice of your life, like the sun lapping at the dark night. Do you believe it? Will you reach out with faith and receive it? Let me wash you with my presence and infuse you with my grace. This is the day that I have made for you!

Set your heart on me as you begin your day. Don't allow your thoughts to drift back to the things that stole your peace. Release the cares of yesterday. The enemy wants to invade your thoughts and hijack your peace today. Don't let him! Set your heart and thoughts on me. Let me be your holy obsession. Thoughts of me have a way of wiping away the slimy weight of disappointment. My glory is alive—ready to hold you near. I am the Lover of your soul. The Healer of every tattered heart. Find me now—in these moments before busyness steals you away. We will face the day together in joyful anticipation.

At each and every sunrise you will hear my voice
as I prepare my *sacrifice of* prayer to you.
Every morning I lay out the pieces of my life on the altar
and wait *for your fire to fall upon my heart.*

PSALM 5:3

Seek the confirmation of my Spirit.

As you seek me first in all things, you will be challenged. At times, you will be tempted to heed the counsel of those around you, instead of the wisdom of my Spirit that rises within you. You must always be humble and teachable, honoring those I've placed in your life as leaders, but you must also have an intimate, personal relationship with me. My voice must be the deciding factor. My Word must be your foundation.

The truth is, you cannot please everyone. You cannot expect to always have man's approval. Some issues are too deep for others to understand. Some instructions that I give you won't make sense to anyone but you. Sometimes they won't even make sense to you! There is safety in the multitude of counselors, and very often I guide you through them. However, sometimes the restrictions of religious mindsets will try to suffocate my voice. This is why you must have a relationship with me first. Run to me before you run to the counsel of man. Cry out for my wisdom, for my guidance—more than any other—and I will make your steps plain. Follow the peace within.

If only today you would listen to his voice.
Don't make him angry by hardening your hearts,
as you did in the wilderness rebellion.

HEBREWS 3:15

I will establish you in my name.

Let my Son be your example. He didn't seek to dine with the religious celebrities of the day; He ate with sinners and sat with the broken. He was more concerned with reviving the weary than acknowledging the proud. Compassion drove Him to unpopular places, stirred the hatred of those who misunderstood Him.

All He did, He did because He saw me do it. He followed the path that would lead to death, in order to win your soul. His life was love—a perfect sacrifice. A lowly, humble journey of the greatest power. This is the life I call you to. A life that flows from the stirrings of your heart and enables you to love the way I do. Don't ignore the compassion that rises within you. Don't brush aside the nudges of my Spirit to step away from the limelight and reach into darkness with my glory. Ask me, each step of the way, which path I would take, who I would talk to, and how I see the people you encounter. Don't build a name for yourself. Build my kingdom, and I will establish you in my name.

"I speak to you timeless truth. The Son is not able to do anything from himself or through my own initiative. I only do the works that I see the Father doing, for the Son does the same works as his Father."

JOHN 5:19

Sing louder than the pain.

I know there are times when the last thing you want to do is to praise me. But beloved, in my presence, as you sing my songs of holy devotion and total reliance, you will find sweet release. You will find healing. I know it hurts. I see every word that you barely choke out of your tightened throat. But sing, my beloved. Sing!

Yes, sing! Do the opposite of everything your broken spirit wants to do. I will come. I will heal. I will restore. These are the moments that define you. This is when the enemy loses. When victory lifts you high. This is when my angels come to restore you. When my strength becomes yours. My grace is enough to get you through. I am coming with hope. I am coming with healing in my wings. Don't give up! Sing louder than the enemy's lie. Sing at the top of your lungs until your explosions of unrelenting trust become louder than the pain. I will breathe strength into your fainted heart. I will be your song. I will fill your life with joy once again.

He has not despised my cries of deep despair.
He's my first responder to my sufferings,
and he didn't look the other way when I was in pain.
He was there all the time, listening to the song of the afflicted.

PSALM 22:24

Come with me on a holy adventure.

I want to fill your life with holy adventure. Not the kind you find on pathways of worldly exploration. I am bigger than your dreams. Greater than your most outrageous imagination. I move on the wind. I whisper without words. My very being is three in one. My holiness dwells in the fragility of human flesh. My suffering love is enough to save the entire world. Why would you limit the way I can encounter you?

Fix your eyes on the unexpected. Release yourself fully into the vastness of my love. Get ready to soar on wings of glory and to step into my unexpected ways. Climb mountains, simply because you're standing upon my Word. You cannot conceive my greatness with your limited understanding, but that doesn't mean you can't experience it. Lean in. Better yet, dive in without hesitation. My mysteries are there for you to discover. Like treasures of priceless jewels that I've hidden for you to find. Let your heart leap with childlike wonder. Come with joy and expect the unexpected.

Arise, my darling!
Come quickly, my beloved.
Come and be the graceful gazelle with me.
Come be like a dancing deer with me.
We will dance in the high place of the sky,
yes, on the mountains of fragrant spice.
Forever we shall be united as one!

SONG OF SONGS 8:14

Pain is healed in my love.

In the safety of my love. This is where pain heals. Some wounds, I heal slowly. With gentle warm breath that won't quench a sacred ember of hope, I bring you back to life. Cradle you safely in my arms. Other times, I come roaring with such passionate might that you're healed in an instant.

No matter how I heal you, I *do* heal you. But you must let me. You must free fall off the edge of despair, into unreserved trust in me, and let go of this pain. Place it in my hands. My nail-scarred hands. Choose to relinquish the identity of your pain that you have connected with. Remember who I am. Who you are. It's okay to feel pain, but it cannot define you, beloved. Give me your reasons. Give me your reasons for holding on to the pain. Surrendering doesn't make you weak. It makes you brave. Though it's scary at first, I will knock down those walls you've erected to protect yourself. Don't worry, I will be right by your side.

The Lord is close to all whose hearts are crushed by pain,
and he is always ready to restore the repentant one.
Even when bad things happen to the good and godly ones,
the Lord will save them and not let them be defeated
by what they face.

PSALM 34:18–19

Your battles have become mine.

The enemy has come like a flood to drown you in heartache and disillusionment. It has felt like a never-ending battle. You have stood. You have prayed. You have done all you know to do. Yet you're not seeing the breakthrough. Beloved, I have come to tell you: though you are weary, do not faint. Though your heart aches, release the pain to me. I am planning the victory.

The enemy comes to steal, kill, and destroy, but I have come to give you life in abundance. Your battles have become my battles. Don't be deceived by what you see. The enemy wants to trick you into thinking he's won. That nothing will ever change, unless it gets worse. But he's a liar! Stop listening to him! Look at me, beloved. Just because you don't see what I'm doing, doesn't mean I'm not orchestrating your breakthrough. You're staring at the circumstances, but I'm calling you to rise above them and declare your victory in advance, even if you've done it a million times. Right now, I'm breathing hope into you again. I have gone before you with a roar, and I'm breaking open the way.

You've kept track of all my wandering and my weeping.
You've stored my many tears in your bottle—not one will be lost.
For they are all recorded in your book of remembrance.
The very moment I call to you for a father's help
the tide of battle turns and my enemies flee.
This one thing I know: God is on my side!

PSALM 56:8–9

My promises are true.

My promises are more faithful and true than you have ever imagined. The power of my Word has sustained you through your life and holds you near my heart. Even now, your heart beats because of my promise to you when you were conceived: "You will live." My words are the very power of life. They are worth believing. They are strong enough to stand on. They must become your profession when every dark and trying circumstance comes against you.

Walk upon the water of my Word, and trust in my promises more than sight or human skill. My Word is your strength. I have never failed to keep every promise I have given to you. My Word is more tangible and real than anything you see with your physical eyes, for all that you see has been made by my Word. I call you to step into living by faith through my Word and let all that distracts you fade away. Never underestimate the power of the Word upon your lips. It is alive and true. It is your sword and shield. A mighty weapon of *dunamis* power.

We have the living Word of God, which is full of energy, and it pierces more sharply than a two-mouthed sword. It will even penetrate to the very core of our being where soul and spirit, bone and marrow meet! It interprets and reveals the true thoughts and secret motives of our hearts.

HEBREWS 4:12

I will supply with abundance.

Trust in me and rest in my promises. Am I not the God of abundant supply? Do I not provide for the birds, for the animals of the field, and for every one of my sons and daughters? You are the most valuable and costly part of all my creation. Sacred blood dripped from the tree to show my love. If I have given the blood of my Son to redeem you, will I not also give you everything you need as you walk with me?

When I open doors of opportunity, they will usher you into a new season. Sometimes they seem insignificant and sometimes like a dream come true. But every open door from me is worth going through. My provision doesn't always come the way you expect. I am not limited to natural means. At times, I will surprise you and cause you to stand back in awe and wonder. I am the same God that sent manna from heaven and multiplied the loaves and the fish. My miracle power hasn't changed. My love for you hasn't diminished.

"People everywhere seem to worry about making a living, but your heavenly Father knows your every need and will take care of you. Each and every day he will supply your needs as you seek his kingdom passionately, above all else."

LUKE 12:30–31

My Promises for You.

Speak my promises over your life today. Read the words I have promised you in my Holy Book. Make them real by faith. Place your hands upon my Word, for they are tangible. Trust me. I will not fail you, for I am your Father and Great Shepherd. Believe, my child, even when all around you is contrary, for then you will demonstrate the power of faith.

I invite you to dive into my Word like never before. To seek me for specific promises that I want you to come into agreement. To align your thinking with truth. Not truth as the world interprets it, but truth that is living and unfailing. Truth that you can feel in the depths of your spirit. Truth that makes you feel alive when you hear it and speak it. I can even whisper words of hope and secret treasures that are tailor made for your situation. I can lead you to the answers when you seek me with all your heart and long for the true promises of my Word.

Their pleasure and passion is remaining true to the Word of "I Am,"
meditating day and night in the true revelation of light.
They will be standing firm like a flourishing tree
planted by God's design,
deeply rooted by the brooks of bliss,
bearing fruit in every season of their lives.
They are never dry, never fainting,
ever blessed, ever prosperous.

PSALM 1:2–3

I am reviving you.

Can you feel the breath of wind blowing upon the embers of your faith? I am reviving you so you can believe again. Release the frustration. Relinquish the right to try and understand spiritual matters with your mind. They must be embraced from a much deeper place. They are light, and life, and truth. They are not confined by earthly measures. Faith is outside the limit of time and space. Faith stands in contrast to natural laws, doctors' prognoses, and demonic attacks.

I reward everyone who comes to me in faith—my promise completed, and my presence sealed upon your life. I respond to every movement of faith. Rise now upon this new wind of faith, and you will not be disappointed. Take the steps that I call you to take. Believe, as you hold my promises. Faith is the victory you need, and my promises are the seeds of that victory. Overcome in faith, and you will see with your eyes the kingdom of heaven before you. I am faithful for eternity. I am reviving you.

Search your hearts every day, my brothers and sisters, and make sure that none of you has evil or unbelief hiding within you. For it will lead you astray, and make you unresponsive to the living God.

HEBREWS 3:12

Come to me first.

Beloved, when trials darken your path and trauma threatens to swallow you, reach for me. In the rush of emotion and exasperation, I am the peace that surpasses all understanding. I am all and fill all. I am the answer you need. I am the healing. I am the wisdom. I am the safety. I am the breakthrough. I will lift your head and bring you hope. Come to me, and I will steady you.

I alone am your Savior. No one else has the power to save you from the utter confusion that tries to plague you. Though I give you others to glean from, and those who demonstrate my love, I want you to come to me first. To depend on me more than any other. To believe that I truly am enough. Though I often speak through vessels of clay, I also speak to you from the place of stillness—the place of my presence—when you come to me. Don't reach to others first. Don't broadcast your need to the world before you have sought my wisdom. Come to me. First.

"Above all, constantly chase after the realm of God's kingdom and the righteousness that proceeds from him. Then all these less important things will be given to you abundantly. Refuse to worry about tomorrow, but deal with each challenge that comes your way, one day at a time. Tomorrow will take care of itself."

MATTHEW 6:33–34

Trust my love for the wayward one.

You believe I am powerful enough to save all of humanity through the gift of my Son, and you are correct. My love and wisdom set a plan in action that could not be defeated by the hordes of hell. The blood of Jesus is an unbeatable weapon. My love conquered death itself. Bridged the gap between heaven and earth.

If I knew what it would take to save the entire world, then why do you doubt that I can save the one you've been praying for? Why do you doubt? Trust my wisdom—it's an ongoing force that sees what you see, but knows exactly what to do. Trust that I love them even more than you do. I created them. I know what makes them tick. I know how to woo them back to me. Just because you don't see change yet, doesn't mean I'm not working on them. It doesn't mean the enemy has won. If I am wise enough to save all of humanity, I certainly am wise enough and loving enough to save the one you love. Keep an attitude of expectancy and faith. Keep believing!

"The Son of Man has come to seek out
and to give life to those who are lost."

LUKE 19:10

You are powerful.

Beloved, have you realized how powerful you are? Not because of the volume of your voice, the number of times you fast, or the hours you spend in prayer. You are most powerful when you fully believe in my love for you. You are unbeatable when you fight from a posture of rest.

The weapons of your warfare are powerful through me, through your unshakable confidence of your position *in* me. When you're fully convinced in my love and understand my character, fear won't push you to react. Instead, you will respond with faith. You will believe I am who I say I am. You will find that place of stillness that contradicts warfare, when you trust my love for you. You are powerful when you believe that I am aware of the battle and am fighting for you and alongside you. Rest is one of your most powerful weapons because it reveals the absence of fear in you. Out of the place of rest, I reveal, *through peace*, exactly what you need to do or what you don't need to do. Find your strength in the place of intimacy with me.

Suddenly, as they were crossing the lake, a ferocious tempest arose, with violent winds and waves that were crashing into the boat until it was all but swamped. But Jesus was calmly sleeping in the stern, resting on a cushion.

MARK 4:37–38

Live from the inside out.

My child, I want you to live in such confidence in your relationship with me that nothing moves you. I want you to walk so aware of my presence that you and I carry on a constant conversation. I want you to feel my nearness every moment of the day. I want to draw you into the depths of my heart, day and night.

This is the place I've called you to live—from the inside out. I offer you the chance to know me. To really know my character and to believe in my generous nature. I want you to know me as Savior, Friend, and Overcoming King. I offer you the chance to live in the way you've always dreamed. To be fully aware of the direction I'm leading you. To notice the gentle tug that excitedly and spontaneously pulls you toward your destiny. I want you to be so confident in my Spirit within you that the realm of my kingdom is just as real, or more real, than the situations around you. I want you to live from the inside out.

Jesus responded, "God's kingdom realm does not come simply *by obeying principles* or by waiting for signs. The kingdom is not discovered in one place or another, for God's kingdom realm is already expanding within some of you."

LUKE 17:20–21

I will give you my perspective.

L ife comes at you from so many directions. Whether you're in a season of busyness or a season of waiting, it can be hard to decipher exactly what I've been teaching you. Often, you're so consumed by the details of life that you cannot see the big picture. It's like the saying, "You can't see the forest for the trees." Beloved, I want you to take time to step back and see from my perspective.

Take time to step away from everything on your plate and invite me to show you what I'm teaching you in this season. Get ready; have pen and paper on hand, because when you ask for my perspective, I will surprise you. There are lessons you're learning right now that you cannot learn in any other season of your life. These are truths you will carry with you for all eternity. These are golden nuggets that no one can steal from you. Treasure for you to share. Wisdom that has been unlocked for you, but you haven't taken the time to tap into it. So come, ask me to show you, and I will!

"I counsel you to purchase gold perfected by fire, so that you can be truly rich. Purchase a white garment to cover and clothe your shameful Adam-nakedness. Purchase eye salve to be placed over your eyes so that you can truly see."

REVELATION 3:18

I want you to think like me.

I have called you to be light, love, and wisdom. Sometimes that simply means having a positive attitude in a negative world. It's easy to point out everything that's wrong, but when you see from my point of view, you are able to unmask that truth to those who come across your path. Don't be sucked into the enemy's trap by hanging around negative people. And when you find yourself around them, be the voice of truth. Show them what I see.

It's easy to gripe and complain when you only notice the bad things. But I want you to stop and purposefully look around to find the beauty. To see the good. This doesn't mean you ignore the facts, it means you aren't ruled by them. It means you think like me and discover the good hidden in every situation. Look intentionally for what is right. And if all you see is darkness and corruption, and it weighs heavy on your heart, those may be the very places I've called you to be the light and the answer.

"My thoughts about mercy are not like your thoughts, and my ways are different from yours. As high as the heavens are above the earth, so my ways and my thoughts are higher than yours."

ISAIAH 55:8–9

August

This is what I want for you.

Today, no matter what comes your way, I want you to find me in the midst of it. It's my desire that you become steady and unshakable, in every situation, because of your awareness of me. I want you to pay attention to the stillness of my Spirit inside of you, more than the swirling storms around you.

Anchor yourself in my peace, by processing everything with me—great or small. You don't need to have ups and downs that throw you off course. I want you to enjoy the confidence that comes from the reality of my presence. I want you to experience that presence, with you and in you, every moment of every day. I want your faith to be unmovable, your walk with me to be unwavering and steady. I desire that you experience continual communion with me that becomes your daily practice. When you cultivate our relationship and pay attention to me in every circumstance, no plan of the enemy will keep you down for long. Though at times you will be caught off guard by trials, you will always know that my hand is firmly grasped around yours.

"Do not yield to fear, for I am always near. Never turn your gaze from me, for I am your faithful God. I will infuse you with my strength and help you in every situation. I will hold you firmly with my victorious right hand."

ISAIAH 41:10

I have given you my words.

My beloved, I have given you my words so that you may appropriate them and triumph in every aspect of your life. My words are powerful and alive, able to revive anything in your life that is dead. My words have the power to heal the sickness and disease that afflicts the body. My words are full of peace to silence any storm. My words are full of light, causing darkness to flee.

If you listen to my voice and confidently believe, I promise that my words will come to pass. Feast on my promises. Let my Word be your daily source of life. Only in me will you find joy and abundance. Only in truth will you experience breakthrough. Take time each day to search my Word and know my heart. When you listen and position yourself in trust, faith, and love, you can expect to see my words come to pass. Your love moves my heart, and I long for you to enter into your inheritance today. My Word has the final say.

Your extravagant kindness to me
makes me want to follow your words even more!
Teach me how to make good decisions,
and give me revelation-light, for I believe in your commands.

PSALM 119:65–66

Let my love overflow.

My love for you is vast and endless. It will open your heart to true understanding of my ways and how I work in the hearts of individuals. To love is to see with clear vision. Without love, you will stumble in the dark. But selfishness dies when my love fills your heart. The tests you face are tests of love—to give freely even as you have freely received. Love will win your battle and subdue what troubles you.

Even as my generous love has been given to you, now you are to give and give and give again. My love is an endless fountain. A never-ending spring of life. It is alive. It never fails. It always reaches into the dark messes of troubled souls and does a profound work. My love is the healing balm that cannot be bought. Never underestimate the power of walking in love. When you share my love, especially with those who are difficult to love, the enemy loses his grip. Beloved, let love fill your heart so it will overflow everywhere you go.

Tolerate the weaknesses of those in the family of faith, forgiving one another in the same way you have been graciously forgiven by Jesus Christ. If you find fault with someone, release this same gift of forgiveness to them. For love is supreme and must flow through each of these virtues. Love becomes the mark of true maturity.

COLOSSIANS 3:13–14

Let love rule.

The revelation of truth can only come through love. As you live in my love, I will show myself through your life and through your words. Many are those around you who need me; love them, and they will see me. I have not given you a spirit of fear, but the spirit of love. My holy presence will spill from your heart as you overflow with my love. Many will attempt to distract you from this treasure, but your eyes are fixed on me, and I will hold you fast in my love.

Let all other things become supplemental to love. Love must rule your life, words, actions, and mindset. Loving must become the primary motive of your life. The deepest desire of your heart must be to know and love me first, then to pour that love out to others. Let love compel you. Let compassion lift you. Let wisdom lead you, and the enemy will never be able to trick you into guilty service. See what I'm doing and remain in sync with my Spirit, and you will never be sucked dry or step outside the healthy boundaries of love.

Anyone can say, "I love God," yet have hatred toward another believer. This makes him a phony, because if you don't love a brother or sister, whom you can see, how can you truly love God, whom you can't see?

1 JOHN 4:20

Be transformed by my love.

T he greatest treasure you will ever receive is my love. Drink deeply from this fountain until you are lifted above every distraction and every temptation. Heaven is open to all my lovers to come and drink all that you desire. Come, my child. Be lifted up in my love until all else becomes secondary. Live in this place of perfect love. Love is my nature revealed in perfection.

The demands of the world are silenced by my love—there is an endless supply to satisfy. Love brings peace and confident trust, because it reveals my character. Love releases my mercy. It is the power that cannot be defeated. I have promised to transform you. To change you from the inside out, until you look and sound like me—the Person of Love. Allow my love to work deeper and more thoroughly within you. The change you long for will happen before your very eyes. My love has power to subdue and to conquer what troubles you. Today, I renew my promise: I will transform you by my love.

Jesus knew that the night before Passover would be his last night on earth before leaving this world to return to the Father's side. All throughout his time with his disciples, Jesus had demonstrated a deep and tender love for them. And now he longed to show them the full measure of his love.

JOHN 13:1

I've come to knock down walls.

Your walls shall crumble before me. The seemingly impossible situations that have wounded you and caused you to barricade yourself in, are nothing but paper to me. I can easily flick them away, if you'll invite me. I don't want you to fear being exposed and vulnerable. I created you with emotions that you don't need to be ashamed or embarrassed about.

Though you've hidden behind this protective barrier, I desire to draw you out. To make you comfortable in your own skin. To know how to trust. How to love. To knock those walls down and set you free. You don't have to hold it all together. You don't have to appear to be something you're not. And you don't need to protect yourself. Let me protect you. Let me heal you with the holy oil of my presence. I want you to walk in awareness of my presence, but I also want you to be aware of your own heart. To give yourself time to get to know yourself and to find the greatness of me, inside of you. To know the truth that extinguishes fear. To let my glory be your only enclosure.

We will build a tower of redemption to protect her.
Since she is vulnerable,
we will enclose her with a wall of cedar boards.

SONG OF SONGS 8:9

Just breathe.

You don't have to strive to hear me or feel my presence. You aren't required to do anything—no conjuring emotions. No stressing about whether you've heard my voice. All you need to do is believe I'm with you. That's it. That's all I require—for you to believe, despite what you see or feel. To simply let go and exist in this moment with me.

Be still. Know I'm right there with you, even if you don't feel me. I know how to move the hearts I've created. You were made for my love. You were created to know my voice. You are destined to see my face. Only, don't try and push to make it happen. Lean back into my arms that are holding you right now, embracing you. Rest in this present moment with me. I am the center of everything. I am the truth that holds it all together. I am already with you, currently exploding with love in the very center of your being. You don't need to do a thing. Just be. Just breathe.

Lord Yahweh, the Holy One of Israel, says: "Come back to me! By returning and resting in me you will be saved. In quietness and trust you will be made strong."

ISAIAH 30:15

I am the Prince of Peace.

I am the Prince of Peace. I rule and reign over stress and turmoil, when you set me as the King over your every thought. I hold everything together in perfect harmony when you bow before me and yield to me—spirit, soul, and body. Anxiety and peace cannot coexist.

Though your busy mind unwittingly pushes me away, I know your heart yearns for me. Don't fret, my beloved. I always respond to hearts that reach for me. Exalt my presence by lifting me higher than the cares that plague your mind. You are powerful enough to choose what you think about. Offer me the sacrifice of praise, by placing those cares on the altar. Give them to me. Force those concerns to bow low before my majesty. Make them submit to the glory that rushes through your veins. Say my name. Sing your songs of love. Sink deep into the stillness of my peace. Leave every single care in my hands. Name each one if you must; then trust me to take care of them. Let me be the only thought that consumes you.

"I leave the gift of peace with you—my peace. Not the kind of fragile peace given by the world, but my perfect peace. Don't yield to fear or be troubled in your hearts—instead, be courageous!"

JOHN 14:27

Search for me.

To love me with all of your heart means to bow before my glory. Many sing the songs of my glory, but when I bring the fullness of my presence to you, it requires you to bow before me in sacred reverence. I dwell in light unapproachable. Transcendent. Different from anything you have known on this earth. Search for me, and you will learn what it means to fear the Lord.

Live in the awareness of my omnipotence and majesty. Know me as Savior and Friend, but humbly yield to me as the King of kings and the Lord of lords. As you live from the place of awe and reverence, I beckon you closer. I purify you and make you more like me. Remember that I have called you to be a vessel of my holy presence. All of my greatness dwells within you. To fear me doesn't mean you stand far off, eyes averted, heart pounding, and the awareness of your sin screaming for its punishment. Instead, fearing me humbly reminds you of the power of my love, extended in mercy. Not pushing you away, but pulling you close.

After this, the church all over Judea, Galilee, and Samaria experienced a season of peace. The congregations grew larger and larger, with the believers being empowered and encouraged by the Holy Spirit. They worshiped God in wonder and awe, and walked in the fear of the Lord.

ACTS 9:31

You are a beautiful dwelling place.

Make your heart a citadel of worship, a castle of praise, where only what is holy and pure can dwell. To love me in my holiness is to have a wall around your garden, a wall of protection and blessing. In this place of sacred intimacy, you will find no deceit of darkness and the lies that have influenced your heart. Surrounded by my glory, you will renounce the self-absorption of your life.

Come closer to me and be lost in my love. We will delight in one another, and I will help you keep your garden fruitful and pure. As you remain in sweet fellowship with me each day, sin loses its grip. Temptation is meaningless. Righteousness and purity are the norm. You are my garden. My joy. My delight. The reflection of my glory. See yourself the way I see you. As you live in this place of continual communion, your fullness becomes a feast for others. A loving example of my total and unwavering devotion to them. You are my beautiful dwelling.

"Loving me empowers you to obey my word. And my Father will love you so deeply that we will come to you and make you our dwelling place."

JOHN 14:23

Embrace the mystery.

R ise up and come away with me. Live in mystery, with no full understanding of what I am doing in your life. Faith will provide the insight you need, to know where I am taking you and what I am doing deep in your soul. Many still feed on the Tree of Knowledge of Good and Evil, but I will feed you from within, where the Tree of Life has been planted.

The fruit of my Spirit will satisfy you. Feast on this tree that was planted by the springs of my Spirit. Do not turn away from the unknown. Be like my faithful one, Moses, who turned aside to gaze on the fire of my presence. I will draw you into secrets where dancing flames bring revelation and wisdom to your soul. Lean in to my presence, and I will pour out the fragrance of divine love. Come closer, and you will taste the mystery of our sweet union. See beyond the veil. Forsake the confines of your understanding, and embrace the mystery of life with me.

You are my dove, hidden in the split-open rock.
It was I who took you and hid you up high
in the secret stairway of the sky.
Let me see your radiant face and hear your sweet voice.
How beautiful your eyes of worship
and lovely your voice in prayer.

SONG OF SONGS 2:14

Delight yourself in me.

C ome close to me and sit with me on my mercy seat, where love is enthroned. Dwell with me in the cloud of mystery. Delight in my mercy. Drink your fill of the wine of my Spirit. The new and life-giving way into my presence has been dedicated for you. Enter, feast, and be delighted in my love. Steep yourself in my love, until every fiber of your being is saturated.

My secrets are reserved for those who fear me and bow in worship at my throne. I seek those whose greatest desire is to know me. Whose heart longs for me in holy wonder. Whose soul thirsts for the Living Waters. Who desires purity in their deepest parts. As you surrender all, I fill you with *my* all. I infuse you with wisdom, glory, and strength. Here, in this place of sacred surrender, you will find your destiny. You will taste eternal pleasures that begin here on earth and continue forevermore. Delight yourself in me, and you will feel the warmth of my radiant smile upon your life.

Who is this one? Look at her now!
She arises out of her desert, clinging to her beloved.
When I awakened you under the apple tree,
as you were feasting upon me,
I awakened your innermost being with the travail of birth
as you longed for more of me.

Song of Songs 8:5

Exchange your thoughts for mine.

t's easy to know exactly where your focus is. If you listen closely to what pours from your lips, you'll understand what's on your heart. I long for you to walk in a continual state of confidence, peace, and joy. But when your mind leads the way, highlighting everything that's upsetting you, it will overwhelm your spirit.

You must seek to live in the awareness of my nearness. It's not enough to forsake complaining or to resist the enemy. You must stay close to me. Confidently embracing my perspective. Constantly inviting my presence to rule your atmosphere. No one says in my presence, "I am afraid." It's never heard in my glory, "I am poor." In my presence all cry, "Glory!" Come into the shelter of my shadow, where all my lovers are washed, robed, crowned, and seated with me. I care deeply for you, and nothing can disturb you here in the safety of my glory. Come and exchange your thoughts for mine. You have the mind of Christ.

Those who live in the Spirit are able to carefully evaluate all things, and they are subject to the scrutiny of no one *but God*. For Who has ever intimately known the mind of the Lord Yahweh well enough to become his counselor? *Christ has*, and we possess Christ's perceptions.

1 CORINTHIANS 2:15–16

You were created for the significant.

Y ou are not defeated. You are not destined for a mundane, pointless, hollow life. I created you for a meaningful, fruitful, satisfying, and significant life. I created you to walk with me in a way few have ever known. I created you for glory. But in order to enjoy the life I've fashioned for you, you must believe. You must seek me as your *ultimate* goal. You must set time aside to be with me and hear my instructions. You must agree with *me* when everything in your life feels out of sorts.

Ask for more faith and seek a courageous heart. Knock on my eternal doors, and they will open to you. Watch the miracles come forth from your proclamations of faith and victory! Nothing will turn you aside when you walk with me by faith, seeing the invisible, loving the eternal, and living for the supernatural. Rise up, mighty one, and take your place with my overcomers. I am with you, and that will always be enough.

You are not forgotten, for you have been chosen and destined by Father God. The Holy Spirit has set you apart to be God's holy ones, obedient followers of Jesus Christ who have been *gloriously* sprinkled with his blood. May God's delightful grace and peace cascade over you many times over!

1 PETER 1:2

I am the contentment you seek.

Become a disciple—a learner of my ways. There is still much more to learn of how I bring you into the highest realm, the place where love prevails. The happiness of life is not found in circumstances; it is discovered when you know that my hand of love is guiding and leading you, even in life's darkest valleys. The contentment you seek cannot be found outside of me.

There is a stability that will keep you strong and focused, and it comes from knowing the triumph of love in every moment of your life. Set your heart on me, rely on my victorious grace, and you will be an overcomer. Then you will know me, not from hearsay, but from heart-deep experiences of intimacy with your God. Come to me and let me teach you. I will sit with you and unveil truths that few dare to hear. When I become the treasure you seek, more than any other, you will find joy and contentment in ways you've never dreamed possible.

"I offer peace to those who are far from me,
and I offer peace to those who are near,
and I will heal their deepest wounds," says Yahweh.

ISAIAH 58:19

You will know a deeper love.

A deeper place in me is calling out to a deeper love in you. I will bring you beyond the shallow and superficial and take you deeper into my endless love. Love that heals. Love that sets you free from guilt and pain. Love that cannot be found in the arms of any other. Love that is alive, calling out to you.

When you yield yourself to me without reservation, seeking to grow more and more into the person I desire you to be, shackles break. Wounds are healed by the power of my love. Areas that you need to grow in, become things we tackle together. Excitement for the deeper things of my kingdom, stirs the longing of your heart and sets you free to run after me. The façade of having it all together is stripped away, and you discover that the real you is perfectly loved. Fully known and accepted. The walls that surround you will crumble and fall down to the victory of my love. When everything else fails you, my love will win the day!

My deep need calls out to the deep kindness of your love.
Your waterfall of weeping sent waves of sorrow
over my soul, carrying me away,
cascading over me like a thundering cataract.

PSALM 42:7

I will carry you.

When you are weary and cannot seem to find a way to connect to my presence, reach for me, and I will carry you. When all you can do is bow low and whisper with faint surrender, I am there. I never dismiss your cries for help. I hear every movement of your heart toward me. I'm here, beloved. Lay back into my arms and give me every care. Every worry. All of your pain. I am here, and I will carry you straight into my presence.

In your weakness, I am strong. I don't fault you for being affected by these trials that have sought to take you out. Instead, I smother your weakness with my strength and draw you near. I hold hope in my hands and will massage it ever so gently into your heart. In my presence, you will find relief. In my arms, you will find comfort. I will pour out my love so profusely, you will be consumed with peace again. I will carry you beyond the threshold of pain into a beautiful place of victory.

"Are you weary, carrying a heavy burden? Then come to me. I will refresh your life, for I am your oasis. Simply join your life with mine. Learn my ways and you'll discover that I'm gentle, humble, easy to please. You will find refreshment and rest in me."

MATTHEW 11:28–29

Find your balance in me.

Disappointments will come, but you mustn't allow them to distance you from me. Blessings will most certainly be poured out, but don't forget me when they do. Though nothing can separate you from my love for you, distractions can dull your awareness of this love. Both sorrow and joy can either catapult you closer to me or cause you to drift away. In all things, you must maintain your constant awareness of me. Seeking me above all else.

Busyness is normal, but it's also something the enemy tries to use to get you off track. He wants to keep you so busy, you lose sight of me. Delight in me, the way I delight in you. Keep me as the center of your heart, and I will help you navigate through every season of the soul. I will teach you how to balance family and friendship, work and play, dreams and goals. Set aside time to connect with me each day. Linger with me. Separate yourself to come away with me. Talk to me throughout your day, and I will help you balance the details of your life.

Stop imitating the ideals and opinions of the culture around you, but be inwardly transformed by the Holy Spirit through a total reformation of how you think. This will empower you to discern God's will as you live a beautiful life, satisfying and perfect in his eyes.

ROMANS 12:2

Remember who you are.

Come closer, and let's talk about who you truly are. You are not only my beloved child, but my beautiful bride. You are the mouthpiece that I speak through. Say my name, and all heaven and hell take notice. You are the hands that I heal through. Watch how I will lead you to others who need my touch. You are my partner in ministry. Together, we release light into darkness. The dwelling place of my Holy Spirit.

The same Spirit that raised me from the grave, lives inside of you. Don't you see how powerful you are? And you are inside of me—living, moving, and existing in the wonder of mysterious union. In me, you lack nothing. My glory can revive you from weariness. It's like a pep talk for your soul. My divine passion restores your soul and causes you to roar with confidence against the enemy. You were worth the price of sacred blood. So stand tall. Be confident and humble, my anointed one. Remember who you are.

My old identity has been co-crucified with Messiah and no longer lives; *for the nails of his cross crucified me with him*. And now the essence of this new life is no longer mine, for the Anointed One lives his life through me—*we live in union as one*! My new life is empowered by the faith of the Son of God who loves me so much that he gave himself for me, and dispenses his life into mine!

GALATIANS 2:20

Your worship is beautiful to me.

Your worship leaves me undone. I have watched the way you pour out your love in the midst of pain. In the seasons of confusion and frustration, you chose me over all others. I see. I know. I hear the love songs that pour from your lips. Your love is my great delight. It has my attention. It ravishes my heart. Your worship is heard in heaven.

Angels listen for your songs. They are drawn to your melodies of love to me. Your songs of praise awaken their worship and bring forth cries of "Holy!" Give me the deepest place of your spirit, and you will experience the deepest place of my love. I withhold nothing from you. All things are now yours, because you have embraced me. Come within the chamber room of my delight and let me hear your voice, for your voice is sweet and your face is lovely as you worship me. Sing with all your heart, sing your love songs, and the angels will join you in worship and adoration.

I long to bring you to my innermost chamber—
this holy sanctuary you have formed within me.
O that I might carry you within me.
I would give you the spiced wine of my love,
this full cup of bliss that we share.

SONG OF SONGS 8:2

Your words are important.

Beloved one, I want you to watch your words. Pay attention to what you say, because it reveals what lies deep within your heart. Do you continuously talk about things that disturb you? Are you constantly complaining? Or are you giving me all of your frustration, in order to enjoy life with me? You can come to understand more about yourself by acknowledging what you talk about, and then by bringing those things to me so I can purify your heart.

Keep your speech in agreement with what I have declared to be true in my Word. Remind yourself often of what I say. Let my Word sink into the depths of your being, until it becomes a part of you. If you will tune in to the sound of heaven, you will notice when the things you say contradict my truth. Speak words of life and light. Your words will bring a blessing or a curse, depending on which kingdom they agree with. They can connect you to the source of my limitless power, or drag you down into places you should not be. Never think your words are unimportant. I listen to every word you speak.

"You can be sure of this: when the day of judgment comes, everyone will be held accountable for every careless word he has spoken. Your very words will be used as evidence against you, and your words will declare you either innocent or guilty."

MATTHEW 12:36–37

These are not your problems.

B eloved, don't hold so tightly to the situations you cannot fix. Give them to me. All of them. Completely. Do you know what will happen when you fully release those cares? You'll step into a dimension of freedom unlike anything you've ever known. Believe it or not, I don't need you to mentally assess every problem, in order to find a solution. It isn't your job to fix everything. And no amount of worry is going to change *anything*.

Sometimes, I need you to do something. Sometimes, there are steps you must take in order to put things on track. But you won't stumble upon the answers by racking your brain and clenching the problem tightly. They aren't your problems, anyway. They're ours. Together. So release difficult situations into my hands, step back, and quiet yourself in my presence. Then you will be able to hear my instructions clearly and experience the peace that comes with them. And if I don't want you to do anything other than to trust me and find peace, you must believe that I know what I'm doing. Let go and trust me.

Say to the anxious and fearful, "Be strong and never afraid. Look, here comes your God! He is breaking through to give you victory! He comes to avenge your enemies. With divine retribution he comes to save you!"

ISAIAH 35:4

Be free from the snare of unforgiveness.

L ove and forgiveness are a part of my nature. Likewise, they must be part of yours. I want you to reflect my character and to do things that feel contrary to the nature of your flesh. You may have every right to be angry and upset, but those who walk in great mercy are those who have embraced mercy for themselves. I alone judge the hearts of man. It is not your job to condemn and declare judgment. It is your responsibility to forgive. After all, think of the many things I've forgiven you for.

And if you're having a difficult time forgiving, I can help you with that too. Be honest about how you feel and come to me with your pain. Let's walk through the process of healing your heart, so that you can stand whole and healthy, able to release forgiveness. You will gain an entirely new understanding of strength, when you become free and confident in my example of mercy. And ultimately, beloved, this is what I want for you— to be free from the snare of unforgiveness. I even want you to extend forgiveness to yourself.

"When you pray, make sure you forgive the faults of others so that your Father in heaven will also forgive you. But if you withhold forgiveness from others, your Father withholds forgiveness from you."

MATTHEW 6:14–15

Praise your way through.

Praise your way into faith. When you're falling apart and things look bleak, praise your way out of the darkness. Don't go deeper into your pain, come up higher and praise your way into freedom. Praise will open your eyes to my wonders. It will pull me into your situation in a special way, for I cannot resist your love and faith. Praise me in advance for what I'm about to do, for I will do the seemingly impossible.

Remember who I am. I am the God of miracles! And your praise will build a platform for the miraculous. I am the God of triumph. I will give recompense. I will take what the enemy has done and turn it around. I am the Mighty One. And I alone am your vindicator. I will stand up for you. Leave your cares in my hand and turn your eyes to me. Let your praise catapult you over the walls of fear, sorrow, confusion, and disillusionment. Remember what I've done. Praise your way through this!

Lord, I will worship you with extended hands
as my whole heart explodes with praise!
I will tell everyone everywhere about your wonderful works
and how your marvelous miracles exceed expectations!
I will jump for joy and shout in triumph
as I sing your song and make music for the Most High God.
For when you appear, I worship
while all of my enemies run in retreat.
They stumble and perish before your presence.

PSALM 9:1–3

Joy will come again.

I am the God of the brokenhearted. When the pain of life beats you up, I am your safe refuge. Hide yourself in me. Come away and rest in me. I am your Healer, and I am kind. I am merciful, and I am good. I love you, and I know how to heal your tender heart. Don't doubt, beloved. Believe in my healing love. Believe in my mercy. Believe in my mighty power. Believe that I am worth trusting.

I am the King of glory. I am bigger and more magnificent than you can possibly imagine. Even when you fall or disappoint yourself, I am with you. Rest in my finished work. Open your heart to me. Will you? Will you let me flood you with healing and peace once again? I will lift you up and resuscitate your faith.

It's okay to go through seasons of grief and weariness, but after I've strengthened you, take my hand and walk with me back into joy. I will not neglect you! Joy will come again. This is my promise to you.

Do it again! Those Yahweh has set free will return to Zion and come celebrating with songs of joy! They will be crowned with never-ending joy! Gladness and joy will overwhelm them; despair and depression will disappear!

ISAIAH 51:11

It is time for your giants to fall.

Get ready to be undone. Completely and totally undone—wrecked by my outrageous love that is being released in your life. You will be amazed by what I'm about to do for you. It's time for your giants to fall!

I have heard your prayers. I have seen your tears. I have watched as you stood on shaking legs that felt like they couldn't take another step. Though the enemy works to steal, kill, and destroy, my glory has made you strong. It is time for you to see what I can do. Time for you to cross the threshold of opposition and step into the joy of breakthrough. Now is the time to be joyfully expectant. To allow yourself to be filled with anticipation. Confident. Not because I do everything the way you think I will, but because you trust me to do things my way. Anchor yourself in my promises, and soon you'll see the fruit of what I've already put into action behind the scenes. You will be astounded at the victory I am releasing. Bewildered by the way I bring these things to pass.

When I had nothing, desperate and defeated,
I cried out to the Lord and he heard me,
bringing his miracle-deliverance when I needed it most.
The angel of the Lord stooped down to listen as I prayed,
encircling me, empowering me, and showing me how to escape.
He will do this for everyone who fears God.

PSALM 34:6–7

Find me in your pain.

Beloved, I don't want you to experience deep emotion, such as anger, fear, and sorrow, and then sweep it under the rug. I want you to acknowledge it. I want you to listen to your reactions and the things that trigger you, and come to me, so I can nurture you with my love.

Every pain is rooted in something that needs my touch and acknowledgement. You don't have to dig around and poke old wounds, looking for problems, but pay attention when life triggers you. Many of the things that feel like an endless cycle are road signs to areas that need healing. If you will ask me to show you the underlying causes of unhealthy emotions, I will. I not only know everything about you, but I also know how to heal you. I don't want you to live an introspective life, focused on the pain, but to focus on me in the midst of it. To find *me* in the pain, and to hear what *I* have to say about it. Don't run from the things you don't understand, but do acknowledge these issues and trust me to bring wisdom, insight, and freedom.

You draw near to those who call out to you,
listening closely, especially when their hearts are true.
Every one of your godly lovers receives
even more than what they ask for.
For you hear what their hearts really long for
and you bring them your saving strength.

PSALM 145:18–19

I am with you in your time of need.

I've loved you from the beginning. I've held you close even when you were a child. I have always been with you. I haven't left, and I never will. Let me bring you through this. Let go of the questions. They cannot be satisfied with an answer that your natural mind can grasp. My answers will be unveiled, as your heart finds hope in me.

Over time, you will understand. You will see the way I cared for you in your time of great need. My answers are deep wells of wisdom that must be drunk one cupful at a time. Buried treasure that takes time to unearth. In my wisdom and compassion, I slowly and carefully unveil only what you can handle. One day you will see clearly past the shadows. But right now, all you need to know is that I love you. I am with you. We will get through this together. The enemy has not won. He is a defeated foe, and one day you will see his ultimate destruction, while you dance with me in victory. Rest now, beloved. Rest in my arms of love.

You comfort me by your counsel;
you draw me closer to you.
You lead me with your secret wisdom.
And following you brings me into your brightness and glory!
Whom have I in heaven but you? You're all I want!
No one on earth means as much to me as you.

PSALM 73:23–25

Intimacy prepares you for ministry.

Intimacy with me is the precursor for ministry. The very foundation for everything else in life. Out of your relationship with me, ministry flows. Unless you are overflowing, you will depend on your own strength and knowledge to reach others. I have a better way. The way of my Spirit. The way of grace—to be so close to me that you only do and say what I show you.

Plunge yourself into the ocean of my love. Saturate yourself in my presence, and you will drip with my love everywhere you go. When you take up your cross and sacrifice your selfishness for greater intimacy, I move through you mightily. When you make our relationship the priority, ministry will be the natural response. You cannot love me and not love others. You cannot be one with me and not feel my compassion for the people around you. Don't let your fears, attitudes, or opinions get in the way of our holy partnership. Simply submerge your will into the fires of divine passion, and I will purify all that you do.

Out of your innermost being
is flowing the fullness of my Spirit—
never failing to satisfy.
Within your womb there is a birthing of harvest wheat;
they are the sons and daughters
nurtured by the purity you impart.
How gracious you have become!

SONG OF SONGS 7:2–3

Freely pour out my mercy.

I long to be merciful to those who turn to me. My grace has restored your soul, and your life's portion now overflows. I desire for you to be merciful to the guilty, gracious to the unworthy, and kind to those who mistreat you. Freely, you have been given these virtues, now freely give them away and watch them multiply.

Never forget where you've come from. Never take my mercy for granted. Maintain awareness that I alone am the One who has saved you from destruction. I love to take lives and change them with my glory. Now I want you to do the same. I want you to release my presence everywhere you go. Don't ignore my gentle nudges when you see those who need something you have. Don't turn your nose up at those who are in error, or who are different from you. I don't condemn the one who turns to me. I never withhold forgiveness to those who repent. Mercy multiplies when you take what I've given you and pour it out freely to those in need.

"How satisfied you are when you demonstrate tender mercy!
For tender mercy will be demonstrated to you. What bliss you
experience when your heart is pure! For then your eyes will open to
see more and more of God. How blessed you are when you make
peace! For then you will be recognized as a true child of God."

MATTHEW 5:7–9

Let nothing hinder our communion.

To hold a grudge against another is a binding chain to your soul, preventing you from arising and coming away with me. Forgive and watch my victory be released within you. I will heal your body and your thoughts when you release forgiveness to the one who offended you. My grace is flowing, and it will never be stopped. I will give you the glory of grace as you give away mercy.

Let my grace make you stronger than your enemies and wiser than your foes. There are many ways the enemy tries to trip you up so that you are distracted from my presence in and around you. But if you intentionally keep me first and submit every thought, even the fleeting thoughts that stream in the background of your mind, you will stay in the flow of my glory. Pay attention to your reactions to situations and never try to justify wrong attitudes. Love others with a pure love. My love. Ask me to show you people from my perspective, and walk humbly with me throughout your day.

You must catch the troubling foxes,
those sly little foxes that hinder our relationship.
For they raid our budding vineyard of love
to ruin what I've planted within you.
Will you catch them and remove them for me?
We will do it together.

SONG OF SONGS 2:15

September

Do not let the enemy distort your view.

L ife fights to capture every ounce of your attention. Trials maneuver themselves in front of you, in order to shift your focus away from me. The enemy knows that if you're consumed and overwhelmed by what you see, he'll have an entryway to your thought processes. He seeks to smother you in the angst of what you see. But you were created for a higher way.

Set *me* before your eyes. Let *me* be the barrier between you and the problem. Look to me, and then, through the light of my glory, you'll see the trial with heavenly clarity. Filter every situation through the screen of my goodness, power, love, and divinity. When my glory fills your vision, nothing is able to distort your view. Circumstances must not be allowed the opportunity to lord themselves over you. Though trials may factually be present, they must not be allowed to consume your vision. See me standing in front of you. Look through my glory, and you will see these problems through the light of truth. It is only when the light of truth has penetrated deep into your being that you will see with my perspective.

We view our slight, short-lived troubles in the light of eternity. We see our difficulties as the substance that produces for us an eternal, weighty glory far beyond all comparison, because we don't focus our attention on what is seen but on what is unseen. For what is seen is temporary, but the unseen realm is eternal.

2 CORINTHIANS 4:17–18

Pay attention to my presence.

Beloved, I want you to soak in my glory today. To find me in every moment and in every situation. To focus on my truth, when facts slam their fists into your vision. To still yourself in my ever-present love, even when you're busy. To let me love you. To listen with expectation, for all I desire to say to you today. To sense my glory filling you so completely that you drip with my presence everywhere you go.

This is the life I've called you to, every day. A life that remains connected to me. Aware of me. In agreement with me. This is the joy of walking with me—my tangible presence that never needs to dissipate. If something flusters you and tries to suffocate the awareness of my presence, simply turn your attention back to me. When you sense my presence lifting, it's because you've become distracted by something else. I'm always here. Always drawing you to myself. In all you do, pay attention to the glory of my love. Seek me first. Seek me continually.

Where could I go from your Spirit?
Where could I run and hide from your face?
If I go up to heaven, you're there!
If I go down to the realm of the dead, you're there too!
If I fly with wings into the shining dawn, you're there!
If I fly into the radiant sunset, you're there waiting!

PSALM 139:7–9

I want you to dance upon the ashes.

Every place that the enemy has come against you is a place for future victory, a stage set for you to sing of my triumphant love, a launching pad into my magnificent restoration. Every trauma can be turned into a place of exorbitant strength, when you invite me into your pain.

Beloved, the enemy hates when his plans backfire. He'd rather knock you out and keep you out, but when you walk in the highest reality of my love, nothing can hold you down forever. If you take my hand, I will lead you to the mountain peaks, where your laughter will echo into every valley that once held your dry bones. But first, we will stop and dance upon the ashes. We will sow the seeds of resurrection life into what appears dead and desolate. Each step of love, and every movement of grace, will release a resurgence of hope and joy. Though you have witnessed loss and destruction, life will come forth despite it all.

I am sent to announce a new season of Yahweh's grace
and a time of God's recompense on his enemies,
to comfort all who are in sorrow,
to strengthen those crushed by despair who mourn in Zion—
to give them a beautiful bouquet in the place of ashes,
the oil of bliss instead of tears, and the mantle of joyous praise
instead of the spirit of heaviness.

Isaiah 61:2–3

The prodigals will return.

I am calling home the sons and daughters who have forgotten me. You will see a waterfall of love and mercy bring my sons and daughters from afar. I have walled them in—they haven't roamed as far as you expected. They are never outside of the boundaries of my love. I have never left their side. I know how to woo the hearts I created. They cannot find what they need, outside of me. In my mercy, they will be restored with fresh passion to seek me and to know me.

Dry your eyes, and with hope-filled hearts, look with eyes of faith. The lost ones are coming home. Your delight must be in finding them and loving them back into wholeness and dignity. You will remove loneliness from their hearts. You will see them restored. Even within your family, there will be healing and grace as I recapture hearts and ignite their longings toward me. Love well. Forgive completely. You will see the restoration you've prayed for. My will shall be done in their lives.

"There once was a shepherd with a hundred lambs, but one of his lambs wandered away and was lost. So the shepherd left the ninety-nine lambs out in the open field and searched in the wilderness for that one lost lamb. He didn't stop until he finally found it. With exuberant joy he raised it up and placed it on his shoulders, carrying it back with cheerful delight!"

LUKE 15:4–5

Enjoy the freedom of being with me.

Learn to be with me in stillness, without worrying about what you should do. Take time to enjoy my presence and to be refreshed in the depths of your being. I don't always need you to *do* something. It's okay to simply be with me in rest. To quiet yourself and find me as your Source of peace. To feel the waves of my love washing over your soul and reviving you. Existing in the reality of my love and enjoying me is more important than any religious duty.

The same is true of your identity. Who you are in this life isn't summed up by what you do, but in who you are—who you truly are in the depths of your being, out of the life-flow of my Spirit within you. I'm less concerned about you discovering what I'd have you *do*, than about who I've called you to *be*. Once you embrace the essence of your identity in me, you will naturally flow into the things I want you to do. Enjoy the freedom to *be*. Embrace the simplicity of childlikeness, as you find yourself in me.

Lord, you are a paradise of protection to me.
You lift me high above the fray.
None of my foes can touch me
when I'm held firmly in your wrap-around presence!
Keep me in this glory.
Let me live continually under your splendor-shadow,
hiding my life in you forever.

PSALM 61:3–4

Come receive exactly what you need.

The moments you spend in my presence, listening to me and soaking in my love, are moments filled with eternity. This is where I energize your being. Many influences have affected your life and your thoughts, but as you come into my glory, I lavish upon you what you need the most: my love and my strength. You are so easily distracted and disturbed, so you must faithfully come and be with me.

I am always enough. Always exactly what you need. In my presence is fullness of joy. In my wrap-around presence, you will find the wisdom you seek. You will encounter love that has no comparison. Loneliness is nonexistent when the glory of heaven rushes in. Fear does not exist in the presence of perfect love. Healing for your spirit, soul, and body is released as you revel in the beauty of the cross. There is no weakness, no wavering, no doubting in my presence. Never worry about locking the world out and spending too much time with me. Everything else can wait, as we linger together in the beauty of this moment.

Bring me a continual revelation of resurrection life,
the path to the bliss that brings me face-to-face with you.

Psalm 16:11

Praise opens the door.

Walk with me on the highway of praise, and I will remove your unbelief. You have asked for greater faith. I will grant it, but it requires that you walk in the spirit of gratitude for all things. Faith and complaining cannot live together, my beloved. You will either have great faith and gratitude, or you will have great doubt and complaining. Choose to praise, and watch as your faith increases.

Walk with me on the highway of praise, and the prison doors that have held you back will fling wide open, just as they did for Paul and Silas. Your praise is like a portal of glory that connects your will to mine. It enables you to think like me and to see with the clarity of heaven's perspective. Praise receives the finished work of faith, in the midst of waiting. It is teeming with life that is not silenced by contrary circumstances. Rejoice in all that I'm doing, especially when you cannot see it with your natural eyes. Praise will lift you higher. Praise will remove the shroud of unbelief.

Paul and Silas, undaunted, prayed in the middle of the night and sang songs of praise to God, while all the other prisoners listened to their worship. Suddenly, a great earthquake shook the foundations of the prison. All at once every prison door flung open and the chains of all the prisoners came loose.

ACTS 16:25–26

Experience peace in your trials.

The peace I bring to you is not comparable to the peace known on earth. It transcends your mortal life and streams to you from my river of tranquility that pours forth from my throne of grace. Peace like a river will subdue your soul and wash away the words of hopelessness and pain. Come into my river of peace and float on my promises. There you will never be disappointed.

Listen to me and peace will be your pillow on which to rest your anxious thoughts. Yield your endlessly running thoughts to my sovereignty. Be okay with letting go and experiencing what it's like to trust me unreservedly. Peace is much deeper than your mindful understanding. It often contradicts what makes sense, but I want you to become comfortable with allowing yourself to be at peace even during trials. It doesn't feel natural to walk in peace when circumstances are screaming in your face, but this is the life of one who is fully confident in my love and goodness. I want you to walk in that peace, and then release it to those around you.

"I leave the gift of peace with you—my peace. Not the kind of fragile peace given by the world, but my perfect peace. Don't yield to fear or be troubled in your hearts—instead, be courageous!"

JOHN 14:27

I am smiling at you.

Beloved, when the whole world is busy and chaotic, close your eyes and find my face. I'm smiling at you. When things feel out of control, and you don't handle things correctly, I'm still smiling at you. Can you feel my heart for you? You move me in a way no one else does. You are the one I love.

Even when you're weak and feel disconnected from my presence, I'm still here. Still smiling at you. I still see you through the eyes of love. Even in your mess, I still love you. I know you and believe in you, because I know who you're destined to be. You are beautiful in the very depths of your being. Sometimes you get so caught up in everything that's happening around you, the things that fight to be noticed, but I want you to stop and see my smile. And then I want you to smile with me. To be so fixated on my joy for what is to come that nothing can shake you.

Yahweh will comfort Zion, restore her, and comfort all her broken places. He will transform her wilderness into the garden of Bliss, her desert into the garden of Yahweh. Joy and laughter will fill the air with thanksgiving and joyous melodies.

ISAIAH 51:3

Give me your time.

I n my love, you are able to do all things, for I strengthen you with my love. People make demands on your time and your thoughts, but I wait for you to come and draw you closer when you choose me above your friends and family. Come as my dearest one, and I will give you grace for your dearest ones on earth, so you may show them my love.

When you give me your time, I give you my strength. Are you feeling weak today? Then come before me until you are bathed in power. Sit in my presence and come back to the truths I will remind you of. No human being can empower you, for their weapons are puny and helpless. Trust in my strength, not in the affirmation of others. Watch me work in your heart as you "waste" your time in my presence. I will pour you out upon the earth as my gift and my treasure, full of my love. As you sit with me and unite yourself to my heart, you will be filled with all you need to touch the world.

Here's the one thing I crave from God,
the one thing I seek above all else:
I want the privilege of living with him every moment in his house,
finding the sweet loveliness of his face,
filled with awe, delighting in his glory and grace.
I want to live my life so close to him
that he takes pleasure in my every prayer.

PSALM 27:4

Resist worry like a plague.

Never say, "It is my nature to worry," for I have given you a life that is carefree. Has worry brought you any blessings? I will take care of your tomorrow, as I have taken care of your today. Your relationship with me means that I will carry every burden that weighs you down, so that you can take my peace as your own. My love will take you through this momentary difficulty.

Beloved, you were created in my image. Created to look and sound like me. And worry was not a part of that plan, which is why it feels so horrible when you get sucked into it. I want you to choose peace. To resist worry like the plague. Worrying isn't going to make things better. It pushes you far from faith and slows down the process of your breakthrough, because you have trouble hearing me when you're anxious. Rest with me in the green pastures of my peace and drink from the quiet brook of bliss. Let worry be far from you—not one thing can disturb you as you rest with me.

"If God can clothe the fields and meadows with grass and flowers, can't he clothe you as well, O struggling one with so many doubts? I repeat it: Don't let worry enter your life. Live above the anxious cares about your personal needs."

LUKE 12:28–29

Trust me more than your plans.

Beloved, I see your restlessness to make things happen. I love your excitement, but I must warn you against striving to do things in your own strength. Walking in my will releases my grace. Remaining in my timing and trusting me to open doors is the only way this is going to be all you've dreamed it to be. You cannot force my hand. You must not fight so hard to see my will come to pass that you actually step out of my timing and grace.

I'm asking you to trust me with your plans. Make them, but then release them to me in total trust and confidence. Pay attention to the gentle nudges, as I direct you to the right people and places. Don't ignore those spontaneous, random ideas that spark inside of you—often, they are the key you need for the next step of your journey. I love your excitement, but we are in this for the long haul. Wisdom will lead you; you only need to ask and believe.

Dear friends, don't let this one thing escape your notice: a single day counts like a thousand years to the Lord Yahweh, and a thousand years counts as one day. This means that, *contrary to man's perspective*, the Lord is not late with his promise *to return*, as some measure lateness. But rather, his "delay" simply reveals his loving patience toward you, because he does not want any to perish but all to come to repentance.

2 PETER 3:8–9

I will write my name upon your heart.

Come and sit with me. Let me remind you how I see you and the situations you're facing. I will whisper words of encouragement unlike any other. I am a faithful Friend. A kind Lord. An unchanging Savior. I am the Alpha and Omega—I see the end of things from the very beginning.

I have wisdom beyond compare. Wisdom I will share with you. My outlook on your life is from a perfect vantage point. When you spend time with me, your heart beats in harmony with mine. You feel the breath of my Spirit, gently easing you into alignment with my will. You will fulfill your destiny when you stay in tune with me. I want you to see your story through my lens. Each chapter flowing with grace and glory. I want to establish you in my love and give you the courage to dream again. Come and find your strength in me. Come and let me write my name upon your heart.

We are convinced that every detail of our lives is continually woven together to fit into God's perfect plan of bringing good into our lives, for we are his lovers who have been called to fulfill his designed purpose.

ROMANS 8:28

I will heal your heart.

Y ou will be a healer of souls and a restorer of hearts, as I bring you higher in my ways. Give yourself to me, forgive all who wound you, and I will work on your behalf. Let your name be synonymous with mercy and grace. Wrap yourself in my likeness. Pour out forgiveness, the way I have done for you.

I know what pain is like. I understand what it's like to be rejected and misunderstood. But it's this pain that breaks you open, so that you can receive my love like a healing balm. As my glory pours into your wounded soul, it expands—saturating every cell and memory. Soon, anger melts away and is replaced with compassion. Even your greatest pain can be healed, when you embrace mercy for others. You will witness my victory within, when you release freedom to those who have hurt you. Don't hold on to the pain, staring at it like it is yours. I bore your pain and grief. Give me your pain, and I will heal your heart, so you can heal others.

Let the sunrise of your love end our dark night.
Break through our clouded dawn again!
Only you can satisfy our hearts,
filling us with songs of joy to the end of our days.
We've been overwhelmed with grief;
come now and overwhelm us with gladness.
Replace our years of trouble with decades of delight.

PSALM 90:14–15

Do not hesitate to step out.

The sweet taste of joy has filled your heart, but I have even more for you as you leave behind the predictable. Step into all that I have chosen to bring to pass in your life. I will direct you by my glory cloud and with my presence. Faith does not hesitate when my cloud has moved. I delight in you and will never leave you, for you are mine.

Never be afraid to step out, and you will find more of me. I have gone before you to prepare the way, and I will be your peace. When you take risks and let my light shine in the dark places, my glory will explode on the scene. I am with you, for you, and working through you. All that I am in you, I want to pour out through you to others. Step into the newness of what I have for you, and you will see the power of my Spirit released through you. I have equipped you with all that you need, and I will be the grace for every step you take.

Jesus called out to them and said, "Come and follow me,
and I will transform you into men who catch people for God."

MATTHEW 4:19

You have a purpose.

Beloved, I don't want you to get so caught up in searching for what I've called you to do that you miss the bigger picture. The simple yet profound truth about your life can be summed up in this: The purpose of your life is to be with me. To know me. To love me and receive my love in ways you still don't know are possible.

Yes, I do have a blueprint for your life. There are plans to be fulfilled and dreams to be realized, but those aren't as important as our relationship. I want our union to be sweet and full. I want you to be so consumed with me that everything else is secondary. Spouses aren't required to feel loved, and careers and ministry aren't needed for you to find fulfillment. Every blessing is icing on the cake—extra. I want you to find total and complete contentment in our love. Then everything else I have for you will flow freely. Easily. And it won't become an idol or a source of stress. Let's enjoy our union. Nothing matters more than this.

You reach into my heart.
With one flash of your eyes I am undone by your love,
my beloved, my equal, my bride.
You leave me breathless—
I am overcome
by merely a glance from your worshiping eyes,
for you have stolen my heart.
I am held hostage by your love
and by the graces of righteousness shining upon you.

SONG OF SONGS 4:9

The season of change has come.

The season of change you have anticipated has now come. It will be your love for me that will see you through the most difficult times. Disruptive revelation that brings the shocking truth to the media, to the government, and to my church—disruptive revelation that overturns the tables of religious profit—will bring about my righteous ways.

New mission strategies are coming in dreams and through prayer. Great understanding of my mysteries is coming to those who sit with me on my blood-sprinkled love seat. The old order is quickly passing away, and a new breed is arising. Known as day breakers and dawn makers, they belong to me and to me alone. As my fiery servants, they accelerate the changes I am bringing to the earth. They will bring back my ways of holiness and passionate love.

The season of change has come. The time to love me with all your heart and passion. You have heard it before, but I declare it again—you will never be the same, for I have placed my hands upon you, my church, my bride.

The season has changed,
the bondage of your barren winter has ended,
and the season of hiding is over and gone.
The rains have soaked the earth
and left it bright with blossoming flowers.
The season for singing and pruning the vines has arrived.

SONG OF SONGS 2:11–12

Demonstrate my compassion.

Beloved, I want you to release my love and compassion to the world around you. You don't need a title, a microphone, or an endorsement. You already have what you need—the life of my Spirit inside you. Let me unveil my Son within you, the very existence of my perfection in human flesh. It's not wishful thinking. You are a vessel of my holiness.

The lost are looking for an encounter. They want to know that I'm real. That I care. They don't need a pamphlet or for you to point out their sin—they are already aware of it. They need a fresh sample of my reality. A touch from heaven, released through you. A word of encouragement that draws them close, not a lecture that pushes them away. I don't need you to guilt people into repentance. I need you to demonstrate my compassion and lavish them with truth that softens their heart. As you go about your day, be sensitive to the tug of my Spirit within you, and let your attention be drawn to the needs of the people in front of you. Be my hands and mouthpiece, and I will do the rest.

If I were to have *the gift of* prophecy with a profound understanding of God's hidden secrets, and if I possessed unending supernatural knowledge, and if I had the greatest gift of faith that could move mountains, but have never learned to love, then I am nothing.

1 CORINTHIANS 13:2

The help you need begins with me.

I will renew your heart and spirit this day, to know me as the God of heaven. My presence lives within you. Where my presence abides, there is heaven. Where I am, glory is found. Living within you at this moment is the heavenly glory that I have given to my sons and daughters. Many look away to heaven and fail to embrace the eternal life that dwells within them. Everything that makes heaven real lives in you, my child.

The help you need starts with me. Come to me and find rest. Come to me, and you'll have perfect wisdom. Very often, I speak to you through others, but I want you to come to me first. I want you to get into the habit of seeking me before you seek the advice and help of others. Truly, embrace my existence inside of you and encounter me before you run to anyone else. When you start with me, your heart is prepared to hear the wisdom and guidance I speak through others. Trust our relationship above all others. Come to me first.

Arise, my dearest. Hurry, my darling. Come away with me! I have come as you have asked to draw you to my heart and lead you out. For now is the time, my beautiful one. The season has changed, the bondage of your barren winter has ended.

SONG OF SONGS 2:10–11

I offer you heavenly realities.

Beloved, I want you to become more aware of the reality of my kingdom in and around you. I want you to wake up and feel the breath of heaven warm against your skin. Throughout the day, I want you to find the peace and grace of my Spirit, as you turn your attention to my presence within you. When you're protected in surprising ways, I want you to remember that I've place my angels around you. Day and night, I offer you encounters of a reality much more profound than your earthly one. I want to bring you heaven on earth.

Soon, heavenly realities will be made clear. All that is around you will become nothing more than trinkets compared to the glory within you. My endless grace has opened a fountain within, pouring satisfying streams into your thoughts, your emotions, your very soul. This grace-fountain will be the source of life—heavenly life—within you. Love, joy, and peace is my presence in your soul. Presence that is alive and real. Pay attention, beloved, my glory is everywhere.

Feast on all the treasures of the heavenly realm and fill your thoughts with heavenly realities, and not with the distractions of the natural realm.

REVELATION 1:14–16

Heavenly life is your portion.

Heavenly life is my portion that I share with you today. Have I not seated you in heavenly places and enthroned you at my right hand as an overcomer? All that I am, I give to you. Receive more, for there are always greater treasures of revelation. Drink of the water of life, which flows from before my throne. It is my joy to bestow upon you every blessing, paid for with my blood.

This heavenly life doesn't mean you will never face trials. It doesn't mean that you won't ever have a bad day. As a matter of fact, your enemy hates you because you are mine. What it does mean is that during trials, you'll have a place of refuge. When you're having a bad day, you'll know how to tap into my grace. When the enemy rears his ugly head, you have a fountain of joy that makes him mad. For every opposition, you will taste victory. Heaven's gift is yours, this very day. The gift of my Spirit within you. The gift of an overcomer.

Every spiritual blessing in the heavenly realm has already been lavished upon us as a love gift from our wonderful heavenly Father, the Father of our Lord Jesus—all because he sees us wrapped into Christ. This is why we celebrate him with all our hearts!

EPHESIANS 1:3

Set your affections on me.

Focus on what I'm doing. Stop being more in awe of what the enemy does than you are of my limitless possibilities. Let your mind be renewed and brought into a heavenly perspective. Your life, your true life, is now hidden in my realm of glory. This is where your focus must be. Set your eyes and your affections on heavenly things, and watch the healing of your heart be complete.

My children, come into my courts and see what I have provided for my household. I have a heavenly eye salve that will cause your eyes to open to the brightness of my glory. I have pure robes to place upon your inadequacy and weakness. Seek my face, forsake your habits of passivity, and stir your heart to come into my heavenly chamber. Praise me, and I will open doors into greater glory. I am the God who makes you new, strong, and courageous. It's in me that you live, move, and exist fully. Let this knowledge bring you into the fulfilling life I have designed you to have.

"He has done this so that every person would long for God, feel their way to him, and find him—for he is the God who is easy to discover! It is through him that we live and function and have our identity; just as your own poets have said, 'Our lineage comes from him.'"

ACTS 17:27–28

I call you my own.

You are my precious child. Sealed with a divine kiss and brought into the kingdom of light. Like all good parents, I look at you and see perfection. I see the reflection of myself in you. I see the tender musings of your heart as you lean in to my strong arms. I am here for you, and I will never leave.

I am a good and faithful Father. I am gentle and kind, and know exactly how to help you grow from one stage of glory to the other. I never withhold mercy. I always provide for your needs, although sometimes you balk at the way I choose to do it. I give you my strength, I clothe you with my radiance, and I made a way for us to be together forever. I am so happy to call you my own. So enjoy our conversations and the sound of your laughter. There isn't anything about you that pushes me away. Even when the frailty of your human flesh is obvious, I declare you worthy, beautiful, and mine.

So that we would know for sure that we are his true children, God released the Spirit of Sonship into our hearts—moving us to cry out intimately, "My Father! You're our true Father!" Now we're no longer living like slaves *under the law*, but we enjoy being God's very own sons and daughters! And because we're his, we can access everything our Father has—for we are heirs of God through Jesus, the Messiah!

GALATIANS 4:6–7

Trust my timing.

The days of completion are mine, not yours. I will complete the work I have for you as my perfected timing comes to pass. Even as my ways are perfect, so my timing is perfect. For you have said, *It seems I am standing still and going nowhere.* But I say over you, I am unfolding my glory upon you even as you wait on me. I will make it happen and show you my perfection.

What often feels like an endless season of wait, is often a time of preparation. You must believe in things you cannot see. You must trust that even when things seem silent, I am working on your behalf. If you judge my faithfulness by what you see, you aren't in faith at all. Faith believes despite the obvious. It remains tapped into me. Honed in on the promises that I made. Don't let go of those promises, beloved. Don't doubt my love or faithfulness, because it's taking longer than expected. Stir yourself up to believe again. Dig your heels in, take a deep breath, and trust my timing.

Here's what I've learned through it all:
Don't give up; don't be impatient;
be entwined as one with the Lord.
Be brave and courageous, and never lose hope.
Yes, keep on waiting—for he will never disappoint you!

PSALM 27:14

You are stronger than you think.

S hake off that heaviness. Stop agreeing with defeat. Don't align yourself with any reasoning that comes from the pit of hell. I am your Champion, your Hero. I didn't lay my life down for you and then leave you defenseless. You have my Spirit. The same Spirit that raised me from the grave lives inside of you!

Situations may have left you feeling overwhelmed, but it's not the end. I make all things new, and I refresh you in the process. My Spirit is a wellspring of joy when you feel dry and depleted. Rest if you need rest. Cry if your heart is grieving. Talk to me about your anger. Process these feelings with me. But don't stay in this place of weariness. I am not only your Helper, I am your Counselor and Deliverer. Let my love seep into every dry and cracked place. Come away with me, and I will restore you. My strength will become yours, and I will set you on the mountaintop once again.

You will be the inner strength of all your people,
the mighty protector of all,
the saving strength for all your anointed ones.
Keep protecting and cherishing your chosen ones;
in you they will never fall.
Like a shepherd going before us, keep leading us forward,
forever carrying us in your arms!

PSALM 28:8–9

Wholeness begins with me.

I am your safe place, where you can run and find refuge. I also want *you* to be a safe place. To be healthy and whole within yourself—confident in your identity, able to love me, love yourself, and to know how to care for yourself—spirit, soul, and body. Every part of you matters. Every aspect of your life is important. I don't want you to sweep things under the rug that affect you in any way.

Listen to what you need in the deepest part of your being. If it's rest, rest. If it's fun, friendship, or adventure, go enjoy yourself. If it's healing in your spirit, come to me. If it's a healthy body, ask me what changes you can make. If it's learning to set boundaries and finding confidence, I can help you with that too. Wholeness and peace start with me. It's a journey of discovering me inside of you, and then processing your emotions, needs, and desires with me. I want you to be so healthy in every part of your being that each day becomes something to look forward to. When you're healthy and whole, it's much easier to bring healing to others.

May the God of peace and harmony set you apart, making you completely holy. And may your entire being—spirit, soul, and body—be kept completely flawless in the appearing of our Lord Jesus, the Anointed One. The one who calls you by name is trustworthy and will thoroughly complete his work in you.

1 Thessalonians 5:23–24

Lean in.

You were made to experience my perfect love. Love that outshines all others. Love that is completely pure and selfless. Love that paid a price for you that no one else could ever pay so thoroughly. There is no human on earth that will fill your heart so intensely. To continue seeking for fulfillment in everyone else but me, will ultimately leave you empty.

Come away with me. Join me in sacred intimacy, where I can pour out my glory into every area of need. Where we can share secrets, and I can surprise you with fresh revelation. You need more than the occasional conversation with me; you were created for heavenly encounter. Lean in. Separate time to be alone with me. No one holds your heart more tenderly or carefully as I do. I am the love that stepped out of eternity to save you. I love you so much that it is hard for you to comprehend. And though it's difficult for you to understand, it is love that you can enjoy with every fiber of your being.

Arise, my love, my beautiful companion,
and run with me to the higher place.
For now is the time to arise and come away with me.

SONG OF SONGS 2:13

Walk with me moment by moment.

Walking the straight and narrow road isn't as hard as you think. It isn't about the things you give up in order to live in right standing with me. It's about staying close to me, so you don't veer from the path. It's about fixing your heart on me and learning to submit every aspect of your life to me, moment by moment. When your thoughts and silent musings cause you to drift away from the knowledge of my presence, it's easy to trip.

It's vital that you pay attention to the checks in your spirit—those subtle warnings that I give you. Many times, you have dismissed them as your own thoughts, but they are me letting you know not to do something or to go in a different direction than you had planned.

Everyone has their own journey, their own relationship with me. Don't judge what others do when I've asked you not to do it. And don't expect others to do the things I've asked you to do. Be careful to guard your heart at all times. Eyes fixed on me. This is our moment-to-moment walk.

Guard the affections of your heart,
for they affect all that you are.
Pay attention to the welfare of your innermost being,
for from there flows the wellspring of life.

PROVERBS 4:23

I am working in your life.

I am removing all that blocks my free-flowing Spirit from pouring out of your life. You will walk in me with power, in the days ahead, my child. I will baptize your life in my mighty Spirit until everything has changed within you. There will be no limit to the flow of my conquering life. You will know a greater anointing and become the person I have destined you to be.

Growth comes when you live close to me with a surrendered heart. Trust me to highlight the areas I want you to work on, instead of walking around with your focus inward, always looking for things that are wrong with you. I have already rescued you from darkness. Everything you need to walk in victory, power, and might is already yours. When you stay in tune with my Spirit, turning your attention to me at all times, you can rest assured that you are growing more and more like me every day. This is a life that pleases me. This is the way you bear fruit for my glory.

We pray that you would walk in the ways of true righteousness, pleasing God in every good thing you do. Then you'll become fruit-bearing branches, yielding to his life, and maturing in the rich experience of knowing God in his fullness! And we pray that you would be energized with all his explosive power from the realm of his magnificent glory, filling you with great hope.

COLOSSIANS 1:10–11

Release shame to me.

My blood is the fire of purity that washes every sin away. To hold on to shame is to refuse the gift that I've given you—the gift of freedom. Maintaining those feelings of guilt won't make you a better person. Accept my forgiveness and forgive yourself, and I will heal your heart and set you free.

Put sin behind you. Once you've repented for what you've done, or neglected to do, I've forgiven you. If you haven't asked for forgiveness, you only need to ask, and I will pour it out like rain. My mercy is never ending, and there is nothing my mercy does not cover. I don't want you to live with a mindset of *What if I would have . . . ?* or *What if I wouldn't have . . . ?* Don't allow the past to hold such a strong grip on you that you forget the price I paid to set you free. Guilt is a trap of the enemy—a ploy to keep you so focused on yourself and your mistakes that you lose sight of my grace. If you will come to me today and give me your shame, I will heal your heart. Forgive yourself and embrace my grace.

"If the Son sets you free from sin,
then become a true son and be unquestionably free!"

JOHN 8:36

October

I will give you faith.

Y ou are not called to walk this road alone. I am with you. I want to pour out grace for each day of your life. When you're weary and have trouble believing, don't let the enemy torment you with guilt. Simply come to me with your humble and contrite heart, and I will help you. Give yourself to me fully, feast on the truth of my Word, and I will fan the flames of faith.

If I didn't expect that you'd have moments when you'd doubt, I wouldn't have encouraged you to have faith. Believing what you cannot see isn't always easy. If it was, it wouldn't require trust. It wouldn't require dependence on me. Faith pleases me—even faith that sometimes wavers but then runs to me for grace. You are my treasure. My chosen one. Do you hear me whispering words of encouragement? Lean in to my presence. I will rescue you from the bondage of unbelief and fear. I will find you when you feel lost. I will refresh you with hope and strengthen you. I freely give you the courage to believe again. Come and receive.

Without faith living within us it would be impossible to please God. For we come to God in faith knowing that he is real and that he rewards the faith of those who give all their passion into seeking him.

HEBREWS 11:6

Feast upon my Word.

Beloved, I want you to align your thoughts with mine. To feast upon my Word, so that its abundance within you will overflow into your words, actions, and even the atmosphere around you. I have given you the power and authority as my child to create a life of blessing and success here on earth. You no longer have to live in defeat, for I have given you the power to create a life of heaven on earth. A life of purpose, as you partner with me to release my glory.

My Word contains all of the wisdom, insight, and counsel you need to live a life of abundance, purity, and fruitfulness. I will teach you how to walk in the power of my Word, so that the world around you flows with love, joy, peace, freedom, health, and prosperity. Choose the righteous posture of faith and expect my goodness to manifest in every area of your life. Let your words stream in harmony with mine. Let your heart meditate on my truth, so it will pour forth my desires and lead you in my will.

Jesus said to those Jews who believed in him, "When you continue to embrace all that I teach, you prove that you are my true followers. For if you embrace the truth, it will release true freedom into your lives."

JOHN 8:31–32

Eternal blessings begin now.

Anything that takes your eyes off of me must be discarded. Worldly pursuits that lure you into temptation must be exchanged for my heavenly purposes. Places in your soul that hold on to unforgiveness will be uprooted and replaced with my compassionate love. The tug of the world will be replaced with the drawing influence of my love. Pleasing others will be replaced with a fiery passion to do my will regardless of the cost. And the temptation to do something in your own strength will be replaced with the awareness that only by my Spirit will you abound and be fulfilled.

For everything you give up, I bless you with much greater. Though it may feel like a sacrifice now, it cannot compare to the joy I will give you in exchange. I offer you a life of abundance, joy, and grace. A life of eternal blessing that begins here on earth. But more than anything, your devotion to me is rewarded with something much more profound than anything earth can offer. You will experience more of my tangible presence, because you will be free from the entanglements of earthly distraction.

You have graced me with more insight than the old sages
because I have not failed to walk in the light of your ways.
I refused to bend my morals when temptation was before me
so that I could become obedient to your word.
I refuse to turn away from difficult truths,
for you yourself have taught me to love your words.

PSALM 119:100–102

Walk in unity with me.

Let your life illustrate the glory of my presence within you. You are a conduit of my Holy Spirit. A releaser of heaven to earth. Don't allow yourself to become stagnant, by resisting what I want to do through you. You are meant to flow with me. To do the impossible, by the limitless power of my Spirit alive inside of you.

My nature has become your nature. When you live in harmonious union with me, continually aware of my voice within you, you do things many others neglect to do. Sometimes, I remind you of someone who you normally don't think about, because they need prayer. Or a friend to reach out to them. Other times, you'll see someone when you're out and about, and be drawn to them, even though you don't know them. Let my compassion flow through you. Maybe they need prayer, a smiling face, or a moment to connect to someone. When you make yourself available to me, paying attention to the thoughts and ideas that rise within you, and then acting on them, you are walking in unity with me.

I'm asking you, my friends, that you be joined together in perfect unity—with one heart, one passion, and united in one love. Walk together with one harmonious purpose and you will fill my heart with unbounded joy.

PHILIPPIANS 2:2

I change you from the inside out.

Without saying a word, your life will speak a message of truth and grace. You will walk in a new level of my power and anointing. You will begin to live as your Father in heaven—holy, pure, and filled with faith. As you set your heart on me, give your thoughts to me, and surrender your cares to me, there will be a new standard of glory operating in your life. Everything changes when you become consumed with the reality of my life working in you.

My presence makes you think differently and act differently, and even changes your physical appearance. My glory transforms you from the inside out. Like the beautifying oils given to Esther, the oil of my Spirit seeps into your spirit, soul, and body—much deeper and more life-changing than anything money can buy. When your heart is yielded to me, you release the fragrance of heaven effortlessly. Many will see the result of my working in your life and know that you have been transformed by the glory of my presence.

God always makes his grace visible in Christ, who includes us as partners of his endless triumph. Through our yielded lives he spreads the fragrance of the knowledge of God everywhere we go. We have become the unmistakable aroma *of the victory* of the Anointed One to God—a perfume of life to those being saved and the odor of death to those who are perishing.

2 CORINTHIANS 2:14–15

Let go and believe.

Beloved, I want you to submit your thoughts to the revelation of the cross. You cannot think your way into salvation, nor can you mentally comprehend my power—the power that lives inside of you. For too long, you've tried to understand how to get a breakthrough, how to overcome the enemy, or how to see the sick healed through your hands. Instead, I simply want you to let go and believe.

Come like a child. Free. Uninhibited. Believe beyond the confines of your brain. That's why I was crucified at the place of the skull—to pierce your mindsets with the power of my resurrection life and with revelation power that is much higher than the mental assent of the world's greatest geniuses. You mustn't lean in to your wisdom, but instead radically accept what is unconventional yet true. I am outside of time, space, and rationalism. I am in you. With you. All around you. I hold the universe, yet can fit all of my glory inside you. Nothing about me makes sense to your limited understanding, so stop trying to figure it all out and enjoy the adventure!

"As high as the heavens are above the earth, so my ways and my thoughts are higher than yours."

ISAIAH 55:9

Your life demonstrates my glory.

Your life will demonstrate that it is not by might, nor by power, but by my Spirit. I will shake the world through a generation of men and women who have surrendered to my ways and have been filled with my Spirit wind. Bring me your tender heart, willing to be changed in a moment, as you gaze into my twinkling eyes of love. I am the God who can be trusted.

When you risk it all to believe that I can work through you, you are stepping into agreement with heaven. The only way to release my glory through you is to move in the ways of faith. To not only know that what I say is true, but also to be courageous and reach out, so that I can reach through you. To open your mouth and speak my words. To touch the sick and release my healing. To walk into the darkness and fill it with light. I love doing miracles through my children. The responsibility to make things happen isn't yours. It's mine. I simply need you to release what's already inside of you.

"You must continually bring healing to lepers and to those who are sick, and make it your habit to break off the demonic presence from people, and raise the dead back to life. Freely you have received *the power of the kingdom*, so freely release it to others."

MATTHEW 10:8

Stop for just a moment.

Beloved, on days when so many things race through your mind that you can hardly grasp one long enough to think it through, stop. Yes, stop. Give yourself permission to sit back and take a breath. Step away from your mental busyness and your to-do list, and find me. I'll help you organize your day, your week, even the next hour, if you'll step away for a moment.

Sometimes, obligations feel more chaotic than they actually are, because you have other internal things vying for your attention. You have duties that must be tackled, but you feel overwhelmed because inside you're dealing with something bigger. Things you haven't taken time to process with me. Situations may be triggering areas inside of you that need to be walked through with me. Or perhaps anxiety is trying to suck you into its debilitating vortex. Either way, you have my permission to let the chores go for a little bit longer. To sit in my presence and be still, while I minister my peace to you. When you come away, you'll have clarity of mind and peace of heart to do all that you need to do in less time.

Don't be pulled in different directions or worried about a thing. Be saturated in prayer throughout each day, offering your faith-filled requests before God with overflowing gratitude. Tell him every detail of your life, then God's wonderful peace that transcends human understanding, will make the answers known to you through Jesus Christ.

PHILIPPIANS 4:6–7

Find your safety in me.

B eloved, it's okay to feel that things are out of control. I'm very aware of what's going on in your heart and how uncomfortable obscurity and waiting can be. When you can't make everything go the way you want and life seems like it's slipping through your fingers, I need you to trust me. This is what faith is all about.

I never asked you to fix everything. I don't want you to take the weight of the world, or even the weight of your own life, and place it on your shoulders. I already did that on the cross. The reason you feel frazzled and anxious is because you can't fix this. And *if* there is anything for you to do, you won't discover it by racking your brain. You'll only hear my wise instructions by handing those things over and soaking in my presence. Releasing control may feel scary and unsafe, but I assure you, it's the only way to be free. To let me do what only I can do. Life has never been in your control, even when you thought it was. I alone hold all things. You must find your safety in me. Let go and trust me.

"Refuse to worry about tomorrow,
but deal with each challenge that comes your way,
one day at a time.
Tomorrow will take care of itself."

MATTHEW 6:34

I am watching over you.

I will deal swiftly with every plan of the enemy to defeat you or to slow down your advance in my ways. There is nothing hidden from my eyes. I call you to walk with me in light and never fear the darkness. Shadows will not harm you. Even if you were to walk through the darkest valley of despair, still I am there. The brightness of my presence will chase away every shadow and remove every fear. I am your Shield. I will protect you from the fiercest foe who rises up against you.

My Spirit is in you. My angels are with you. My love surrounds you. My glory is a wall of protection encircling you. I am your ever-present help in times of trouble. I will never leave you. Abide in me, and the reality of this nearness will infuse you with courage. You are more than a conqueror! You are more than able to overcome! My victory has become yours. Come and sit at my table in the presence of your enemies and feast on my love. I am watching over you.

Lord, even when your path takes me through
the valley of deepest darkness,
fear will never conquer me, for you already have!
You remain close to me and lead me through it all the way.
Your authority is my strength and my peace.
The comfort of your love takes away my fear.
I'll never be lonely, for you are near.

PSALM 23:4

Stay close to me.

Come closer to me. Live close to my heart, my child. I will bring you into the secret place and give you rest. Let nothing trouble you. The enemy is a defeated foe. My presence will be your peace. Lay your head upon my shoulder and rest with me. Entwine your heart with mine until we are one. It is the slanderer who will always wound you in your weakness. But I will strengthen you until you stand complete, wearing my robe and my armor.

You were created to live in my presence daily. To be more aware of my love for you than your shortcomings and weaknesses. It's only when you get distracted and lose sight of my love, faithfulness, and power that anxiety grips your heart. It's okay to not understand everything. It's okay to get lost in the mystery of it all—remembering my ways are greater than yours. It's okay to stand in my presence and be filled with wonder. You don't have to do anything but enjoy me, and when you do, the power of the enemy won't impress on you any longer.

You have kept me from being conquered by my enemy;
you broke open the way to bring me to freedom,
into a beautiful, broad place.

PSALM 31:8

You are beautiful.

I have known all about you and your struggles, and still, I call you my own. My dear one, I am faithful, even when you see your weak and frail heart—I am faithful until the end. Did I not come and wash the feet of those I love? The filth of this world may smear itself on you from time to time, but it will not stain you. My blood was enough to take care of that.

I will wash away the sting of your past and the defilement of your life until even your former ways are forgotten. In me, all things are new. Did you ever consider that you are harder on yourself than I am? Your life is a story of mercy and grace. Each chapter written through the eyes of your Creator. The One who loves you and believes that you are worthy. Knows that you are desirable. Beautiful. Holy. Perfected before time began, when I held you in my heart. Come away with me into the places I've longed to show you. There is no veil between us.

Yes, we will follow your ways, Lord Yahweh, and entwine our hearts with yours, for the fame of your name is all that we desire. At night I yearn for you with all my heart; in the morning my spirit reaches out to you. When you display your judgments on the earth, people learn the ways of righteousness.

Isaiah 26:8–9

You are the echo of my heart.

By passing into my presence, you will enter the realm of divine love that will cast out every fear. Choose the place nearest to my heart, the place of deepest love, and I will reveal my glorious secrets to you. I will cast out loneliness from your heart. I will draw you deeper into my ways. I will meet every need you have. I will be your holy Friend and faithful Lover. You will never be alone, for when your life is consumed with me, you discover that I am enough.

Enter into my cloud-filled chamber, and I will give you the wine of my love, the joy of my heart, the peace of my kingdom, and the power of my Spirit. You will become the echo of my heartbeat. My masterpiece of sacred devotion. Come and sit with me on my mercy seat, where my love is enthroned. Sacred union will make you a dispenser of mercy to those who mistreat or misunderstand you. You will become like me when you quiet yourself in the chamber of my presence.

Revive me with your tender love and
spare my life by your kindness,
and I will continue to obey you.

PSALM 119:88

Live from the depths of truth.

Beloved, why are you more impressed by the things you see than the invisible things of my kingdom? Why are you reacting to your life circumstances as if they are the final word? They are only temporary. Though you feel them and are affected by them, they must not be allowed to rule you. I want you to live from a different perspective.

I want you to live from the perspective of heaven. To engage with truth that navigates you through the difficult times. To be more aware of what I'm doing in the midst of chaos and conflict than what the circumstances merit. This is not denial in a negative sense, it's denial in the most holy and effective way—denying the world more access to your heart than my truth. It may be *normal* for some people to yield to the pressure, but it is not *your* normal. At least it shouldn't be. Not for you. Not for those who call themselves mine. Instead, live higher. Deeper. From the depths of living truth inside of you that replaces fear with joyful anticipation of what I'll do. This is the life I've called you to.

The way you counsel and correct me makes me praise you more,
for your whispers in the night give me wisdom,
showing me what to do next.
Because you are close to me and always available,
my confidence will never be shaken,
for I experience your wrap-around presence every moment.

PSALM 16:7–8

Sing in opposition to your pain.

Let your praises find true expression as you come before me with singing and a thankful heart. True worship is the highest and most sublime form of gratitude, because in your songs of worship, you are proclaiming my goodness.

The most beautiful expression of your heart comes when praise stands in full opposition to what's happening around you. Worship rises before me as a sweet offering of love. Beloved, I want you to know that I don't simply receive your praise, sit back, and enjoy it without an awareness of what it costs you. I don't turn a blind eye to your pain. This devotion to me, in the midst of your pain, moves me. You have my ear. You have my heart. You have my full attention. The streams of affection that rise from your lips pull me close. I come and weave myself into the substance of your offering. How beautiful it is. Pure and real. I see your tears. I know you need me. I'm here. I cannot resist you when you offer me such love.

"You are my Maker, my Mediator, and my Master.
Any good thing you find in me has come from you."
And he said to me, "My holy lovers are wonderful,
my majestic ones, my glorious ones,
fulfilling all my desires."

PSALM 16:2–3

Be free with childlike joy.

t's time to enjoy the freedom of childlikeness. To dance without reservation. To sing at the top of your lungs. To trust with such simplicity that it makes no sense. To look in the mirror and love yourself. To befriend everyone without worrying about what they think of you. To forgive quickly. To celebrate wildly, until you collapse on the floor with joyous laughter.

A childlike heart brings joy, and when you possess joy, you possess the atmosphere of glory and breakthrough. When you wear the garments of praise, you are clothed in victory. Come like a child and put on your Father's robes. Robes of righteousness and grace. Array yourself in my splendor. Dance in garments of praise that have existed from the beginning of time. As you view yourself as my child, the garments of shame are taken, and you sit enthroned with me. Together, we will laugh at the plans of the enemy. There is no need to be depressed when I have brought you my greatest gift of all, the gift of my Son who brings release to every captive.

"Yes, Father, your plan delights your heart, as you've chosen this way to extend your kingdom—*by giving it to those who have become like trusting children.*"

MATTHEW 11:26

Victories are won through praise.

S inging praises will bring deliverance into reality. Many are the victories that have been won by praise. The overflow of grace in your life will bring you a merry heart and a cheerful countenance. When praises rise before me, burdens are lifted.

Do not be one of those who withhold their praise until they have their way. When you praise in freedom, my beloved, my will is done in your life. All that you long for will be fulfilled. Faith praises in the dark—even my servants, Paul and Silas, praised me in their prison cell until the sounds of joy shook the earth and broke open the way. Not only that, but angels are released as you praise. Heaven on earth greets your circumstances with might and power, shifting things into heavenly alignment.

This is the day to bring your joyous gratitude as your love offering to me. I give you my peace and open before you a way into my glory, for you are the heir of my promises and the child of my joy.

Let everyone thank God, for he is good, and he is easy to please!
His tender love for us continues on forever!
Give thanks to God, our King over all gods!
His tender love for us continues on forever!
Give thanks to the Lord over all lords!
His tender love for us continues on forever!
Give thanks to the only miracle working God!
His tender love for us continues on forever!

PSALM 136:1–4

All I have asked for is your heart.

I've seen your struggle. I've heard you crying out to know me more. Noticed that you want to please me, but feel as though you just can't get it right. Beloved, we are in this together. True, meaningful relationships are raw and genuine. Each one, free to be themselves. I want you to be yourself. I want you to be okay with who you are, because I'm okay with who you are. You don't have to perform for me or behave with what's considered proper Christian etiquette. I simply want you to get to know me. To know me not only as Lord and Savior but to enjoy me as Friend.

Let me smooth out the rough edges. Let me teach you how to walk as my child. Don't worry if you mess up. Just stay close to me with a tender heart and admit when you notice I'm tapping on areas that need to change. Growing into my image isn't a duty; it's something you desire to do when you get to know me on a deeper level. Stop putting so much pressure on yourself and relax. All I've ever asked for is your heart. Completely.

Stop imitating the ideals and opinions of the culture around you, but be inwardly transformed by the Holy Spirit through a total reformation of how you think. This will empower you to discern God's will as you live a beautiful life, satisfying and perfect in his eyes.

ROMANS 12:2

I am peace.

Beloved, it isn't a lack of problems you need. In fact, as long as you're on this earth, you will face uncomfortable situations. What you need is peace in the midst of them. Problems will come and go, but you must not allow your emotions to be dictated by them. You can search the entire world to find something to ease your stress, but to truly experience the peace you crave, come to me. For I am peace.

Draw near to me, and I will draw near to you. Exchange your anxiety for the healing power of my presence. Offer up the worry and fear and allow me to go deep enough to pull them out by the roots. Take time to rest with me and to heal your heart. As long as you're willing to let go of any need for control, I can be the Lord of peace that you need me to be. Put those cares in my hands and leave them there. I offer you peace that goes beyond understanding. I offer you myself.

This is the one who gives his strength and might to his people.
This is the Lord giving us his kiss of peace.

PSALM 29:11

Let nothing hold you back.

Give me the burden that holds you back, my child. Untie the cords to this world and come away with me. You are destined for so much more than you've known. Let go of everything that divides your heart. Give me all of the questions, fears, and doubts. I love you, and I want every part of you—spirit, soul, and body. Hold nothing back from me, for I've held nothing back from you.

I am the King of your heart—ruling with passion that is stronger than death. The heavenly realm is prepared, awaiting those who are no longer chained to this earth. Greater deliverance comes to my ascending ones, for as you enter my world, all that contaminates and hinders love is removed from you. In my presence, everything that doesn't reflect my glory falls like lifeless leaves to the ground. Unanswered questions are satisfied by my love. Free from the entanglements of worldly pursuits, you're free to worship me in spirit and truth. I have come into your world, now come into mine.

Trust in the Lord completely,
and do not rely on your own opinions.
With all your heart rely on him to guide you,
and he will lead you in every decision you make.

PSALM 128:1–4

Remember who you are.

When you become side-tracked by your imperfect love, you believe that I'm just as concerned about it as you are. Beloved, your frailty and weaknesses aren't a surprise to me. I don't see you the way you see yourself. All I see is your beauty. You are radiant. More beautiful to me than any other. Let my kiss upon your life awaken you to hope. You are not defined by your shortcomings or sins.

Come closer—let me kiss you over and over and over again, until the memory of your past holds no more pain. I've torn the veil that has separated us and paid the price to set you free. Turn to me—I will pour out my love that heals every wound. Your burdens aren't too heavy for me; I don't mind taking them from you, if you'll let me. Will you let me?

And if you ever feel lost, confused about your identity, close your eyes and know that I am with you. I will lead you and remind you who you are.

O my beloved, you are lovely.
When I see you in your beauty,
I see a radiant city where we will dwell as one.
More pleasing than any pleasure,
more delightful than any delight,
you have ravished my heart,
stealing away my strength to resist you.
Even hosts of angels stand in awe of you.

SONG OF SONGS 6:4

Ascend with me.

The confusion that comes into your soul is because you have yet to ascend into a higher place—my hiding place—where I have placed you in the secret stairway. Heaven calls you, heaven pulls you. Exchange your thoughts for mine and take my heart and my mind as the heavenly gifts I give to you. In my realm, all things are possible, and nothing can defeat you. In my realm, there is no striving or pushing yourself forward, only resting near the fountain of the Lamb.

Come to me, and I will tuck you underneath the safety of my wings until you are strong again. You were created to soar with me, ascending over these mountains of defeat. Close your eyes. Remember the way that the warm breeze feels against your skin. The freedom of life when you ascend with me. I won't forsake you. The sweetness of my touch will revive you. My glory will illuminate the darkness that felt as if it would never lift. I am the King of glory. Your faithful King, full of power. Overflowing with love for you.

Because I am innocent I will see your face
until I see you for who you really are.
Then I will awaken with your form and be fully satisfied,
fulfilled in the revelation of your glory in me!

PSALM 17:15

I am so happy you are mine.

I love you. I want you to soak in the revelation of my love, today and every day. I want you to know that the way you love me moves my heart. You are my delight. And the offering of your life has my full attention. I've never overlooked one tear, as you bowed low and surrendered your will to mine over and over again. I'm so pleased with the cry of your heart to be fully mine and to be consumed with my love.

So now I will consume you. The fiery passion of my love for you will blaze upon your life in ways you've never known. Even now I am working on your behalf. I am planning beautiful surprises that will bring you to your knees in thanksgiving and joy. I can't wait for you to see what I have in store for you! I cannot resist those who so freely and unreservedly give themselves to me, trusting me, even in the darkest valleys. Thank you for receiving my love. I am so happy that you are mine.

I found the one I adore!
I caught him and fastened myself to him,
refusing to be feeble in my heart again.
SONG OF SONGS 3:4

Come into my glory.

Will you take my glory to be more valuable than anything you possess on this earth? Will you choose to esteem what is precious in my sight? The reality of my glory makes all else dim and seem insignificant. As I shine my light of truth upon your soul, you will know how earthbound you have been. Come into my chamber room, and you will see your life as I see it, as the expression of my glory.

I am the King of glory. Invite me to illuminate your life, and the shadows will flee. Darkness doesn't stand a chance when I pierce it with my light. I will surround you with my glory until the atmosphere around you radiates with my presence. As you soak in my light, it not only penetrates deep into your spirit, soul, and body; it also bursts from the mystery of my Spirit within you. The enemy hates exposure. He cannot be where the light of my glory exists. My glory is alive and powerful. Always overcoming darkness, because light *always* dispels darkness. Always!

This Living Expression is the Light that bursts through gloom—the Light that darkness could not diminish!

JOHN 1:5

I am right here.

When your soul is bowed low and the shrill voice of fear challenges your faith, remember my love. Choose to fill your mind with thoughts of me and refuse to give into the lies the enemy sets like a trap. If you've already lost your peace and have fallen down that black hole of anxiety, find me. Beloved, I am right there. You don't have to fight fear, you only need to focus on me.

Even if dread has clouded your thoughts, and you're having trouble finding me, I'm still with you. Don't start questioning why you can't feel me. It is only fear holding your attention. Ignore it and breathe. Let memories of all I've done for you in the past flood your racing, tired mind. Remind yourself of the times you saw the giants fall and the walls of opposition crumble. If I've come through for you before, why don't you think I'll do it again? Things may be out of your control, but they're not out of mine. Do you remember my touch? Have you seen my faithfulness? Yes, you have. I haven't changed, so don't worry. I'm right here.

Perfect, absolute peace surrounds those whose imaginations are consumed with you; they confidently trust in you.

ISAIAH 26:3

It all begins with me.

Your greatest protection is to be united to me. Nothing will harm you in my burning presence. Here you are safe. Don't search outside of me for what you need; begin with me. Come to me when fear nips at your heels. Talk to me about the things that concern you, and I will give you clarity. Let me be your all, and I will consume all that seeks to separate you from me.

Outside of me, danger lurks. The enemy cannot reach into the flames of my glory, so remain inside of me. Connected and aware of me at all times. My glory is your shield. I am your strong tower. My presence is perfect peace and incomprehensible joy. There's no need to run to and fro, seeking what can only be found inside of me. So come to me. Be with me. Wrap yourself in the warmth of my deliverance. No one cares for you more than I do. I still the raging storms and release the rains over your dry and weary soul. When you feel restless and alone, begin with me.

God's glory is all around me!
His wrap-around presence is all I need,
for the Lord is my Savior, my hero, and my life-giving strength.

PSALM 62:7

Give me your undivided heart.

My beloved, surrender your life's purpose to me. In my realm, there is no place for a divided heart, for all has been given to me. All that you hold in your hands and all that distracts you, lay it down before me. You will arise and not fall; you will ascend into my glorious flames, where passion and purity unite. Come away, my true friend, and make my world your home. This is what you were created for. A life of uninterrupted union with me is the foundation for a truly blessed life.

When you step into the glory of my presence, you will not fear the dividing of your soul and spirit with my sword of light. I slice away the tumors of complacency, shame, and hatred. My love is passion, and I passionately reveal all that seeks to isolate you from my presence. I speak light into the darkness. I unmask religion's lies and pour out liberty so you can freely enjoy me. Give me your undivided heart, and you'll never be the same.

I've made up my mind.
Until the darkness disappears and the dawn has fully come,
in spite of shadows and fears,
I will go to the mountaintop with you—
the mountain of suffering love
and the hill of burning incense.
Yes, I will be your bride.

SONG OF SONGS 4:6

Wholeness is my gift to you.

Beloved, I don't want you to be afraid of pain. I know how badly it hurts, but if you'll let me, I'll teach you things you won't learn during any other time. Don't ignore your emotions and stuff them so deeply that you're afraid to face them. Acknowledging this pain, and coming to me with it, will open the way for healing to begin.

When you feel pain, anger, hurt, or any negative emotions, lean in to me and bring that pain with you. Don't dismiss your reactions to life's uncomfortable moments. Together, we will get to the root of what's triggering you, so you can find freedom from its crippling effects. I am the God of wholeness—spirit, soul, and body. Your emotions, feelings, and thoughts are important to me, and I want them to be important to you too. They can alert you to areas of pain and trauma that need my healing power. Draw near to me to and discover what I want to heal inside of you. Ours is a journey of joy, and wholeness is my gift to you.

"I am the Gateway. To enter through me is to experience life, freedom, and satisfaction. A thief has only one thing in mind— he wants to steal, slaughter, and destroy. But I have come to *give you everything in abundance, more than you expect—* life in its fullness until you overflow!"

JOHN 10:9–10

Know the way you move me.

I want you to think of the most beautiful elements of nature—the ones that have caused you to gasp in wonder and left you in awe. The brilliant sunsets that paint the sky are merely a token of beauty compared to you. Even the wispy mystery of the aurora borealis fails in comparison to you. Bask in the splendor of my beautiful creation as a reminder that you are more radiant still, and nothing moves my heart the way you do.

Don't let the trees stand taller and more confident than you. You are royalty. A true reflection of infinite glory. *You* move my heart. Not just humanity as a whole, but *you* specifically. You are the apple of my eye, my treasure, my bride. Turn your heart to me, and I will enrapture your soul. I am in awe of your love—imperfect yet birthed from faith. Let this revelation of unlimited, unmerited acceptance sink deeply into your heart. Let the bliss of perfect love consume you. You are mine.

Listen, my dearest darling,
you are so beautiful—you are beauty itself to me!

SONG OF SONGS 4:1

Receive my grace.

Your failures cannot remove you from my heart. Your weakness only attracts my grace. Come to me when you fail, beloved, and watch my smile of compassion wash over your soul. I see it all—you cannot hide from me. I know every desire, motive, and impure thought, yet I love you just the same. Seek my grace in your defeat, and victory will be yours.

Throw off the voice of accusation, rest in my saving love, and your faith will be strengthened. Nothing—not sin, failure, not even the times you've questioned or doubted me—will separate you from my eternal love. Though there have been times you've rejected yourself, I have never rejected you. I accept you unreservedly. Faith, in this love, will slay your discouragement and remove the weapons from the hands of your enemies. It is only he who reminds you of your failure. But I release hope. Hope that gives birth to joy. Even when you don't see my glory, it's there—with you. Entwining itself with you. Receive this grace. Receive my love.

I am sent to announce a new season of Yahweh's grace and a time of God's recompense on his enemies, to comfort all who are in sorrow, to strengthen those crushed by despair who mourn in Zion— to give them a beautiful bouquet in the place of ashes, the oil of bliss instead of tears, and the mantle of joyous praise instead of the spirit of heaviness. Because of this, they will be known as Mighty Oaks of Righteousness, planted by Yahweh as a living display of his glory.

ISAIAH 61:2–3

Burn holy in my presence.

My strength will overcome your weakest flaw until every part of you is filled with the energy of grace. Never let go of your passion to be holy in my eyes. It is a holy obsession that sets you apart from others. I will purify you with this living hope, and you will see the transformation take place in my glory. Burn holy in my presence until faith radiates from your inner being.

Step into my transforming love and expect me to move on your behalf. Each day as you yield to me, you are growing. Every moment, reflecting my glory. You are in me and I am in you. My light, transforming you from the inside out.

As you change and grow, grace will be your song and faith will be your portion. Songs of endless joy will flow from your lips. When the enemy tries to overwhelm you, distract you, or tempt you, the melodies of triumph will be your war cry. You will witness my victory breaking forth, for I hold it in store for the upright and for those who love me. Remain in me and sin will never have dominion over you.

This means that God is transforming each one of you into the Holy of Holies, his dwelling place, through the power of the Holy Spirit living in you!

EPHESIANS 2:22

November

I have the final say.

I see the way the enemy comes after you. It doesn't just feel like the rug has been pulled out, it's like the world has tilted off its axis, leaving you dazed and confused. Things are being shaken, and you're not sure if you have a tight-enough grip on me. My beloved, close your eyes and turn your heart to me. I've got you.

I've got you, but I need you to breathe. I need you to lean in to my Father's heart. Let me sooth your anxiety and heal this trauma. You will not be able to see clearly and hear my instructions until you find your peace. Until you can fully let go and trust me, it will be difficult to move forward. I am your safe place to cry, vent, and even scream. But don't stay in a puddle of self-pity for long. Remind yourself of my promises and put them on your lips. They contain life and power. They are your weapon. Use them! My Word is true, and you can depend on it. No matter what the enemy lies to you about, I will always have the final say.

All who are oppressed may come to you as a
shelter in the time of trouble, a perfect hiding place.
May everyone who knows your mercy
keep putting their trust in you,
for they can count on you for help no matter what.
O Lord, you will never, no never, neglect those
who come to you.

PSALM 9:9–10

Be filled with my healing waters.

I am a never-ending fountain of living water, and I long to pour myself into every dry, cracked, and broken area of your life. Do you feel me now, reaching into your pain with my healing love? Listen, and you'll hear my rushing river flowing through you, as it washes away the debris of confusion and disillusionment, clearing away the dry dusty remains of disappointment, so you can clearly see the joy I have in store for you.

No trauma is too great for the power of my love. The biggest, gaping holes—the areas of your life that feel empty and void—become openings for me to pour myself into, when you invite me. So invite me, and I will come. I will fill you with myself, turn mourning into joy, replace heaviness with hope, and till the soil of your heart, so beauty blooms from the ashes. Drink deeply of my love, and it will transform you—spirit, soul, and body. Set your eyes on me today, and offer me your pain once and for all. Swim in my healing waters and allow the currents of my love to lead you into wholeness.

In the days of desert dryness he split open the mighty rock,
and the waters flowed like a river before their very eyes.
He gave them all they wanted to drink from his living springs.

PSALM 78:15–6

Rest with me.

I care deeply for you, my child. There is nothing that you feel or experience that I don't also experience as I carry you through life. My hand is upon you, and nothing will take you away from my love. Quietly wait on me, and you will feel my nearness. You will hear me whisper into your soul, and my peace will descend upon you.

My little one, there is a hiding place you can find in me. It is a place of my tangible affection, created for you to dwell. The shadow you see over you is the shadow of my wings. Not a shadow of confusion, but a shadow of safety, beside my heart. Here you will be refreshed. Here you will see from my perspective. For I have taken you from troubled waters and lifted you higher, to rest in my presence. No matter how dark the night and how fierce the trial, my kiss of mercy will keep and protect you.

When you sit enthroned under the shadow of Shaddai,
you are hidden in the strength of God Most High.
He's the hope that holds me, and the Stronghold to shelter me,
the only God for me, and my great confidence.
He will rescue you from every hidden trap of the enemy,
and he will protect you from false accusation and any deadly curse.
His massive arms are wrapped around you, protecting you.
You can run under his covering of majesty and hide.
His arms of faithfulness are a shield keeping you from harm.

PSALM 91:1–4

My love provides everything you need.

Everything you need, my love has provided. With passion much stronger than the grave, I gave all I had for you. I gave everything to not only be with you forever, but to pay the price for you to live in victory. Never underestimate the power that was released through the cross. My death and resurrection are the foundation of your faith.

An unlimited supply of my goodness was unleashed through what was accomplished on the cross. Do you need healing? It's yours. Do you need forgiveness? I pour it out without reservation. Are you living in shame? I have washed you clean and brought you to my side. Hope? It's yours. Favor? You can have that too. If I didn't withhold the gift of salvation for all eternity, why would I withhold what you need during your temporary stay on earth? My love is relevant. It applies to every avenue of your life. There is nothing too great, too small, or too mundane that is not affected by the power of my love.

To preach the message of the cross seems like sheer nonsense to those who are on their way to destruction, but to us who are on our way to salvation, it is the mighty power of God released within us.

1 CORINTHIANS 1:18

You are my warrior.

My armies are battle-ready and prepared to fight on your behalf. Step out in faith and watch the miracles break forth. Have I not equipped you? All who rise against you will fall, and those who disgrace my name will be set aside. But your calling is to move forward in faith and bring defeat to the forces of darkness.

Give yourself to me with wholehearted devotion, and the glory within you will shine so brightly, darkness will tremble. Your life of radical obedience will catapult you into my strategic plans that release your breakthrough. You are unstoppable. You have the backing of heaven, and the favor only a child can have. If you could see the angels that have been released to you, you would never be intimidated by the enemy. I have given you everything you need to overcome.

Beautiful one, you are my warrior. Strong and courageous. Anointed and treasured. Cared for. Capable of more than you know. Surrounded by angels who are ready to slay the giants with you.

Bless the Lord, all his messengers of power,
for you are his mighty heroes who listen intently
to the voice of his word to do it.
Bless and praise the Lord, you mighty warriors,
ministers who serve him well and fulfill his desires.

PSALM 103:20–21

Faith is your victory.

Faith is the victory that overcomes the power of this world. Walk in the steps I have chosen for you, and no one will be able to hinder you for long. Faith opens the doors and sets you in the right place at the right time. You will be amazed at the opportunities that greet you as you're led by my Spirit.

Many are my servants who step out with small faith, and witness me working a great work. Never measure your faith by your fears, but insist that your fears submit to your faith. Your enemies fight in vain. Do not be discouraged by what can be seen with your eyes, but be filled with my faith as you set your gaze on me. Faith is the force that lifts you above your enemies, because it enables you to see clearly. Embrace truth as your best friend. Marry wisdom, for she will be your perfect partner. Cherish my peace, and you will be kept far above the fray. Root yourself in my love, and faith will be the natural result.

Every child of God overcomes the world, for our faith is the victorious power that triumphs over the world. So who are the world conquerors, *defeating its power*? Those who believe that Jesus is the Son of God.

1 JOHN 5:4–5

Thankfulness connects you to my truth.

I have created a clean heart within you. The virtues of my Spirit are being born in you. As righteousness covers your heart as a breastplate, it creates greater strength and boldness. The time has come for you to praise me with all of your heart, for my overcomers are arising and will not be defeated. Praise me for the impossibility that I am changing into victory. My armies are set in place, so begin to praise me with all of your heart!

I want you to focus on maintaining a thankful heart. For every negative thing that comes against you, find something good to fill your thoughts. Put praise on your lips and remember the many ways I've blessed you. A grateful heart is one that remains in harmony with the ways of my Spirit. Thankfulness and praise not only clear away the cobwebs of anxiety and depression; they also make it almost impossible to focus on the negative. Thankfulness washes your heart and makes you feel lighter, because it connects you with the power of my unchanging truth. This is my desire for you today—for the power of gratitude to set you free from heaviness.

Let your heart be always guided by the peace of the Anointed One,
who called you to peace as part of his one body.
And always be thankful.

COLOSSIANS 3:15

Process your emotions with me.

Process with me. I've never asked you to push down your feelings when things go painfully wrong. I never said that it's error to experience a gamut of emotions. In fact, I gave them to you, so you'll know what's going on inside of you. So that you can step into communication with me and get my perspective. To discover areas of mistrust, incorrect mindsets, and wounds that need healing.

I allow you to feel. I actually *invite* you to become aware of your deepest emotions. I've never forbade your feelings. Even I got angry when they set up shop in my Father's house. I've experienced the pain of betrayal. I've cried out with the sting of loneliness and what seemed like abandon when my Father turned away from me on the cross. It's okay to be disappointed. To feel anger. To not understand and have no idea how to make things right. But in all of your emotions and processing, I want to make you whole. To present you with a side of me you may not have known yet. Sit and talk to me. Let's process these things together.

Pour out all your worries and stress upon him and leave them there, for he always tenderly cares for you.

1 PETER 5:7

I want you to have limitless faith.

Where do the limits begin on your faith? Because I am limitless in my ability. Restricted by nothing other than the scope of your belief. No matter where your faith ends, it isn't a reflection of what is true and possible. Nothing is impossible for me, even if you choose not to believe it.

If you are able to believe that my love is enough to save your soul, why do you stop there? I care about your day-to-day life. Lack of faith will hinder you, but I have invited you to grow in your faith. To believe that anything, absolutely anything, is possible with me. It's risky and scary to put your faith out there, because you're wondering how you'll feel if I don't answer the way you want or in your timing. But, beloved, you have placed your life in my hands. I know how to take care of you. I haven't asked you to force my hand; I've only asked you to believe in my love. To fully and absolutely trust me. Take the risk of believing for greater. I'm with you every step of the way.

> Jesus put his hands over their eyes and said,
> "You will have what your faith expects!"
>
> MATTHEW 9:29

Face fear with me.

Sometimes confronting your fear means facing it head on with me. It means not hiding behind denial or shoving that fear down deep. When you find yourself smackdab in the middle of the battle, don't stand behind me. Stand next to me. Grab my hand and let's forge forward together. Be honest about your fears. Invite me into every one of them and make me Lord over them.

One of the biggest challenges you face is the dread of what may come. The fear that something may or may not happen. The terror that the enemy implants inside of you—that I may not be as good as you've believed me to be. He kills hope. He works to steal your trust in me. More than anything, *he is a liar*! I am good. Even when it seems I haven't answered, I have. One day, you will gain clarity regarding these difficult challenges. For now, remember—when trouble is staring you in the face, that's when you realize how strong you really are. It is these confrontations with fear that draw my power like a magnet. I am with you. We'll get through this, together.

"Do not yield to fear, for I am always near. Never turn your gaze from me, for I am your faithful God. I will infuse you with my strength and help you in every situation. I will hold you firmly with my victorious right hand."

ISAIAH 41:10

You will get through this.

David was a man after my heart. A man who was honest about how he felt. Who knew I wouldn't be offended by his questions. A man who went through trials and pain, but found me on the battlefield. It was out of tremendous opposition that he came to know my faithfulness. But that doesn't mean that he didn't occasionally question it.

Your character and resilience are forged from the trials you face, when you face them with me. Like a diamond whose beauty is birthed out of pressure, so is your beauty coming forth from the trials that feel like they're squeezing you. It's okay to be honest with me. I can handle it. Out of the testing of your faith, trust is born. It's only when you need me to step in as your Savior, that you truly understand what it is to be saved. The enemy thinks he's drowning you with problems, when really, he's presenting the perfect opportunity for me to step in and prove my faithfulness. Beloved, I know it feels hard right now, but you will come through this shining with the brilliance of my glory.

Say to the anxious and fearful, "Be strong and never afraid. Look, here comes your God! He is breaking through to give you victory! He comes to avenge your enemies. With divine retribution he comes to save you!"

Isaiah 35:4

Your sacrificial love is beautiful to me.

My beautiful one, I've seen your unrelenting devotion to me in the secret chambers of holy devotion. The way you rest with me and enjoy the sweetness of my comfort ravishes my heart. You will always need the refreshing of my presence, and I will lead you beside still waters throughout your entire life. Our sacred relationship is anchored in our holy union.

This awakening of your heart in my presence must continue to be cultivated on the battlefield. It is vital that you remain connected to me during times of great warfare. To glue your lovesick eyes to me when everything tumultuous clamors for your attention. You must carry the secret place within your heart. The time for true apostolic Christianity is coming. It will be seen in sacred intimacy, sacrificial ministry, and faithfulness in suffering.

The empowering of my glory is not for you only. It is meant to be shared. It is designed to mature you and bring you into the beauty of our partnership. To teach you to love others, to remain strong, and to see beyond yourself.

I admit that I haven't yet acquired the absolute fullness that I'm pursuing, but I run with passion *into his abundance* so that I may reach the purpose that Jesus Christ has called me to fulfill and wants me to discover.

PHILIPPIANS 3:12

I am speaking to you.

Listen to the words I speak into your being, for my words will bring life and power. I long to train you to hear my whisper and know my voice. You belong to me, and I will speak to you. Search for my truth and ask me for wisdom, and I will give it. I will open your mind and heart to know my secrets as you come closer to me and sit with me.

Don't doubt what you hear stirring in the quiet of your soul. I believe in our union, and your ability to discern my voice, that's why I don't shout to get your attention. You are one with me. I have made my home inside of you. Don't depend on others for the guidance you need, more than you depend on me. As you lean in to faith and expect my secrets to alight upon your heart, revelation comes. My life flows into every word, inspiring you to greatness. Releasing wisdom. Igniting hope. I am speaking to you. It's time to believe it.

The Lord Yahweh has equipped me with the anointed, skillful tongue of a teacher—to know how to speak a timely word to the weary. Morning by morning, he awakens my heart. He opens my ears to hear his voice, to be trained to teach.

ISAIAH 50:4

Come further into love.

Quiet now, my child. Still your restlessness in the warmth of my embrace. This is the place I have created you for. The invitation for peace and total release from stress, is always available. There is only one reason why you have days when you can't seem to shake the relentless thoughts—it's because you haven't gone far enough into love. Fall deeper, past the shackles of this world that bind you to the cares and concerns that plague you, into my arms. Become so focused on me, so filled with my love that all fears, insecurities, questions, and frustrations cannot be found.

My love is powerful enough to drown out all that clamors for your attention, but you must let me overtake you. You must set time aside for first-love encounters. Only you can choose how much you will release to me. Only you can decide how far into my presence you will go. There is always more available, and I will never block the way. Trust me. Come further into my love.

"Even if the mountains were to crumble and the hills disappear, my heart of steadfast, faithful love will never leave you, and my covenant of peace with you will never be shaken," says Yahweh, whose love and compassion will never give up on you.

ISAIAH 54:10

Step behind the veil.

There is a well of life that springs from my presence. No other love can delight your soul; no other sound will move your heart. Come and be prepared in my fullness. All that is broken, I will heal, for I am the God of mercy, and I sit upon a throne of grace. You have only discovered a portion of my forgiveness and love—there is still much to learn as I take you deeper into my ways. As you come into my light, you will see even more of my love. I am the God who heals you, the Father of endless mercies.

As you step behind the veil, you will find me. I do not hide myself from you. I am always available. Come in faith and set aside distractions. The closer you come to me, the more my glory dispels the darkness. You don't need to live in the shadows of obscurity, when I've invited you into the light. My love will pierce every mindset with unavoidable truth. Focus on me, beloved, and you will experience my tangible presence.

It was now only midday, yet the whole world became dark for three hours as the light of the sun faded away. And suddenly in the temple the thick veil hanging in the Holy Place was ripped in two!

LUKE 23:44–45

My voice will satisfy you.

Will you open your heart and listen to my voice? For my voice is full of life, truth, and wisdom. They are words, whispers, and substance, which are unmistakable. Everlasting. All consuming. Trust my Spirit inside of you and listen. The sound of a stranger will not satisfy you like the sound of my voice.

Your heart, your lips, and your life need to be surrendered to me. Rise up and be drenched in my glory. The new comes, as the old fades away. This is the season of my splendor. The signs in the heavens and on the earth will multiply, showing you that a new day has dawned. Might and power are available to all my holy ones. Both destruction and revival are coming, a day of darkness and a day of brilliant light. But, if you listen for me, you will know what I am about to do and how I will use you. My faithfulness will be your shield and protection. I will come closer to you as you draw closer to me, beloved. Fear will be swallowed by love.

While Peter was still speaking, a radiant cloud composed of light spread over them, enveloping them all. And God's voice suddenly spoke from the cloud, saying, "This is my dearly loved Son, the constant focus of my delight. Listen to him!"

MATTHEW 17:5

I am freeing you from the lies.

Beloved, I want you to pay attention to what you're thinking about. Both the obvious thoughts and the subtle musings of your subconscious. Nothing must go unchecked. Every thought must come into alignment with my truth. It's time to be honest with yourself. It's time to become aware of your thoughts and feelings, so that you can bring them to me.

Hidden fears, areas of unforgiveness, and incorrect ideas about who I am or how I want you to live and behave must come into the light of my holiness. It is the only way to be free. My grace will expose lies that you've believed. Don't be afraid of what's on the inside. I've already seen every belief, even the ones you haven't realized are there. I care about every thought. I know how to address the distortions that have wedged themselves into the dark crevices of your mind. This is your season of breakthrough. I am doing a deeper work and drawing out the infestation of lies, so that you can be truly free.

Lord, you are my secret hiding place,
protecting me from these troubles,
surrounding me with songs of gladness!
Your joyous shouts of rescue release my breakthrough.

PSALM 32:7

I want you to love yourself.

I want you to love yourself. To be absolutely crazy about the *you* I created. To look in the mirror, see all of the flaws and imperfections, and love yourself anyway. To learn to laugh about your quirks instead of being embarrassed by them. To feel comfortable in your own skin and to remember that it is the home I have chosen for my Holy Spirit. No one spends more time with you than you do, so make the time enjoyable.

Until you have fully embraced my love for you and actually believe that I think you're amazing, you won't be able to love yourself—not to mention loving others correctly. So first, let the reality of my unrelenting, unstoppable love for you seep in. Lose yourself fully in this awareness. Then, if for no other reason, love yourself because I do. Honor me in this way. Stop being so hard on yourself. If there are changes to be made, we'll make them together. But first, believe you deserve to be happy, healthy, and whole. Take care of yourself. Let my love for you, combined with your love for yourself, lead you on a journey of wholeness.

You leave me breathless—
I am overcome
by merely a glance from your worshiping eyes,
for you have stolen my heart.

SONG OF SONGS 4:9

Live with expectation.

What if I designed this very moment to be a moment of encounter? A moment of victory. A moment of breakthrough. What if you lived with the anticipation of good, every single instant? What if you paid attention more? Believed that every second of your life was an opportunity for something greater. Could it be that if you stilled your thoughts for just a few seconds and turned them to me, something amazing might happen?

To live with this expectancy means you have embraced my goodness. It means you've made a practice out of being thankful, and naturally believe there will be something new to be thankful for. It means you aren't dreadfully peering around every corner, wondering what new scheme the devil has up his sleeves. You're confident because you trust my love. You're walking in tune with me. Standing hopeful, because your eyes are constantly on me. From now on, I want you to expect my goodness to overtake you! My love is an unstoppable force. Stay in my love.

Why would I fear the future?
For your goodness and love pursue me all the days of my life.
PSALM 23:26

Find fulfillment in me.

Find your fulfillment in me. In the reality of a life saturated with the knowledge of my love. In the reality of holy union. Let our relationship make you feel complete. Relish in the truth that I see you. Know you. Appreciate every move you make that reflects my goodness, faithfulness, compassion, and joy.

What you will experience with me is far greater than the temporary gratifications of fame, fortune, or dreams coming true. I want you to be happy on the deepest level. I love satisfying the desires of your heart and giving good gifts to my children, but there is indescribable contentment and unspeakable joy, which can only be found in my presence. Let me be your desire, more than anything else. In the secret place of my love, when no one else is around, you will experience the substance of profound fulfillment. It is a living force that you cannot obtain through any other avenue. Start with me. Be consumed by me. No matter what else I bless you with, all will fail in comparison.

My heart and soul explode with joy—full of glory!
Even my body will rest confident and secure.
For you will not abandon me to the realm of death,
nor will you allow your Holy One to experience corruption.
For you bring me a continual revelation of resurrection life,
the path to the bliss that brings me face-to-face with you.

PSALM 16:9–11

The answer you need is found in me.

The reason you've been heavy and overwhelmed is because you've been seeking the answer for your problem in multiple places. Yes, you're looking at me and seeking me, but you're also stuck in your head, trying to reason things out. Instead of allowing your thoughts to drag you around in vicious circles, let your spirit lead you to me.

I want you to walk in singleness of heart. Meaning, fix your attention on me and me alone. When all of your attention is on me, you'll tap into the breakthrough, because everything you need is found *in me*. You'll find the peace and joy you've allowed the enemy to steal, because in me is perfect peace and mystifying joy. Release the duty of finding a solution, so that I can show you my solution. You aren't operating in grace and peace when you're striving to figure things out. Stop relying on yourself to discover the key that will get you to the other side. Tether yourself to me with unyielding determination. Become so fixated on me that the heaviness and frustration cannot hold on. Stay consumed with me and breakthrough will come.

Jesus said to them,
"Why are you fearful?
Have you lost your faith *in me*?"
LUKE 8:25

Let heaven invade your brokenness.

It's okay to feel the desperation of hunger for me. Let your discomfort lead you into my presence. I see the weariness that has landed so heavily upon you. It will always find you when your focus is on duties, obligations, and disappointments. Instead, stand in my presence. Again and again. Let your hunger and thirst thrust you before me—the only One who will satisfy.

I know how to brush away the dusty debris of your distracted mindset. Come closer to me and heaven will invade the brokenness. My glory will explode every chain of heaviness. I'm standing beside you. In you. I created you, and I know how to heal you and refresh you. I am your wisdom. I speak life into every dead thing. I resurrect the joy that grief has stolen. Resign that weight to me and receive my grace. You don't need to carry what I've already paid the price to free you from. I encapsulate all you need. I am enough. Rest in me, and I will fill you so completely, there will be no room for any contrary thoughts.

I long to drink of you, O God,
drinking deeply from the streams of pleasure
flowing from your presence.
My longings overwhelm me for more of you!
My soul thirsts, pants, and longs for the living God.
I want to come and see the face of God.

PSALM 42:1–2

You are capable.

Why do you doubt the greatness within you? You are more capable than you know. I breathed the breath of mystery into you. Molded you to be a unique expression of my creative power. I fill you with the majesty of heaven and call you mine.

If you only understood how much you look like me. How much power lives within you. All of heaven rejoices at the miracle I've done within vessels of human flesh. Hell trembles when you walk in your identity. You are a carrier of my glory. A creator, just as I am the Master Creator. The wisdom that I used to form all that you see and the profound things you don't see, resides within you. Believe in what I've place inside of you. Stop doubting and start taking chances. You don't need another word from heaven, you already have it. Take steps and trust me for open doors. If one door closes, keep your eyes on me, and I will lead you to the right one. It is my will for you to live your dreams.

"Come and join me," Jesus replied.
So Peter stepped out onto the water
and began to walk toward Jesus.
But when he realized how high the waves were,
he became frightened and started to sink.
"Save me, Lord!" he cried out.
Jesus immediately stretched out his hand
and lifted him up and said, "What little faith you have!
Why would you let doubt win?"

MATTHEW 14:28–31

I am your compass.

The road has offered you many twists in turns. Taken you in directions you didn't think you would go. But when you realize that life's path has led you through an unexpected journey, don't fear. I am with you. No path is beyond the scope of my radar.

I am your compass. I know how to lead you through the blazing desert to the waters of refreshing. This journey may not have gone exactly as you would have chosen, but beloved, we're not done yet. Continue hoping in me. Walking with me. Holding my hand. I am the Way Maker. I am the Way. Trust me beyond the scope of your perspective. I have a much higher vantage point. I see not only your glorious future, but your past and present, and I will weave them together to create something beautiful. I have already laid out a path that is better than you imagined. Things aren't always going to turn out the way you expect, but when you continue on with me, I always bless you with the best.

"I will walk the blind by an unknown way and guide them on paths they've never traveled. I will smooth their difficult road and make their dark mysteries bright with light. These are things I will do for them, for I will never abandon my beloved ones."

ISAIAH 42:16

Do not let failure stop you.

Every time you attempt something and fail, I'm still cheering you on. Like a proud father, I watch you with excitement and confidence, even when you fall. Get up! Get up! Brush yourself off, refuse that discouragement, and try again. Then again. And again. Of course it doesn't feel good to mess up or to have doors slam in your face that you expected to be great opportunities, but it's okay—I'm making you into an overcomer. I want you to have the desires of your heart.

Failures may be embarrassing and disheartening, but they don't define you. Each step of the way you're learning, growing, finding out what doesn't work, and becoming more skilled. Ask me, and I will give you the resources you need to hone those dreams, skills, and ideas. One day, they will transform into the beautiful fulfillment you desire. It's going to take courage, but I can give that in abundance. It's okay to be a dreamer, but don't live under the illusion that it should be easy. Your dreams are worth it! Take risks, work hard, and don't let failure stop you.

I know what it means to lack, and I know what it means to experience overwhelming abundance. For I'm trained in the secret of overcoming all things, whether in fullness or in hunger. And I find that the strength of Christ's explosive power infuses me to conquer every difficulty.

PHILIPPIANS 4:12–13

My plans for you are outrageously good.

Y ou have no idea how obsessively good I am or how inconceivably amazing my plans are for you. You cannot separate me from love, faithfulness, or goodness. I am their very definition. It was my goodness that led you to repentance, and it is my goodness that continues to be unveiled in your life.

Don't listen to the lies of the enemy that tell you I'm good to others but not you. Waiting seasons are not the same thing as seasons of my denial. However, you do need to have patience. And you must yield to my ways, over and over again. Sometimes, trusting me hurts, because it means you must become more dependent upon me than on yourself or others. But it's always worth it. Faith is the ingredient that causes my outrageous blessings to rise! Remember the many times I've come through for you. If I've done it before, what makes you think I won't do it again? Believe in my absolute power and my unflinching love for you. I have beautiful plans and joys unspeakable in store for you!

For this reason the Lord is still waiting to show his favor to you so he can show you his marvelous love. He waits to be gracious to you. He sits on his throne ready to show mercy to you. For Yahweh is the Lord of justice, faithful to keep his promises. Overwhelmed with bliss are all who will entwine their hearts in him, waiting for him to help them.

ISAIAH 30:18

I am the friend you have always wanted.

I am the True Friend you have always wanted. So many times when you called to me, I answered, and I was with you. Though you are delicate, I have made you strong. Do you remember how I set your heart on fire and gave you the grace to love me and seek me with your whole heart? I am your wraparound Shield, your strong Protector, and your True Friend.

My voice will comfort you and bring you peace. Remember the comfort I poured out upon you when your heart was broken and you did not know what to do. I was there in that hour to mend your broken soul and restore you to myself. I am drawn to your weakness, my beloved, like a river is drawn to the lowest places in the valley. I will fill you with my peace to sustain you and my love to empower you. Remember this, my beloved: I am your True Friend.

Some friendships don't last for long,
but there is one loving friend who is joined to your heart
closer than any other!

PROVERBS 18:24

Remember my promises.

Remember the promises that I have spoken to you. Do not let them go. I promised you life, strength, healing, and power. My words will be the armor to empower you when doubts assail you from every side. Keep coming to me and never forget the destiny I have promised you, for your inheritance is received by faith.

Take my Word and let it become your foundation. Stand upon it. Wrap it around your thoughts and let it rise from your lips. It will increase your faith. Even the promises I have made to you personally are to be trusted. Don't look to the right or the left, but keep your heart fixed on me. Judge every prophetic word that comes to you, by the witness of my Holy Spirit inside of you. Let your hope be stirred by the words that I give to you. Don't be afraid to believe me fully and to invest yourself in my promises. Every word I speak is alive and brings light to every dark chasm.

What a God you are! Your path for me has been perfect!
All your promises have proven true.
What a secure shelter for all those
who turn to hide themselves in you!
You are the wrap-around God giving grace to me.

PSALM 18:30

Accept a new picture of faith.

If the very thing you've been praying for came to pass today, how would you feel? Stop for a few moments and imagine it. Let your mind run wild with the excitement and activity that moment would have. You've spent so much time rehearsing negative things today. I want you to run with full force into the positive.

Put yourself into that moment right now. How would it feel? Allow yourself to feel it now, as if it's happened. Who would you tell? How would you celebrate? The smile on your face would be the smile I've given you. The joy rising within you would be the joy I created you for. You'd feel the weight lift from your shoulders.

Today, I want you to do more than just imagine it; I want you to accept that picture. I give you permission to celebrate and feel the emotion of that moment, because after all, that is what faith is. It's receiving what I have for you before you've actually seen it manifest in the natural. Start getting excited and praising me today, as if I've already answered, because I have.

Let joy be your continual feast. Make your life a prayer. And in the midst of everything be always giving thanks, for this is God's perfect plan for you in Christ Jesus.

1 THESSALONIANS 5:16–18

Do not be influenced by negativity.

Your enemy knows how to wound you. He will even come through the voices of those you love the most. But I want you to be alert to my voice, more than any other. I have taught you to follow my voice. You know what it sounds like and feels like. Now I want you to stand strong and not permit the voices of negativity to matter.

My voice sounds like peace. My voice explodes with hope. My voice is encouraging. It's full of wisdom. It imparts confidence. It infuses you with expectancy and optimism. It reminds you who you are and how beautiful, worthy, and strong you are. Though the enemy tries to silence truth, you are powerful enough to embrace it. Though society may measure you by what you do and how you look, that is not how I measure you or how I want you to measure yourself. Always measure yourself by my grace—the grace that was poured out for you, because you are worthy. Don't be influenced by any other voice but mine.

I'll listen carefully for your voice
and wait to hear whatever you say.
Let me hear your promise of peace—
the message every one of your godly lovers longs to hear.
Don't let us in our ignorance turn back from following you.

PSALM 85:8

December

Invite me into your unbelief.

I want you to be honest with yourself about how much you trust me. If you say you trust me, and then follow it up with a sigh or walk around with heaviness, it's a good indication that you're not trusting me. I don't want you to feel guilty about your lack of faith, but I do need you to invite me into that fear and disbelief. I want you to walk in a higher dimension of trust. That means letting go of control.

I am God, and you are not. That means I can do what you can't, and I can do things you haven't even considered. It's not your duty to fix everything and everyone. If you truly believe that I am God, then let me be God for you. Let me be the miracle-working God that you say I am. When you're really trusting me, fear isn't present. You can say with absolute confidence and a smile on your face, *I'm trusting God to take care of that*, then walk away knowing I will.

Trust in the Lord completely,
and do not rely on your own opinions.
With all your heart rely on him to guide you,
and he will lead you in every decision you make.
Become intimate with him in whatever you do,
and he will lead you wherever you go.
Don't think for a moment that you know it all,
for wisdom comes when you adore him with undivided devotion
and avoid everything that's wrong.

PROVERBS 3:5–7

I will bring people to support you.

In your weakness, you discover my strength. You learn that many times I pour out that strength through the encouragement and counsel of others. Though I want to always be the first one you run to, I also want you to pay attention to those who truly care about your heart with no agenda for themselves.

When you are at your lowest, remain before me, and I will bring people to you who carry my heart. I will place them around you to help you. I know exactly who you need in your life at the precise time you need them. Even if you haven't found them yet, they will come. They may not come in the way you expect. Sometimes their counsel will flow through their teaching, ministry, or a prophetic encounter. Some you will never meet in person. Some will hold you as a dear friend or spiritual parent. Regardless of how encouragement and counsel come, if you are willing to receive, I will bestow. Reach out to receive my strength and ask me to lead you to people who will support you.

Listen well to wise counsel
and be willing to learn from correction
so that by the end of your life
you'll be known for your wisdom.

PROVERBS 19:20

Today is my gift to you.

Don't fear the future. Stop living in the past. Neither of these things must have lordship over your life. I am the God of timeless eternity, but I give you one day at a time. I release the time you need to heal, to laugh, to ponder, to work, to rest, to love. Today is my gift to you.

Let me work out tomorrow's details. All I ask is to be present with what's before you today. If there are details to be ironed out, do it with me, in my peace. Don't become so focused on tomorrow that you miss the grace I've given for today. Today is my gift to you. Embrace it fully.

If today is meant to bring healing for the past, then you must submit to the healing that today has. Don't live in yesterday's trauma. Don't yearn for yesterday's blessing. Laugh for every reason you can find today. Dance like a child. Love more intensely. Forgive quickly and unreservedly. Time will continue passing, but if you'll take it one day at a time, my grace will meet you.

"Refuse to worry about tomorrow,
but deal with each challenge that comes your way,
one day at a time.
Tomorrow will take care of itself."

MATTHEW 6:34

Give me the start of your day.

Before your mind starts running with a million little things, set it before me. Make time for me before you start your day, and you'll notice how much more enjoyable your day will be. When you have a long list of time-sensitive things that must be done, pause and find my presence before you rush about. You'll find that you'll get more done with greater grace when you do. It contradicts the laws of nature. My grace is ready to meet you and speed up everything you set your hands to, when you honor me at the beginning of your day.

Just as lovers enjoy each other in the small moments throughout the day, but also need to spend time alone together, so do we. You were created to take joy in our moment to moment conversations, but you must savor my love in the secret place of your heart—in these set-apart times when you honor me first. I have created you with a need for these love encounters, and you will feel the difference when you do this. I am calling you aside, beloved. You can have as much of me as you want.

Let the sunrise of your love end our dark night.
Break through our clouded dawn again!
Only you can satisfy our hearts,
filling us with songs of joy to the end of our days.

PSALM 90:14

Focus on me today.

Today, instead of getting sucked into the world around you, stay focused on me. Center your heart in my presence, where it can be kept safe from the swirling chaos. Choose me first. If you truly want to hear from me, put down your phone, set aside social media, ignore those emails and texts for a while, and tune in to me. Wait for the instructions of heaven. Bless me with your attention. Be more aware of what's happening in you, than what's happening around you.

When you're tapped into me, you become light in the dark world. You bring peace into the arguments. You are able to mend the division, because you hear my wisdom and compassion. When you can stand outside of the confusion and look at it from the context of peace, you'll know how to pray, and those prayers will be full of power. You'll be able to love the contrary ones, because you understand their words and actions stem from things within them that only I can heal. Keep your mind focused on me today. Invite me into every thought and every emotion.

Feast on all the treasures of the heavenly realm and fill your thoughts with heavenly realities, and not with the distractions of the natural realm.

COLOSSIANS 3:2

Your brokenness can be beautiful.

Don't be afraid of your brokenness. I will use it for my glory. I will take what the enemy has used to break you and breathe strength into you like you've never known. Though it hurts to be broken, it makes you relatable. It gives you understanding and empathy for the hurts of others. It becomes the birthing ground for extraordinary miracles, because your brokenness brings you to me in absolute honesty and complete surrender. This is the place of abandon that I cannot resist.

When you are broken open—raw and undone—I walk straight into that wound and flood it with my love. I know how to heal you. I know to mend your broken heart in a way no one else can. I pour myself into your brokenness, so that you can be whole in the depth of your being. Your life becomes fertile ground for the seeds of glory to grow. For the miracle of healing to transform you. Your brokenness is beautiful, when it brings you to me in total surrender. I will not forsake you.

When holy lovers of God cry out
to him with all their hearts,
the Lord will hear them and come to rescue them
from all their troubles.
The Lord is close to all whose hearts are crushed by pain,
and he is always ready to restore the repentant one.

PSALM 34:17–18

Hold nothing back from me.

I want to be Lord over every part of your life. Over your joys and sorrows, hopes and fears, goals and disappointments. I don't want you to hold anything back. Beloved, come face-to-face with me. Stand in my presence and ask for my Spirit to reveal the areas that you haven't fully surrendered to me. It's time for you to release control in those parts of your life that you've held on to.

Let the searching gaze of my Spirit into the secret caverns of your heart. There are situations and people that I will gently bring to your remembrance. It's important that you don't push the thought back down but acknowledge it and bring it to me. Any pain, fear, trust issues, bad habits, wrong attitudes, or areas that you're still in control of, instead of letting me be in control, must be addressed. I love you, and I will lovingly correct you and draw you into the place of safety, where you can lay these things at my feet, once and for all. It's time for you to rise to a new level of freedom.

My old identity has been co-crucified with Messiah and no longer lives; *for the nails of his cross crucified me with him.* And now the essence of this new life is no longer mine, for the Anointed One lives his life through me—*we live in union as one*! My new life is empowered by the faith of the Son of God who loves me so much that he gave himself for me, and dispenses his life into mine!

GALATIANS 2:20

Be infused with my vibrant life.

I am the God of resurrection power. I infuse every dead and lifeless thing with vibrant life. Do you have loved ones who've turned from me? Call upon my resurrection power over their deadened hearts. I know how to woo the hearts of those who I've created. Do you have dreams that have been buried in the grave of disappointment? Let me give those dreams newness of life. I will reawaken them and dust them off. I will season them with fresh wisdom, creativity, and favor.

I alone am a miracle-working God. When you stand in faith, believing nothing is too hard for me, I meet that faith and show myself strong. It doesn't matter what it looks like on the outside. Get a new understanding of my power. I formed the earth, stars, and seas. I breathe life into every wind. I sculpted your frame. Made pathways for every vein. Wove your flesh from the substance of love. Let me be the God whose very name is alive. I will show my resurrection power in your life.

We are permanently grafted into him to experience a death like his, then we are permanently grafted into him to experience a resurrection like his and the new life that it imparts.

ROMANS 6:5

Lift your attention to my love.

Fasten yourself to eternity and remain there. Don't lower your gaze to your situations. Every time the enemy throws the situation that stirs your anxiety in your face, resist him. Choose to lift your attention to my love, my faithfulness, and my goodness. I know you're trying to stay at peace. I hear your cry for my help; I've already given it to you.

Beloved, I'm not only with you, I'm alive inside of you. If you're feeling overwhelmed, heavy, and stressed, it's not because you don't have the ability to shake it off. It's because you haven't fully released this problem to me. You're not totally trusting me yet. You know me. You know my love. You know I'm all power-ful. But you're agreeing with the fear that I won't come through. You're agreeing with the weightiness of this problem, more than you agree that I can and *will* come through for you. I know it's been a long time of waiting, but you don't see the whole picture. The days will pass anyway, so instead of spending them in wor-ry, spend them getting to know me better. Spend them enjoying every ounce of good that the day gives you.

"Are you weary, carrying a heavy burden? Then come to me. I will refresh your life, for I am your oasis."

MATTHEW 11:28

My Word withstands the tests.

This battle you're in is trying to shake the foundations of your faith. I don't want you to crumble under the weight of it. I've given you what you need to overcome. It's time to pick up the sword of my Word and slice through the lies and the darkness. Wrap yourself in the light of my Word. Stand and declare the truth! You don't have to scream it, you don't have to repeat it like a magic charm, but you do need to soak in its truth and keep it in your mind and on your lips.

My Word is faithful and true. It is tried in the fires of affliction. Proven in times like this, so put it to the test. The enemy will flee when you do! Yes, you are in a battle. But righteousness will win the battle. My Word has the power to redeem any situation. It shines into dark valleys and exposes lies. It illuminates areas in your life where you haven't let my light shine before. It reveals areas of doubt. It purifies. Beloved, apply the truth of my Word. Put it to the test.

Every word God speaks is sure and every promise pure.
His truth is tested, found to be flawless, and ever faithful.
It's as pure as silver refined seven times in a crucible of clay.

PSALM 12:6

Set aside time for glorious encounters.

I am an endless fountain of love, mercy, and provision. You will never find the end of my love for you. Regardless of how long you have walked with me, there are always new pathways to discover. Ask me, and I will lead you into greater encounters of glory, revelation, and holy bliss.

Tangible realities of my nearness are available to those who dare to believe; who are willing to take the time to search for my face; and who aren't content with occasional encounters, but desire something more. Think of the most radical stories you've heard when heaven invaded earthly lives, then take to heart the fact that I want even more for you. There is no limit to my love. No limit to how deep you can go. Impatience will try to squeeze you into an awareness of time, but you must come to me and stay in my presence. Stay there until all sense of time and space fade into the distance and you're swept into the currents of my glory. Beloved, set time aside for me. Make our relationship your priority.

We have come into an intimate experience with God's love, and we trust in the love he has for us. God is love! Those who are living in love are living in God, and God lives through them.

1 JOHN 4:16

Step into the flames of first-love passion.

D o you remember the joy that filled your heart when you started walking with me? When you realized how absolutely crazy I am about you? Do you remember the way you hungered and thirsted to know more of my truth? Or the way I greeted you each day, because you were so consumed with getting to know me? I do. I remember the passion that awoke your heart.

Beautiful one, I invite you to step into first-love passion again. I want you to finish this year strong. I am stoking the flames of sacred desire within you. Can you feel them rising higher right now? It's my desire for you to end this year so consumed with sacred love for me that nothing can ever quench it. I want you to dive into times of prayer and devotion that consume you. Change you. Saturate every fiber of your being. Launch you into an entire year of sacred encounters. You don't have to wait until January. I want you to experience the bright, glorious, all-consuming glory of my love today. Step into the flames of first-love passion.

Fasten me upon your heart as a seal of fire forevermore. This living, consuming flame will seal you as my prisoner of love. My passion is stronger than the chains of death and the grave, all consuming as the very flashes of fire from the burning heart of God. Place this fierce, unrelenting fire over your entire being.

SONG OF SONGS 8:6

Discover my heart.

I have prepared a place for you to rest, an oasis of my presence. Never be discontent with seasons of stillness and waiting. It is here, in the quiet of inactivity, where you are refreshed and made ready for the upcoming season. I hear your cry to walk in my ways, but first, I want you to discover my heart. And here in this sacred place, I will impart to you all that I am.

Keep on asking, for I will keep on fulfilling every longing you have. It is my desire for you to release what I've imparted to you, but I don't want this to be the main thing you long for. Long for my heart and to know me in greater depth, and ministry will be a natural by-product of our relationship. Keep on seeking me for the new expression of my Spirit, and you will possess my kingdom in fullness. Keep on knocking on the door that's in front of you, and it will open up and bring you into my chambers where all cry, "Glory!"

"Ask and you'll receive. Seek and you'll discover. Knock on heaven's door, and it will one day open for you. Every persistent person will get what he asks for. Every persistent seeker will discover what he needs. And everyone who knocks persistently will one day find an open door."

LUKE 11:9

You need to laugh.

I created you with great joy. I dance over you. Sing over you. Brood over you with a Father's heart for His child. You move me and bring me more pleasure than you know. Beloved, it's time for you to embrace my joy. To live a higher life. To let me peel back the layers of heaviness that life has covered you with. Embrace my joy.

I am not a heavy-handed, legalistic chastiser. I am the epitome of joy. I created you to have fun. Laughter is like medicine, and I offer it to you without measure. Don't take life so seriously that you forget to enjoy it. Don't be afraid to enjoy life because you're scared of what you may lose. I want to fill you with unspeakable joy! Tears of joy to replace tears of sorrow. Joy that unlocks the chains that have weighed you down. But you must not only receive it, you must interact with joy. Beloved, that means you must laugh. Yes, laugh out loud! Heaviness doesn't want you free. Pride wants you to feel embarrassed. But joy is the key you need to get free today. Laugh on purpose today!

The meek will overflow with fresh joy in the Lord Yahweh, and the poor will shout their praises to the Holy One of Israel!

ISAIAH 29:19

Let me teach you again.

My child, I want to teach you things you've never known. I want you to relearn the lessons you thought you grasped. Just because I revealed myself to you and poured out revelation, doesn't mean you've mastered the fullness of it. Allow me to unearth the hidden gems of my wisdom for you. Dig into them with me, and I will teach you greater things.

I want to enlighten your understanding. For you to find me living inside of you. To be so complete in your identity that trials don't knock you out. I want you to learn how to conquer the battles of the earthly realm, by staying fixated on the substance of my Spirit within in. Embrace the mysteries of my kingdom. Be comfortable with the mysteries of creation, the wonder of my mercy, and the absence of time as you know it. Dive into the mysteries of the heavenly realm. Come up higher, and I will train you in the ways of inexhaustible and unfathomable faith. There is more to learn that you can possibly imagine.

By the time Jesus finished speaking, the crowds were dazed and overwhelmed by his teaching, because his words carried such great authority, quite unlike their religious scholars.

MATTHEW 7:28–29

Extend grace.

I remind you today, give others the grace you need for yourself. Extend mercy, because you understand what it's like to be misunderstood. When those who should celebrate you, belittle you, ask me why. You may be surprised to learn of the pain they're carrying. The words of those who berate you are indications of their own self-hatred. A person who withholds love is often a person who isn't receiving the love they need. Will you love them for me? Will you look past their actions and find my heart?

Be careful about judging the hearts of those around you. It's easy to justify your anger and pain, but I'm calling you to a higher lifestyle. If I've placed you in dark places, it's because I know you are full of light. Will you shine for me? Will you allow mercy and kindness to soften hard hearts? You see the outside, but I see in the hidden caverns of their hearts. I see their greatest need, and I'm asking you to pray for those who speak ill against you. Let me fill your love tank, so you will overflow everywhere you go.

"Refuse to be a critic full of bias toward others, and judgment will not be passed on you. For you'll be judged by the same standard that you've used to judge others. The measurement you use on them will be used on you. Why would you focus on the flaw in someone else's life and yet fail to notice the glaring flaws of your own?"

MATTHEW 7:1–3

You must learn to rest.

There are seasons to fight and seasons to rest. In these seasons, when peace seems like nothing more than a dusty artifact and you can't find the right words to pray, let alone remember how to raise a battle cry, you must rest. You must let me be your fierce Protector. You must trust that you'll be safe in my arms—the ones that were spread wide in full surrender to the Father, just as you must surrender to me. Will you let me fight for you?

I'm not telling you to lay down and give up. I'm telling you that you must be okay with stillness in the middle of a battle. You must listen when I encourage you to rest. You must trust me enough to release yourself to rest. To give yourself permission to stop thinking. To find refreshing in my presence, so you can receive a new strategy that is going to look totally different than what you expected. I want to be for you what you cannot be for yourself. You know when to push, to declare, to fight, and to dance over pain, but you must also learn to rest.

His left hand cradles my head
while his right hand holds me close.
I am at rest in this love.

SONG OF SONGS 2:6

Find joy in something new.

These are the days of discovery. You will discover me in hidden places and in previously unknown ways. I am calling you into new experiences. Into adventures of life and spirit. Life isn't meant to be boring and monotonous. It is yours to enjoy! I want you to ask me to lead you into these times and places of adventure—both great and small.

It's time to step away from the security of what you've known. Do something new. Embrace radical change. Challenge yourself and become comfortable with discomfort. Look at fear and laugh in its face. Do things you've been too afraid to attempt. Separate with procrastination once and for all. Take the risk. You may find exactly what you're looking for in the very places you've been afraid to go. Do you feel me prompting you? Don't ignore the nudges of my Spirit. You will find me in the most unlikely places. You will find joy in the unknown. Be bold and do something new!

"Stop dwelling on the past. Don't even remember these former things. I am doing something brand new, something unheard of. Even now it sprouts and grows and matures. Don't you perceive it? I will make a way in the wilderness and open up flowing streams in the desert."

Isaiah 43:18–19

I created you to know joy unspeakable.

I have created you to be happy, which is why it feels so bad to be stressed, worried, and anxious. You cannot manage the actions of others, but you can, with my help, manage yourself. You can learn to find peace in storms. You can find joy, regardless of your circumstances. You can learn to let the opinions of others slide off of you. I alone am the one who defines you.

I want you to experience a life of radical joy and peace that isn't dependent upon your circumstances. I want you to look for the best, to see things from my point of view, and to go after a fulfilling life. Joy is much deeper than what happiness brings. Joy defies trials. It dares to laugh, even when hell is closing in. It trusts in my love. It is free. It lives in radical anticipation of good. A life of joy is a life that doesn't ignore pain, but it is sourced in the reality of my presence in every situation. It is this joy—my joy—rising within you that makes you strong.

Now may God, the inspiration and fountain of hope,
fill you to overflowing with uncontainable joy
and perfect peace as you trust in him.

ROMANS 15:13

Get to know my Holy Spirit.

I want you to cultivate friendship with my Holy Spirit. Become totally and completely dependent upon this part of my personality. Get to know my Holy Spirit, because He knows and loves you with undeniable passion. Embrace the fact that we, the Triune God, planned your relationship with Holy Spirit from the very beginning. The gift of the cross released the blessing of my Spirit to you. For you to have this part of me is a gift of unmeasurable love. It cost us everything.

I want you to sense my presence at all times. To feel me wooing you from within. To know me as your Helper, Teacher, and Bringer of Peace. Call on me when you need me; when you need the awareness of my presence; when you need wisdom, grace, peace, and strength; when you need—anything! It's an honor to need me. You don't have to be embarrassed about your total dependence upon me. It leads you into a lifestyle of holy communion with me. Lean in and listen. You will hear the voice of my Holy Spirit.

Allow the healing words you've heard from me to live in you and make them a model for life as your faith and love for the Anointed One *grows even more*. Guard well this incomparable treasure by the Spirit of Holiness living within you.

2 TIMOTHY 1:13–14

Exchange your thoughts.

Pay attention to what you're thinking about. I want to be the Lord of every thought, both conscious and subconscious. Don't let thoughts run through your mind without noticing if they are based on truth or a lie. And don't ignore flashes of painful memories of situations because acknowledging them and talking to me about them are keys to unlock healing. Stressful thoughts that bombard you or won't leave you alone have lies attached to them. Come to me, and let's expose every lie.

Exchange your thoughts of worry or pain to mentally fix things, and become fixated on me. Let your mind settle on the truth of my Word and the power of my love for you. Don't settle for less than all of me. I know how to cleanse the mind that I created. Tune in to my voice. Renew your mind by saturating it with my Word. Engage with my Spirit in times of stillness and contemplation. Stay in my presence, and I will expose the lies you've been thinking.

Now it's time to be made new by every revelation that's been given to you. And to be transformed as you embrace the glorious Christ-within as your new life and live in union with him! For God has re-created you all over again in his perfect righteousness, and you now belong to him in the realm of true holiness.

EPHESIANS 4:23–24

Always long for more of me.

There are many who are content with so little, when I have so much more to give to them. Because you have longed for all that I have, you will have it all. Your desire for me has captured my heart, beloved. And now, you will see me do more for you in this season than you ever experienced before. Because you love me, I will pour out my heart into you and merge you into my glory.

You were created for all of me. You are a carrier of my glory. Destined to experience my presence in new and unprecedented ways, as you press in for more. You can have as much of me as you desire. Just come close, day after day. Believe in my desire to bless you. Relish in the tangible awareness of my presence, but realize that there is always more. Always deeper encounters for you to enjoy. Always beautiful discoveries for me to unveil. Your hunger for greater intimacy with me is pleasing to me. You shall have it!

God conceals the revelation of his word
in the hiding place of his glory.
But the honor of kings is revealed
by how they thoroughly search out
the deeper meaning of all that God says.

PROVERBS 25:2

I am unlocking destiny.

I am about to bring you into a place where you have never been before. A place of contentment and peace that the world cannot impart. A place of favor and stability. A place of joy. I have prepared you, all your life, for this day of destiny. Every setback, every time that you yielded your heart in unpleasant circumstances, has set the stage for my imminent blessings.

The coming season will be extraordinary and filled with delight. Answers to prayers that were prayed long ago will soon be coming. What looked like delay after delay will make sense to you, as the clouds part and the light of glory shines through. I've held you all along, especially when it's felt like you've lost your footing. Align your thoughts and your expectations with my promises, and don't allow yourself to be afraid of believing. Shake off doubt and choose to embrace radical faith. I am greater than your dreams, greater than your plans, and greater than your thoughts could ever be.

Never doubt God's mighty power to work in you and accomplish all this. He will achieve infinitely more than your greatest request, your most unbelievable dream, and exceed your wildest imagination! He will outdo them all, for his miraculous power constantly energizes you.

EPHESIANS 3:20

I will give you the eyes of faith.

Many look at the horizon filled with clouds and expect only a coming storm, but your eyes of faith will see the clouds of glory. Ezekiel saw the clouds, yet within the storm was the Man of Fire, surrounded with lightning and glory. What do you see in the storm? If all you can see is darkness and chaos, ask me to adjust your vision. I will help your eyes to focus on a higher reality, so you will see that I am at work in the storm.

A soaring faith will bring you into my ways. A sagging faith will bring you down into the ways of men—seeing only what man sees and believing only what man believes. Never let your faith be set on the words of men, but on the living words of God. When you feel the winds, expect me to reveal myself within them. My Word is greater, my strength is stronger, and my purpose is more glorious than anything found on earth. It's possible to see from my point of view and live with eyes of faith.

Faith brings our hopes into reality and becomes the foundation needed to acquire the things we long for. It is all the evidence required to prove what is still unseen.

HEBREWS 11:1

Family is my outrageous love gift to you.

The cry of my heart rings from one end of the earth to the other. It echoes throughout eternity. Within the miracle of my birth, I have released a simple yet profound message—I want you to be a part of my family. No matter what you have done, I love you, and I have called you to find your home in my presence.

I was sent to the earth to open the way for you to come close. To realize the impact of radical love upon your life. You have my permission to come like a child—completely unhindered in our relationship. To be with me without inhibitions. For your heart to expand and take in more of my love—and then even more. I want you to feel comfortable in my presence. To giggle. To dance. To kick back and feel at ease. To know I'm even better than any earthly family. Your place in my family will give you purpose. No matter what, I won't reject you. Embrace my outrageous love gift. Take my name for yourself.

Those who embraced him and took hold of his name were given authority to become the children of God!

JOHN 1:12

Your surrendered life will awaken others.

You are an awakener of others. As they witness what I am doing in your life, many will see and trust me. They will be drawn into a deeper place with me because of your surrender and your obedience to my call. Move your heart closer to me, and the shadow of my power will rest upon you. Do not be passive in this hour but passionate to pursue all that I hold in store for you.

Never underestimate the power of your surrendered life. Many will tell you to stay where you are. To stay in the safety of what you've known. To fear stepping out of the boat to walk on the water. Keep your eyes on me and step out in faith. I've got you. Your story will ignite passionate faith in the hearts of others. Come closer, and I will immerse you in the realm of my glory until all that is seen in you is my splendor. Your life of passionate pursuit sets you apart from those who have settled for less. Thank you, beloved, for never settling for less than my best.

"Rise up in splendor and be radiant, for your light has dawned,
and Yahweh's glory now streams from you!"

ISAIAH 60:1

You are free to be yourself.

Don't compare yourself to others. I want you to be secure in the person I've created you to be. You have freedom to be led by my Spirit, instead of following the current trends. Free to do what's right for you. For your family. For your group. For your business. The way others live isn't the only right way. Step outside of what's expected, when you know I'm the one leading you. The rules of others aren't necessarily my rules for you.

You are safe with me. Free to be yourself. The expected norm changes over time, but I don't. Grasp truth for yourself. My truth. Truth that is perfect for you and your life. People may try to convince you that their way of living is the way to go. That they're happier because of it. While that may be true, I don't want you following others simply because they appear happy. They have their own struggles. I want you to seek *me* for your path. To know the way that I want you to live, eat, exercise, and worship. Be comfortable in your uniqueness. Know what makes you a happier person, by seeking me in every choice.

You are so intimately aware of me, Lord.
You read my heart like an open book
and you know all the words I'm about to speak
before I even start a sentence!
You know every step I will take before my journey even begins.

PSALM 139:3–4

I want you to go after your dreams.

Beloved, I have placed destiny within you. When you feel dreams stirring and you cannot escape them, run with that desire. Stop making excuses for why your dreams haven't been realized. Seek me for wisdom. If you truly want to see those dreams come to pass, it's going to take effort and commitment. It's time to be the best version of you that you can be. Make a habit of diligence. Make a habit out of running after your dreams. You're worthy and capable!

It's up to you to choose the greater desires over the temporary distractions. Walk away from social media and the things that waste your time, and choose to go after what you most desire. I have created you to succeed. That doesn't mean you won't fail. It means that there are lessons you will learn along the way. Failing pushes you to dig further in prayer. It drives you into my presence for greater wisdom. Roadblocks only serve as an alternate route. They give you a different perspective, by causing you to walk around them to see what you've missed. They can be launching pads to a different dimension of your dream that you haven't considered.

You know that when your faith is tested it stirs up power within you to endure all things. And then as your endurance grows even stronger it will release perfection into every part of your being until there is nothing missing and nothing lacking.

JAMES 1:3–4

It is important that you find your tribe.

I want you to surround yourself with people who encourage and support you. Those who not only see the gold in you, but call out the hidden treasure. Beloved, you deserve to have people who will walk alongside of you to support you, to walk with you through difficulties, and to help make you a better person.

You are worthy of deep and meaningful friendships and mentors. You also have much to share with others. If you are in a place where you don't feel valued or supported, if you haven't found your "tribe" of like-minded people, ask me for direction. I will lead you to those who I know you'll love getting to know. I'll also need you to do your part to step out and interact with them. Don't neglect the opportunities I have and will place before you. There are seasons when you may feel that no one understands you. Seasons when I've set you apart, in order for you to come away and grow in me, but there are also times for you to dive into community and friendships. It's time to find your "tribe"!

Some friendships don't last for long,
but there is one loving friend who is joined to your heart
closer than any other!

PROVERBS 18:24

My silence serves as a lesson.

Even when you cannot sense me, I am here. I hear every prayer and see every sigh of your heart. I know every thought you think. I am with you right now. I promised to never leave you. It may feel like I've stepped back, left you without direction or the sound of my voice, but I haven't. My seeming silence is a lesson. A reminder to be still. To find me by embracing the quiet I want your mind to find.

It isn't that I'm not speaking. Often, I'm just speaking in a way you don't recognize. Pay attention to the cues of life all around you. I speak in many ways and through many different instruments. Remember the countless times I led you to an answer in surprising ways. I know how to get you where you need to go. I have never failed you, and I never will fail you. Always remember that I am faithful. If all you hear is silence, yield to that silence. You will find me there.

I am standing in absolute stillness, silent before the one I love,
waiting as long as it takes for him to rescue me.
Only God is my Savior, and he will not fail me.
For he alone is my safe place.
His wrap-around presence always protects me
as my champion defender.

PSALM 62:5–6

I have made you to be powerful.

I t's time to be the best version of you that you can be. It's time for you to take a stand and embrace happiness. It's time to stop blaming others for what you have or don't have. It's time stop wondering why I'm not providing things that I've given you the power to go after yourself. It's time to laugh more. To stop making excuses. To stop looking at your situation as if it's hopeless. To take steps, no matter how small, toward your dreams. I have made you powerful!

I want you to take charge of your life, with me as your Leader. I want you to find balance in your life. To seek me for wisdom on how to manage your life. I want you to have time for work, play, family, friends, hobbies, and to enjoy me. I want you to love your body. To believe in yourself. To get to the root of issues that are hindering you. You are not a victim. You are a perfect package of unlimited power and glory! I am on your side. Step past every limitation and realize how powerful you are!

I find that the strength of Christ's explosive power infuses me to conquer every difficulty.

PHILIPPIANS 4:13

About the Authors

D r. Brian Simmons is known as a passionate lover of God and the lead translator of The Passion Translation, a new heart-level Bible translation that conveys God's passion for people and His world by translating the original, life-changing message of God's Word for modern readers. Brian and his wife, Candice, travel full time as speakers and Bible teachers.

G retchen Rodriguez has coauthored three books with Brian Simmons: *Prayers on Fire*, *The Divine Romance*, and *Ever Present Love*. Her heart burns with one main message: intimacy with Jesus and discovering the reality of his presence. She and her husband invested nine years as missionaries in Puerto Rico, along with their three daughters, and now make Redding, California, their home. For more about Gretchen, see her website: gretchenrodriguez.com.